EDUCATION IN A COMPETITIVE AND GLOBALIZING WORLD

KNOWLEDGE ENGINEERING

PRINCIPLES, METHODS AND APPLICATIONS

EDUCATION IN A COMPETITIVE AND GLOBALIZING WORLD

Additional books in this series can be found on Nova's website under the Series tab.

Additional e-books in this series can be found on Nova's website under the e-book tab.

EDUCATION IN A COMPETITIVE AND GLOBALIZING WORLD

KNOWLEDGE ENGINEERING

PRINCIPLES, METHODS AND APPLICATIONS

ALFONSO PEREZ GAMA
EDITOR

nova publishers
New York

Library of Congress Cataloging-in-Publication Data

Library of Congress Cataloging-in-Publication Data

Knowledge engineering principles, methods and applications / editor, Alfonso Perez Gama.
pages cm. -- (Education in a competitive and globalizing world)
Includes index.
ISBN 978-1-63463-909-5 (hardcover)
1. Expert systems (Computer science) 2. Artificial intelligence. 3. Education, Higher--Effect of technological innovations on. I. Perez Gama, Alfonso., editor of compilation, author.
QA76.76.E95K5777 2015
006.3'3--dc23
2015000086

Published by Nova Science Publishers, Inc. † New York

CONTENTS

Foreword: The Crossing of the Knowledge

Development of the Information Society

It is well known the information age began since the invention of written language 3500 years BC, marking an important conservation, the oral language, a milestone; but it was not until Gutenberg's printing press (around 1500 AD) in which the new demands for information processing, storage and retention purposes, future reference and dissemination, marked the launch of the information Society. The mass circulation publications then began opening a space for the democratization of information. It was not until the birth of the computer, 500 years later in 1946, preceded by important contributions of Boole, Turing, Shannon and others, that the real boom of the information age was beginning; it was minted the term of electronic data processing, pari passu with modern systems. Changes occur constantly in all social and economic spheres. Since then telecommunications overflow showing the elimination of distance and adding a new ingredient evidenced by communications between systems, people and the same computers. The era of automation demanded new infrastructure: the global information networks to enable mass communication and real-time enterprises.

Paradoxically, it was also recognized, the computer as the most important sincethat of Gutenberg technological change, and much was written about its intrinsic power, predicting and verifying major changes and redefinitions in the lives of individuals and the social and economic progress of the countries which were advanced in computing. New computer science marked a milestone in the historical development: it has drawn their its own side of knowledge and today it´s an important place in all disciplinary knowledge so it is essential to continue studying the phenomenon of the computer, not only as a mass medium of communication but as something indispensable in everyday life as non-neutral in the educational process, and even unparalleled in educational technology. A long process of computerization began in our countries supported by the new science of computing and, obviously, the same Operations Research (OR).

We do not intend to make a full review of what happened in this new space, but if you contrast that time with today: nowadays we have the new role of the computer: it left office single data repository, calculator, simple typewriter to become a cognitive tool, a mental mirror and, why not say so: an intellectual colleague.

Today we know that the Train was for the Industrial Society, what the Computer meant for the Information Society and already accepted what the e-Commerce and Intelligent Businesses are for the Knowledge Society.

ASSUMPTIONS OF THE KNOWLEDGE SOCIETY

Countries that were not rode on the train on computers, continued, to lag behind. The rapid development of information infrastructures generated greater demand for contents and knowledge. In the early 80s, V Generation Project of Japan, or the U.S. Strategic Computing almost marked the final launch of the new Knowledge Society, and, it´s not unreasonable to say that. We already have expert systems with new satellite communications, with the very personal computer and CD ROM.

Data, is one of the multiple determinations of a problem, so in a systematic way, the transition to information, which is the input to a Decision Making Process, which in turn responds to Management Styles; given its strategic importance means the, fuel, to achieve development and socio-technical progress; refers to descriptions of the information into a new dimension: the knowledge that seals a revolution: the Knowledge Society. In the same way, the databases, towards a new generation: the knowledge bases that burst as the new immaterial asset in the organization: the intellectual Capital.

KNOWLEDGE, represents the expertise, the problem solving, the shortages face, the managing complexity, how to do a task, how to represent cognitive skills, and how to enhance the new competences of the intellect that include Intellectual Capital, and is required for, survival business, if you want to compete successfully in the Third Millennium. Knowledge among others, refers to the How to do? Which is correct? How to proceed?

ENTERPRISE is the magnifying of human endeavor: it remains unresolved, it is a "living" system that has the added value to your MIS (management information system), so that if it is supported on knowledge, it becomes an intelligent company.

INTELLIGENCE is the systematization and processing of knowledge that increases the efficiency of a system in a way more than proportional, and providing further autonomous performance; is the main added value for the organization, which enables the company to stand out, to survive with success remaining competitive; Intelligence, refers to How to do more with less which is the challenge of today most economies.

WISDOM, is the systematization and the processing of the intelligence, allows transcendence as a system effect on the organization, increases the efficiency of a system, is the main added value for the society, makes it more significant, is the Cultural Intelligence process for the organization by applying judgments and values to the understanding of the social, economic and technological problems. Wisdom will be designated as the coming revolution: Society of Wisdom

FEATURES OF THE KNOWLEDGE SOCIETY

By centering on scientific and technological activities, which in turns are already part of the national development plans in most advanced countries;

Because information and knowledge act as elements of integration and social function;

Because it has been recognized, that knowledge is the main input of an intelligent system, based essentially on educational activities;

Because the knowledge economy is the new third millennium economy, with growing needs of skilled jobs which are intellectually demanding;

Because most of these jobs demand ICT (Information Communication Technology);

Because the democratization process of knowledge will enable the cyber-society of the knowledge and the wisdom.

Finally, because the computer replaced the role of energy: the new wealth of nations which are products of the mind: intellectual assets. From the artifacts and hand labor of the old Industrial Society we passed to the mind-facts and minds-work.

And the DEPARTMENTS OF OPERATIONAL RESEARCH?

It was thought-provoking, old databases we projected in the 60s with so little intelligence remembering dinosaurs. Its use was limited to finally some statistics and graphs. In fact, with the flowering of the Informatics the OR disappeared of the MIS core. Today we have the decision support systems (DSS) as part of the structure of a management information system that supports the difficult task of the executive to reduce the complexity of modern business and its purpose is to confront problems from the daily practices: DSS provide space to solve organizational problems.

The data warehousing technology enables the integration of dispersed and scattered information on the organization and also link databases that are geographically distant and not required to have a copy in situ. That is, business intelligence BI which is producing another realignment of companies in the world, as happened with the information in the two past world wars.

Now is Big Data: is the expression for large collections of data sets (including discrete, and continuous), so large and complex that it becomes difficult to process it using traditional database management systems. It needs advances techniques as artificial intelligence, AI, (machine learning, natural language processing, Intelligent Maintenance Systems, IMS) on developing advanced predictive tools and techniques to be applicable in this Big Data environment. Recently limits on the size of data sets that are realistic to process were on the order of exabytes (EB 10^{18}) requiring massive parallel software which use to run on several servers (e.g., hundreds). Modern framework provides a parallel processing model and associated implementation to process huge amount of data, and also using e.g., multiple layer architectures and evidently high performance computing.

Extracting value from big data, enterprises are able to optimize logistics and distribution methods, efficiently allocate resources and credits, and robustly combat computer crimes, benefitting consumers as a whole.

COGNIMATICS: THE INFORMATICS OF THE KNOWLEDGE SOCIETY

The informatics was the European neologism, proposed for automatic information processing, methods and practices lexicon. In SISOFT 2001 we proposed the term

COGNIMATICS (from COGNOS, knowledge) so we describe the computational processing of the knowledge, its forms of representation, methods, techniques and practices of the new intelligent processing.

TOWARDS A KNOWLEDGE INDUSTRY

Clearly this industry is a mind intensive work of immaterial type in which labor is an additional component to the artifacts as mentioned before: mind facts to be done by knowledge workers. Also the capital has an additional dimension within intellectual and assets capital. The Knowledge has its own life cycle: acquisition, storage, dissemination, and application. This cycle is a sequence of intellectual tasks by which knowledge workers build their unique competitive advantage for social and environmental benefit. It also comprises a range of strategies and practices used in an organization to identify, generate, display, represent, distribute, and enable adoption of insights and experiences (knowledge).

An economy of knowledge focused on the production and management of knowledge in the frame of economic constraints, is a knowledge-based economy. Said meaning, the more frequently used, refers to the use of knowledge technologies (such as knowledge engineering KE and knowledge management KM) to produce economic benefits as well as job generation.

Various observers describe today's global economy as one in transition to a "knowledge economy," as an extension to a "postindustrial economy". Such a transition requires that the rules and practices that determined success in the industrial economy, need rewriting in an interconnected, globalized economy where knowledge resources such as professional competences -as know-how- and expertise are as critical as other economic resources. According to the analysts of the "knowledge economy," these rules need to be rewritten at all levels: from firms and industries in terms of knowledge management, to public and politics, and also as ICT & knowledge-related topics.

In a knowledge economy society, knowledge is an input/output product (regarding Leontief), while in a KE environment; the same knowledge is a resource and a tool. This difference is not yet well distinguished in the subject matter literature. They both are strongly interdisciplinary, involving economists, computer scientists, software engineers, mathematicians, chemists and physicists, as well as "cognitivits", psychologists and sociologists. KE is an engineering discipline that involves integrating knowledge into computer systems (e.g., expert systems) in order to solve complex problems normally requiring a high level of competences, knowhow and expertise. At present, it refers to the building, maintaining and development of knowledge-based systems. It has a great deal in common with software engineering, and is used in many computer science domains such as artificial and computational intelligence including knowledge based databases, Business Intelligence, knowledge based expert systems, decision support technology, intelligent knowledge based systems IKBS, and many others. Knowledge engineering is also related to mathematical logic, as well as strongly involved in cognitive science and socio-cognitive engineering where the knowledge is produced by socio-cognitive aggregates (mainly humans) and is structured according to our understanding of how human reasoning and logic works.

The new knowledge industry may create new jobs as Knowledge Engineers, Knowledge Software Architects, Knowledge Base Administrators, Knowledge Requirements Analysts,

Knowledge Authoring Teachers and Lecturers, Testing Knowledge Bases Technologists, Data and Knowledge Stewards, Knowledge Technicians Architects, Quality Knowledge Assurance Technologists, Technologist of Knowledge Governance, and others.

WHAT IS THE SUMMARY?

The society has moved between techno-philia and techno-phobia; the first one states the end of the kingdom of necessity, in which a technological change will bring prosperity and better living conditions. The second one relies a bit on technique e.g., the computer as a tool is good, data warehouse, the best complex calculator and typewriter, big data but nothing more.

Our first conclusion is that the high computer technology can no longer be considered as optional or marginal: it is shown that computing is enabling high competitiveness to the enterprises. Otherwise enterprises become marginal an could disappear.

ICT are the major value added for modern organizations i.e., explain the final product of the company. Banks, financial sector, always show high returns benefit from the telecommunications infrastructure and the same Informatics and cognimatics.

This implies that ICT should appear in our countries explaining solutions to big problems and also explaining the electronic and distance learning.

It is not enough to fight to improve the quality of education: much better is modeling a highly competitive education sector and to build national capability to generate knowledge and innovation.

Consequently knowledge is the starting point for deciphering the origin of the universe and the KE is its main technology.

J. Alfonso Perez Gama
Fundación de Educación Superior San Jose,
Bogota, Colombia

In: Knowledge Engineering
Editor: Alfonso Perez Gama

ISBN: 978-1-63463-909-5

Chapter 1

FUNDAMENTALS OF GEOGRAPHIC KNOWLEDGE ENGINEERING FOR TERRITORIAL INTELLIGENCE

Robert Laurini*
LIRIS, INSA-Lyon, University of Lyon, France

ABSTRACT

In a lot of applications from agriculture to zoology, from environmental planning to territorial intelligence, actual systems of artificial intelligence are not very efficient, essentially because of a naïve representation of space.

As spatial knowledge corresponds to conventional geometric and topological knowledge, geographic knowledge corresponds to knowledge about geographic features in the real world even if real features can have spatial relationships between them. In other words, spatial knowledge is based on topological, projective and distance relations; but if applied to geographic features, one must take Earth rotundity and other characteristics (demography, physical geographic, economic geography, etc.) into account.

After a rapid presentation of spatial relations and their properties, this chapter will detail the 12 principles governing geographic knowledge. First emphasis will be given to various forms of geography knowledge, such as located facts, geographic clusters, flows, gradients, co-location rules and topological constraints.

Then, based on ribbon theory, spatial relations and Earth rotundity, geographic relations will be defined. For instance, let us consider two features in the real world associated with a DISJOINT relation; when down-scaling, those objects can be associated with a TOUCHES relation. As a consequence, any reasoning mechanism must be transformed accordingly.

1. INTRODUCTION

Due to the difficulties of modeling geographic analysis and reasoning, knowledge engineering must be revisited in order to integrate space and computational geometry. Spatial

* Robert.Laurini@insa-lyon.fr.

knowledge must be seen as an extension of geometry but also must integrate topology (Laurini-Milleret-Raffort, 1989), whereas geographic knowledge can be defined as spatial knowledge applied to the Earth. In other words, the main difference between spatial and geographic knowledge deals with semantics of all the features which are on the Earth.

Territorial intelligence can be defined as business intelligence applied to any territory ranging from a parcel, to a country and the whole Earth. As it is common to claim that planar geometry can be applied to parcels, for larger features the rotundity of the Earth must be taken into account. Therefore the concept of spatial granularity of interest is very important. Indeed for a city-level politician and a nationwide politician, the interests are different. During centuries, this problem was solved by considering scales. Beyond the strict ratio between the map measures and the Earth measures, a lot of semantics were hidden: for instance at the scale of 1:1,000,000 usually building are not visualized because they representations were too small: the limit of 0.1 mm was generally used according to the following rule "*if the mapped size of an object is less than 0.1 mm, then that object is removed*".

What is the origin of geographic knowledge? For centuries, geographers and urban planners have constructed skill and methodologies to analyze, to assess a territory in order to propose solutions. Sometimes this knowledge can be written in reports and some of them can be accessed by Internet. By text mining some chunks can be extracted. But due to the specific characteristics of this knowledge, for instance the problem of recognizing and extracting place names, special algorithms are procedures have been produced. And then one can run process of geographic information retrieval (GIR).

The objective of this chapter is to present the fundamentals of geographic knowledge engineering. In the next section, an analysis of geographic features will be presented, emphasizing on a new model based on ribbons. Then a difference will be made between spatial relations and geographic relations. In the fifth section, the twelve principles of geographic knowledge engineering will be discussed preceded by twelve prolegomena. Then some various ways of encoding geographic knowledge will be introduced. To conclude this section, application in territorial intelligence will be rapidly sketched.

2. Geographic Objects

The objective of this section is to revisit the modeling of geographic features for knowledge engineering.

A solution will be based only on two types of areas, crisp and fuzzy, but a new sort of areas called ribbon will be used to model what is common to call "linear objects".

2.1. Representation of Geographic Features

A very important aspect when modeling a geographic feature deals with mathematical representations usually taken as attributes. For years, several models for instance for storing a simple polygon exist, but standardization has opted for one of them (OGC). For a street, several models exist depending from actor's vision. Figure 1 illustrates four families of models totally different:

- the first model is based on graph with edges as street axes and nodes as crossroads;
- the second based on two polylines delimitating the private part and the public part (cadastre meaning);
- the third as an area l model for describing the section reserved for traffic;
- and finally a 3D model in order to integrate engineering networks.

Do not forget that feature shapes are always simplified overall at smaller scales: in order to increase readability, lines are generalized i.e., some points are removed thanks for instance to the well-known algorithm designed by Douglas-Peucker (1973). In addition, depending of the context sometimes some cartographic objects must be enlarged or slightly moved.

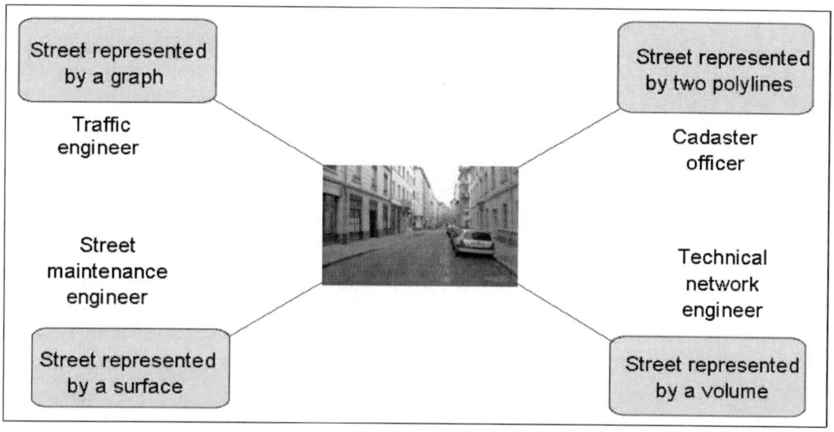

Figure 1. Multiple geometric representations of a street.

For decades, geometric models of geographic features have been based on points (0D), lines (1D), areas (2D) and volumes (3D). But points and lines do not exist really in the nature since all objects are 3D and moving. Geography for its part is mainly 2D.

In the majority of GIS (geographic information systems) software products, rivers and roads are modeled as lines, sometimes with a width, which is strange from a mathematical point of view. To solve this problem, the concept of ribbon will be introduced.

2.2. From Lines to Ribbons

Since lines do not exist in the real world, except perhaps lines such as the Equator, the meridians and the parallels, in a recent paper (Laurini, 2012), I have proposed to use ribbons to model what it is common to call linear objects such as roads and rivers.

Due to curves (circle portions, clothoids), roads are not rectilinear. So the idea of modeling lanes by rectangles is insufficient. In order to deal with this important characteristic, a more general definition is need. From a mathematical point of view, a ribbon can be defined as a transformation of a longish rectangle.

Figure 1 illustrates this principle. Let's call R a ribbon and ρ a rectangle of length l and width w, one can state $R = H(\rho)$, in which H is a taenic[1] transformation.

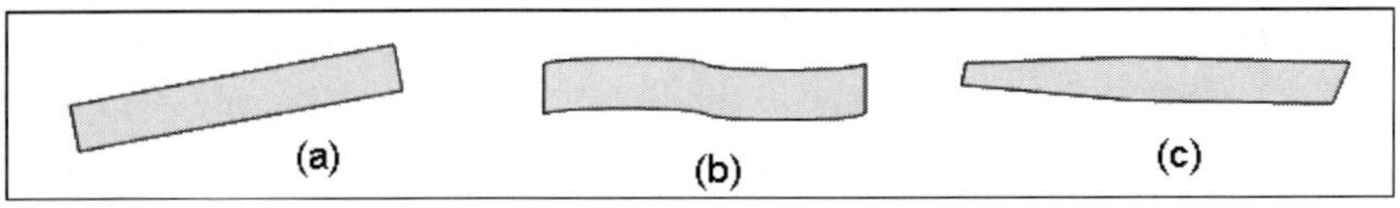

Figure 2. Various types of ribbons. (a) Rectangular ribbon. (b) Ribbon. (c) Loose ribbon.

2.2.1. Rectangular Ribbons

A rectangular ribbon R is a longish rectangle. Let us call ends the two smaller extremities and sides the larger ones.

The width is noted w, the length l and r_l ($r_l = l/w$) the longishness ratio which is supposed to be much greater than a positive value r_L; a possible minimum value is 5 ($r_l > r_L > 5$).

Let us call skeleton the medium line between two ends located at a distance $h = w/2$ from the sides of the rectangle. Let us note *Skel(R), End1(R), End2(R), Side1(R), Side2(R),* respectively, the skeleton of R, its two ends and its two sides.

2.2.2. Ribbons and Taenic Transformation

A taenic transformation (Figure 3) transforms a 1D curve into a 2D area with the following properties. Let us note $y=f(x)$ a curve which is supposed to be continuous and differentiable.

In each point of the curve, let us consider two points U_1 and U_2 at h distance from the curve located at the perpendicular of the first derivative. Let's call them corresponding points. The loci of those corresponding points form two curves C_1 and C_2 respectively. Knowing that $dy/dx = tg(\alpha)$, we can write respectively:

So for C_1: $\begin{Bmatrix} x_1 = x + h \times \sin(\alpha) \\ y_1 = y - h \times \cos(\alpha) \end{Bmatrix}$ and for C_2: $\begin{Bmatrix} x_2 = x - h \times \sin(\alpha) \\ y_2 = y + h \times \cos(\alpha) \end{Bmatrix}$.

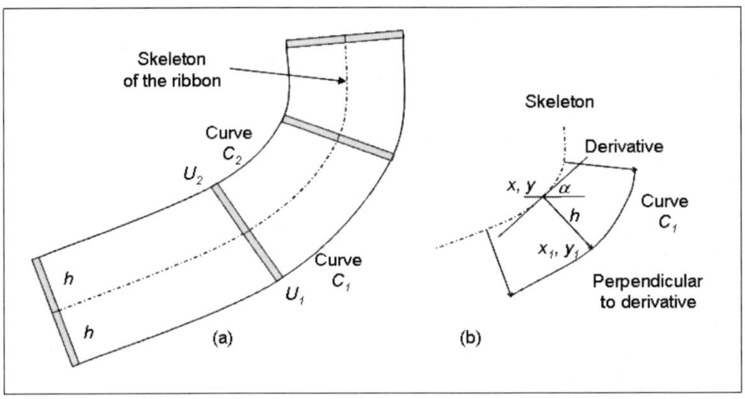

Figure 3. Construction of a regular ribbon with a taenic transformation. (a) Regular ribbon. (b) Details of the construction of a regular ribbon.

[1] From Ταινία, ancient Greek for ribbon.

Consider the derivative at corresponding point U_1, one has:

$\frac{dy_1}{dx_1} = \frac{dy_1}{d\alpha} \times \frac{d\alpha}{dx_1}$ but $\frac{dy_1}{d\alpha} = -h \times (-\sin(\alpha)) = h \times \sin(\alpha)$ and $\frac{dx_1}{d\alpha} = h \times \cos(\alpha)$.

So $\frac{dy_1}{dx_1} = \frac{dy_1}{d\alpha} \times \frac{d\alpha}{dx_1} = \frac{h \times \sin(\alpha)}{h \times \cos(\alpha)} = tg(\alpha) = \frac{dy}{dx}$.

A similar computation can be done for U_2 giving $\frac{dy_2}{dx_2} = \frac{dy}{dx}$. So the consequence is that the derivatives of the corresponding points are equal to the derivative at the skeleton and the angle is the same.

Now, consider a ribbon end. We can write the following dot product between the tangent in U_1 and the end:

$$DP = (h \times \sin(\alpha) \times \Delta x_1 + (-h \times \cos(\alpha) \times \Delta y_1)) = \frac{h}{\cos(\alpha) \times \Delta x_1}(tg(\alpha) - \frac{\Delta y_1}{\Delta x_1})$$

So if $\Delta x_1 \rightarrow 0$, we can see that the dot product tends also towards zero which means that the angle is right. As a conclusion, both ends are orthogonal to the sides.

2.2.3. Loose Ribbons

Starting from any polygon *P*, what are the conditions to consider it as a loose ribbon? Indeed often due to measurement errors (f.i. roads) and other reasons (f.i. rivers), ribbons are not always perfect rectangles. For solving this problem, let us consider its equivalent rectangle.

The first step is to consider all vertices of *P* (Figure 4a) and by the least square method to compute the regression line $y=mx+q$ (Figure 4b). Let us define θ the angle so that $tg(\theta)=m$. Then we make a rotation of $-\theta$ so that the regression line is parallel to the *x*-axis (Figure 4c). Then, we sort all vertices according the ascending values of respectively *x* and *y* coordinates. We determine minimum and maximum according to those orders. Along *x*, the mid values of the two first and the two last will determine ribbon ends; and along *y*, the mid values of the two first and the two last will determine sides (Figure 4d); those value will determine the equivalent rectangle of *P* noted *ER(P)*.

Now, let us compare the areas of *P* and *ER(P)*. Generally speaking, there is a small discrepancy between those values. A solution is to lightly modify *l* and *w* to reach the exact value. Let us note A_1=*Area(P)* and A_2=*Area(ER(P))*. Generally speaking, they are not equal. To get them equal:

$$A_2 = (w + \Delta w) \times (l + \Delta l) = w \times l \times (1 + \frac{\Delta w}{w}) \times (1 + \frac{\Delta l}{l}) = A_1 \times (1 + \frac{\Delta w}{w}) \times (1 + \frac{\Delta l}{l})$$

Let us suppose that we want to impose modification in the same proportion. So we can write $\frac{\Delta w}{w} = \frac{\Delta l}{l} = t$ the modification ratio, so giving $A_2 = A_1 \times (1+t)^2$. Its value is $t = \sqrt{\frac{A_2}{A_1}} - 1$, or $t = \frac{\sqrt{A_2} - \sqrt{A_1}}{\sqrt{A_1}}$. With this modification, both areas will be equal.

If the longishness ratio r_l of the equivalent rectangle is greater than the threshold value r_L then the polygon *P* is considered as a loose ribbon *R =ERR(P)*.

In order to simplify this presentation, one will only consider ribbons as rectangles, i.e., the *H* transformation becomes the identity transformation $R = H(\rho)$ so $R = H(\rho) = \rho$.

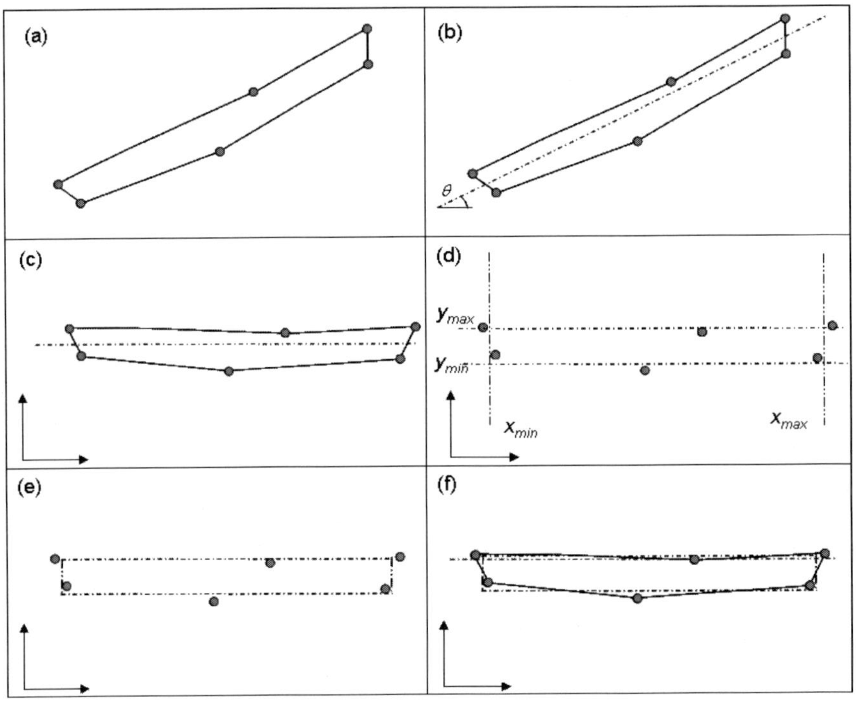

Figure 4. Loose ribbon and its equivalent rectangle. (a) Loose ribbon. (b) The regression line. (c) Rotation. (d) Determination of the two minima and the two maxima. (e) Equivalent rectangle. (f) Loose ribbon and its equivalent ribbon before the back rotation.

In Figure 5, an example of road modeled by ribbons is presented in which one can distinguish several ribbons, namely for bus lanes, bike lanes, median and so on.

Immediately it can be seen that ribbons can have their own relations between them.

2.3. Fuzzy Geographic Features

Usually, two categories of features can be distinguished, crisp and fuzzy. Crisp objects must have well-defined boundaries such as administrative objects (countries, regions, provinces, natural parks, parcels, etc.) and manmade objects such as streets, buildings.

Other objects, for instance some natural features can be defined as crisp objects; but there are difficulties. A river at some scales can be defined as a line whereas sometimes the expressions such as minor bed or major bed are used.

Even some dry rivers can be without water. For seas, according to the tide levels, geometric shapes can be different. One of the more salient examples is "Mont Saint-Michel" which is roughly only 1 km^2 wide at high tide and several squared kilometer wide at low tide.

Where does begin a hill, what is the upper limit of a valley, where does begin a marsh? Those are common questions in which features can be modeled as fuzzy geographic sets.

For those objects, fuzzy sets can be used in which some membership grades can be defined (Figure 6) (Zadeh, 1995). An interesting model (Cohn-Gotts, 1996) is the egg-yolk model with two parts, the core (the yellow part) and the extension, the white part of the egg.

For instance for a river, the "yolk" represents the minor bed whereas the "egg" modeled its major bed. Another example is given in Figure 7 in which the mangrove and the jungle are modeled with the egg-yolk representation.

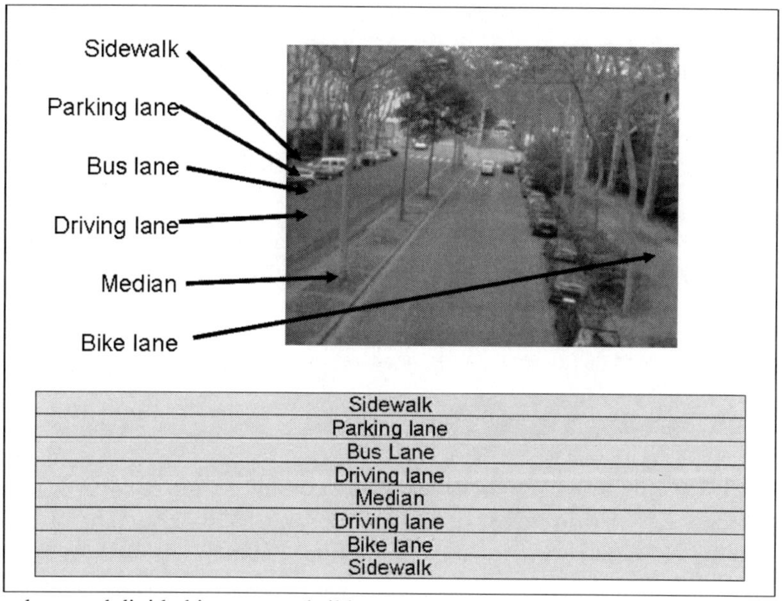

Figure 5. An urban road divided into several ribbons.

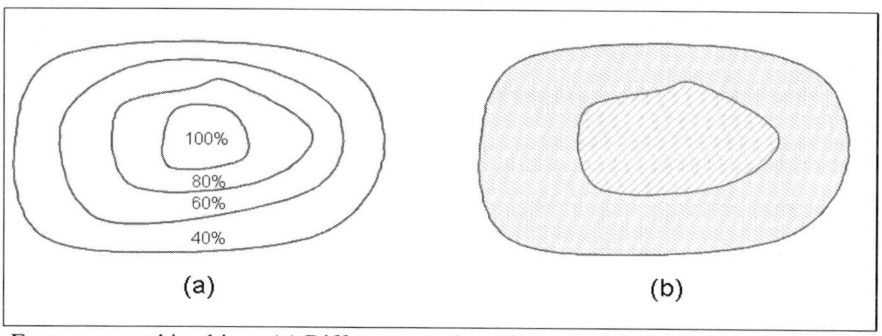

Figure 6. Fuzzy geographic object. (a) Different membership grades. (b) The egg-yolk representation.

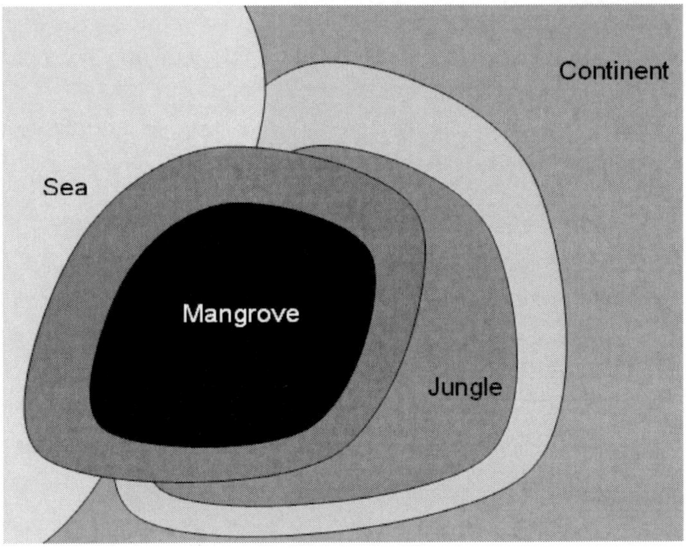

Figure 7. Fuzzy geographic features.

3. Spatial and Geographic Relations

Spatial relations describe relations concerning mathematical objects in space (Laurini-Milleret-Raffort, 1989). But before examining these relations, let us details some aspects of spatial operations.

3.1. Spatial Operations

There are a lot of spatial or geometric operations which can be used in geoprocessing. Only a few will be examined in this text, i.e., minimum bounding rectangles, centroids and buffer zones. Remember that some spatial operations include sophisticated computational geometry algorithms. For more details, refer to (Preparata-Shamos, 1985).

3.1.1. Minimum Bounding Rectangle

For several more sophisticated operations, it is interesting to determine the smaller rectangle encompassing an area, for instance a polygon, which sides are parallel to the coordinate axes. In the list of polygon coordinates, we extract easily x_{min}, x_{max}, y_{min} and y_{max}. Figure 8a shows a polygon *A*, and Figure 8b its minimum bounding rectangle (MBR). But in reality, due to the rotundity of the Earth, the minimum/maximum longitude and latitudes, instead of lines, this MBR is limited by parts of ellipsoids (Figure 8c). Let us encode it `Mbr(A)`.

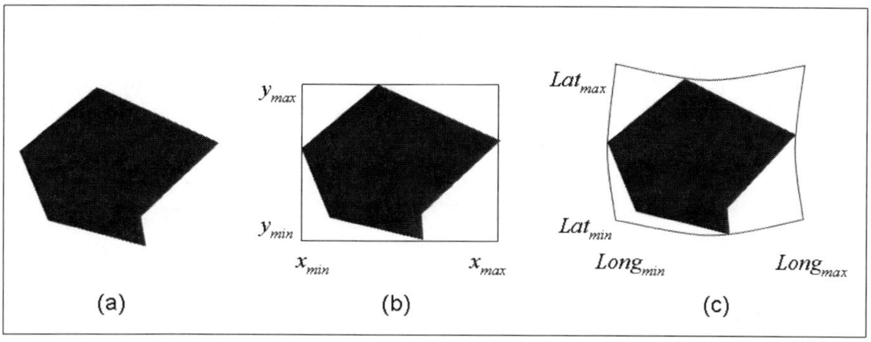

Figure 8. Minimum bounding rectangle. (a) initial polygon. (b) its MBR. (c) an MBR taking Earth rotundity into account.

3.1.2. Centroid

Sometimes, it is interesting to exhibit a point representing an area: let us call it a centroid located in the center of the area. Centroids can be loosely defined as a point in the center of an area. But mathematically several possibilities (Laurini-Thompson, 1992) can be used to define a centroid, for instance (Figure 9):

- the barycenter of vertices (Figure 9a),
- the center of gravity (Figure 9b),
- the center of the minimum bounding rectangle (Figure 9c).

Usually the last one is used because it is the easier to calculate. Let us encode it `Center(A)`. When the polygon is not connected, the center of the MBR of the bigger component is taken; for instance, for the US, only the MBR of the conterminous States is usually used.

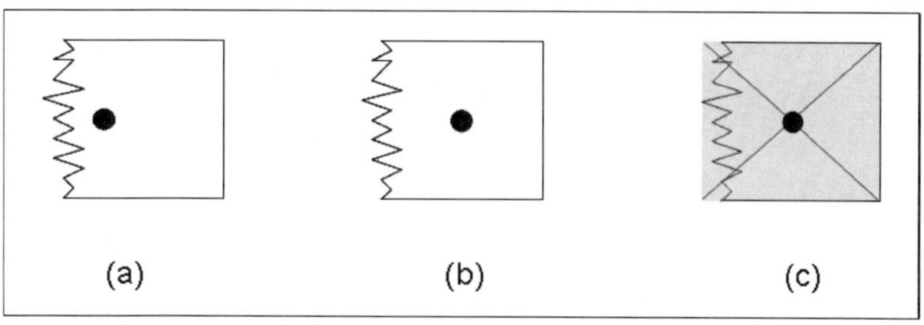

Figure 9. Several definition of a centroid. (a) as barycenter of coordinates. (b) as center of gravity. (c) as center of the minimum bounding rectangle.

3.1.3. Buffer Zones

When one wants to get the number of people living less than 10 km from the borders of a country, he must define a buffer zone. More generally when considering a polygon (Figure 10a) and a distance *d*, two buffer zones can be defined, an inner buffer zone (Figure 10b) and an outer buffer zone (Figure 10c). LET us encode it `Buffer(A,d)` in which when *d* is positive, this is an outer zone and when *d* is negative an inner buffer zone.

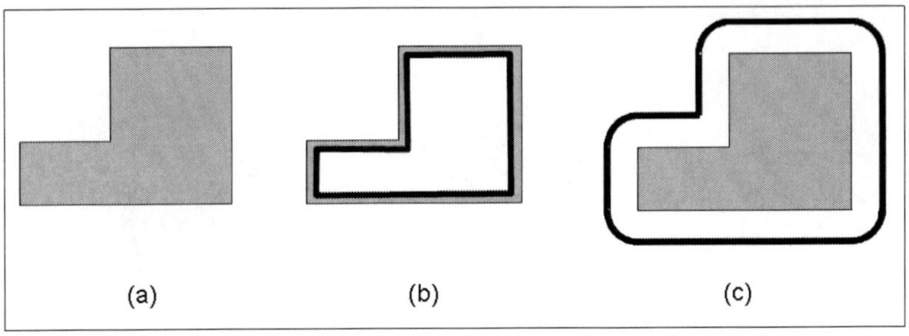

Figure 10. Several definition of a centroid. (a) As barycenter of coordinates. (b) As center of gravity. (c) As center of the minimum bounding rectangle.

3.2. Spatial Relations

First, let me say that spatial relations are hidden in coordinates. In this section, among planar spatial relations, topological and projective relations will be examined. Then, some considerations regarding tessellations will be given.

3.2.1. Topological Relations

Topological relations such as at 1D, interval relations (Allen 1983) (Figure 11) and at 2D Egenhofer relations (Egenhofer, 1991, 1994])[2] are well known (Figure 12).

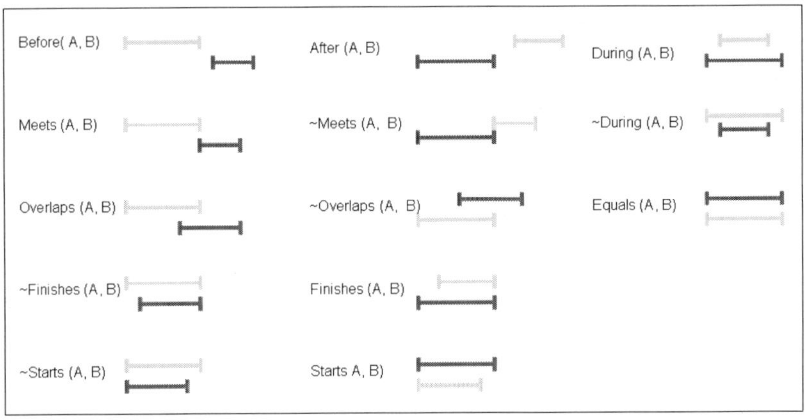

Figure 11. Topological relations at 1D (Allen 1983).

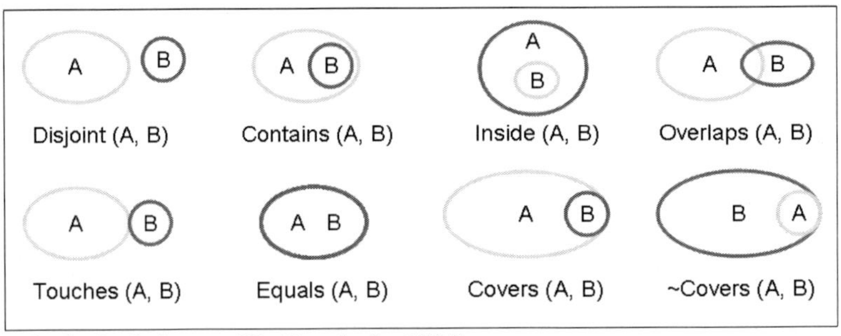

Figure 12. Topological relations at 2D (Egenhofer 1994).

[2] Instead of "TOUCHES", sometimes "MEETS" is used.

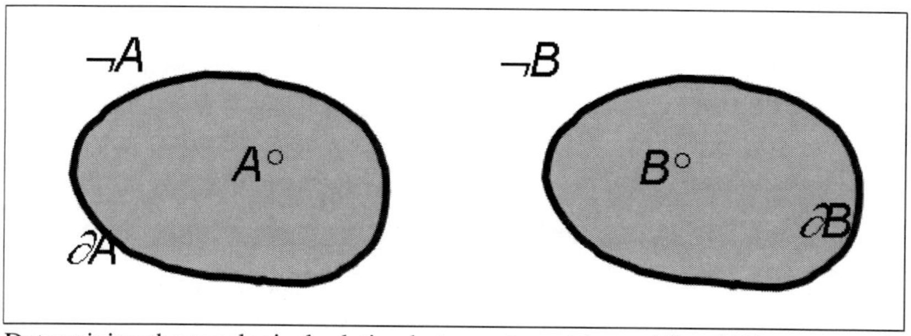

Figure 13. Determining the topological relation between two objects. A° and B° represent the inner parts, ∂A and ∂B the boundaries and ¬A and ¬B the outer parts.

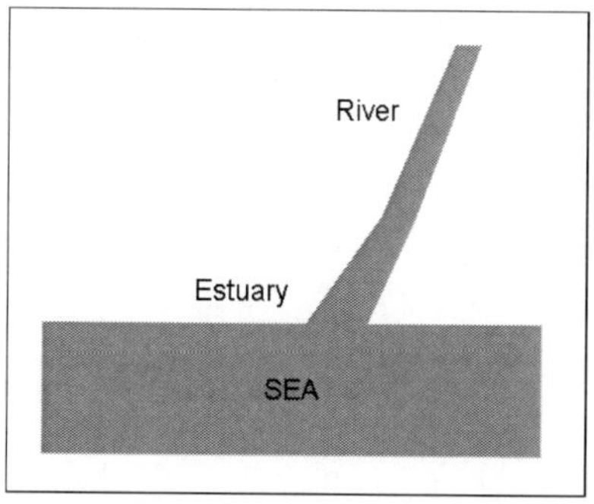

Figure 14. There is a TOUCHES topological relation between river and sea, corresponding to the estuary.

To determine the topological relation between two areas, one solution (Egenhofer et al. 1992, Clementini et al. 1993) is to compute the so-called 9 intersections. Considering a polygon, let us note $A°$ the inner part, ¬A the outer part and ∂A its boundary (Figure 13). The answer is given by the following matrix in which the result of one intersection can be void ∅ or not void ¬∅.

$$R(A,B) = \begin{pmatrix} A° \cap B° & A° \cap \partial B & A° \cap \neg B° \\ \partial A \cap B° & \partial A \cap \partial B & \partial A \cap \neg B \\ \neg A \cap B° & \neg A \cap \partial B & \neg A \cap \neg B \end{pmatrix}$$

For instance for TOUCHES, the result is as follows:

$$TOUCHES(A,B) = \begin{pmatrix} \varnothing & \varnothing & \neg\varnothing \\ \varnothing & \neg\varnothing & \neg\varnothing \\ \neg\varnothing & \neg\varnothing & \neg\varnothing \end{pmatrix}$$

Clementini et al. (1993) have developed this matrix by integrating the dimensions of the intersections (0D, 1D or 2D).

With such topological relations, one can easily define relations for geographic features. For instance Figure 14 presents a TOUCHES relation between a river and the sea.

Another model for topological relations has been proposed independently in 1992, by Randell, Cui and Cohn (1992) which allowed qualitative spatial representation and consistent reasoning. This logic received the name of "Region Connection Calculus" (RCC); this acronym is also the first letter of authors' names. This model is equivalent to the Egenhofer model. The 8 relations have different names: DC (is disconnected from), EC (is externally connected with), PO (partially overlaps), TPP (is a tangential proper part of), NTPP (is a nontangential proper part of), TPPi (inverse of TPP), NTPPi (inverse of NTPP) and EQUAL.

Anyway, these topological relations can be organized in a graph showing the vicinity of all relations (Figure 15).

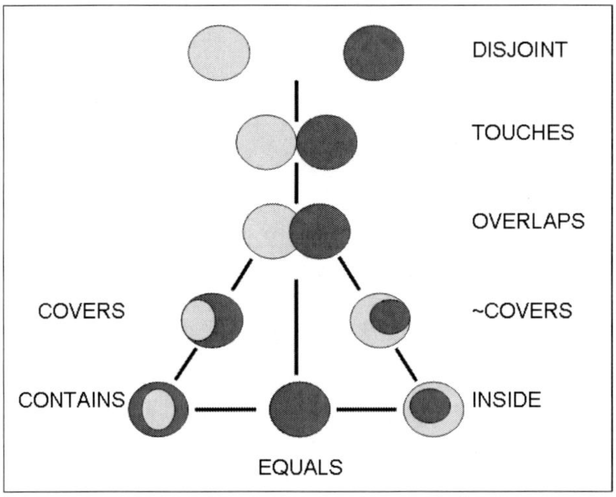

Figure 15. Vicinity of topological relations.

3.2.2. Projective and Other Spatial Relations

But other relations exist such as projective (or cardinal such as North/South, East/west) relations and distance (near/far) relations (Figure 16).

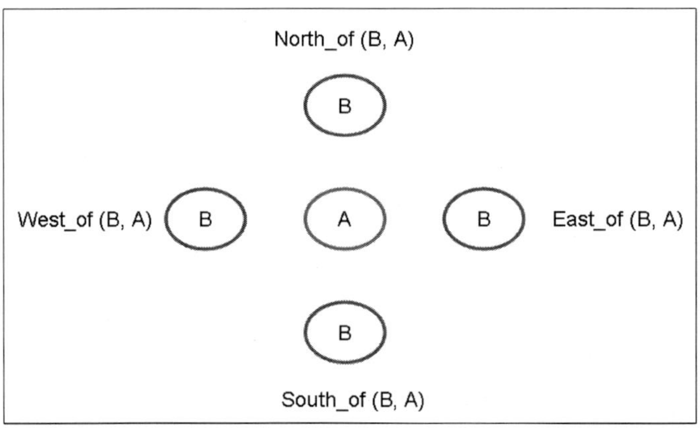

Figure 16. Projective and distance relations.

3.2.3. About Tessellations

By irregular tessellation (or tessellation), one means the total coverage of an area by subareas. For instance the conterminous States in the USA form a tessellation to cover the whole country. Generally speaking, administrative subdivisions form tessellations, sometimes organized as hierarchical tessellations. Let us consider a domain *D* and several polygons P_i; they form a tessellation iff (See Figure 17a):

- For any point p_k, if p_k belongs to *D* then there exists P_j, so that p_k belongs to P_j
- For any p_k belonging to P_j, then p_k belongs to *D*.

A tessellation can be also described by Egenhofer relations applied to P_i and *D*, but in practical cases, due to measurement errors, this definition must be relaxed in order to include sliver polygons (Figure 17b).

Those errors are often very small, sometimes a few centimeters at scale 1. In other words, one has a tessellation from an administrative point of view, but not from a mathematical point of view. Let's call them "loose tessellation".

But the Earth is not a plane and all relations must be revisited taken rotundity into account.

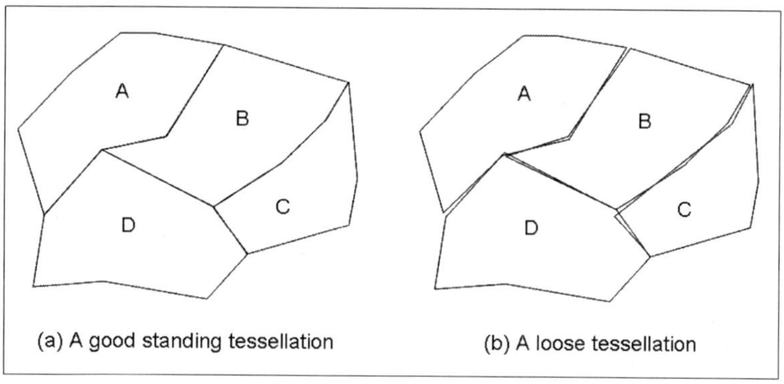

Figure 17. A tessellation with sliver polygons and a good standing tessellation.

3.3. Characteristics of Spherical Spatial Relations

As example, let us consider the relation "North_of" and transitivity.

```
North_of ("Philadelphia", "Boston")
North_of ("Boston", "Montreal") }
=> North_of ("Philadelphia", "Montreal")
```

But for "`East_of`", this is different. Let is first consider the following:

```
East_of ("Philadelphia", "Paris")
East_of ("Paris", "Berlin")      }
=> East_of ("Philadelphia", "Berlin")
```

But for other cases, transitivity is not true:

```
East_of ("Paris", "Beijing")
East_of ("Beijing", "Philadelphia")   }
=> East_of ("Paris", "Philadelphia") // false
```

But:

```
East_of ("Philadelphia", "Paris") // true
```

3.3.1. East_of and West_of Relations

Indeed, the real rule must integrate longitudes: when the transitivity leads to cover more than 180°, this is the converse.

```
East_of (L1, L3) = East_of (L1, L2) => East_of (L2, L3) ∧
((L3.longitude - L1.longitude) < 180°)
East_of (L3, L1) = East_of (L1, L2) =>East_of (L2, L3) ∧
((L3.longitude - L1.longitude) > 180°)
```

A similar transitivity rule can be written for `West_of`.

3.3.2. South_of and North_of Relations

There are no restrictions for transitivity. However, if one says "what is north of North Pole?"

The answer is void; and moreover when one is at the North Pole, all directions are going south! But there is always an easternmost feature for any feature.

3.3.3. Projective Relations and Areas

Projective relations are easy to define for points but it is more complex for areas. Do not forget that areas can be not connected such as countries with several islands.

Moreover some countries can have holes such as Italy with Vatican City and San Marino. Some are constituted of pieces of territory which are very far from the main component: for instance France with Martinique, Guyana, New Caledonia, etc.

Let's consider Canada, the conterminous states of USA (USA for short) and Mexico. As it is easy to claim that Mexico is south of Canada, what is the exact projective relation between USA-Mexico and Canada-Mexico? It is common to claim that "Canada is north of the conterminous states of the USA", but Canadian cities such Ottawa or Toronto are south of Seattle. A solution is to consider centroids of those areas. So but taking this definition, we can claim:

```
North_of ("Canada","USA")

North_of ("USA","Mexico").
```

Moreover, one can claim the `East ("Mexico","USA")`. But is Canada east or west of the USA? By using both centroids, there is an answer, but this answer is not totally convincing.

3.4. Spatial Relations in Urban Space

Considering a city and spatial relations between urban objects, we can make the assumption that the conventional 3D Cartesian approach is still valid. Moreover considering again streets, some observations can be made.

- they are one-way streets and sometimes two-way streets can have several lanes;
- some objects are positioned on the street (pedestrian zebras), some under such as sewerages, and some above such as traffic lights;
- some concrete concepts such as sidewalks, medians, crossroads, T-junction, runabout, road signs, curves, engineering network can be defined with the "*has_a*" semantic relation, but their "topological semantics " are stronger;
- some objects such as engineering networks can be under streets or under sidewalks;
- as previously told, for some actors, streets are defined by the lines with parcels whereas for others the streets are reduced to the asphalted part (Figure 1).

So those observations imply that Allen or Egenhofer relations are not sufficient to describe relationships between street objects. So, the question is "what could be the minimum set of useful relations?"

3.4.1. Binary Other Topological Relations

```
On (street, pedestrian_zebra)
Under (street, sewerage)
Above (street, traffic_light)
Along (sidewalk, street)
On (sewerage_grid, street).
```

3.4.2. Relations Between Urban Features and Places

```
Host (barrack, army)
Host (hospital, health_activity) .
```

3.5. Ribbon Relations

As previously told, ribbons derived from longish rectangles. So the relations between areas can be applied to ribbons. But due to their particular shapes, other interesting relations between ribbons can be detailed. First let us examine basic operations and some new relations.

3.5.1. Operations

Two operations can be defined. Considering that any ribbon can be decomposed into sub-ribbons, either longitudinally or laterally, we can define two operations, longitudinal splitting and lateral splitting (Figure 18). Of course, those operators can be recursively used.

For longitudinal splitting, one has $w1=w2=w$ and $l1+l2=l$, whereas for lateral splitting $w3+w4=w$ and $l3=l4=l$.

In order to solve the problem, Lee and Hsu (1990, 1992) proposed a table representing all spatial relations between two rectangles. They found a total of 169 types in which they number: 48 disjoint, 40 joint, 50 partial overlaps, 16 contains and 16 belongs (= inside). In our cases, disjoint, partial overlap, contains and belongs relations can be considered as outside our goal. More, due to the semantics of ribbon, a lot of them can be discarded. This is not sufficient. Suppose a road which alternates between simple and dual carriageways. In this case, we need to consider three ribbons, corresponding to dividing and merging. Finally, Figure 19 gives the more interesting ribbon relation, namely Side-by-Side, Edge-to-edge, and merging rectangular ribbons, ribbons and loose ribbons. Similarly, other relations can be defined, for instance crossing, T-junctions, etc.

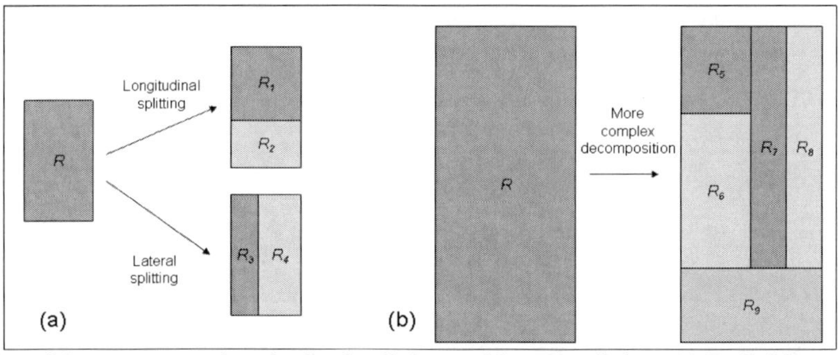

Figure 18. Two ribbon operators, longitudinal splitting and lateral splitting. (a) Definitions. (b) A more complex decomposition.

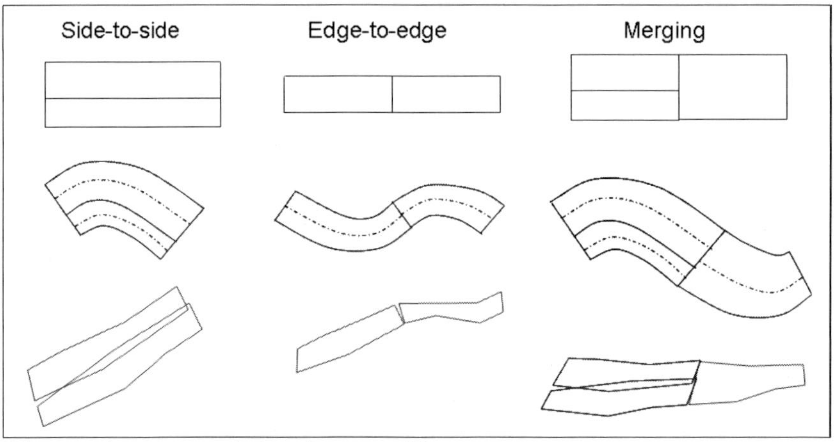

Figure 19. The more interesting relations between ribbons.

For instance, in transportation and along rivers, the following relations can hold:

```
Side-By-Side (Platform,Railways)
Side-By-Side (Bus_stop, Bus_lane)
Side-By-Side (Levee, River)
Side-By-Side (Towpath, River).
```

Initially towpaths along rivers were made for horse-drawn boats; but more and more they are replaced by bike lanes.

3.5.2. Orientation

Since one-way or two-way streets exist, orientation can be defined whereas for some cases of ribbons orientation is not valid. For instance, in a conventional street, the decomposition into ribbons is as in Figure 20.

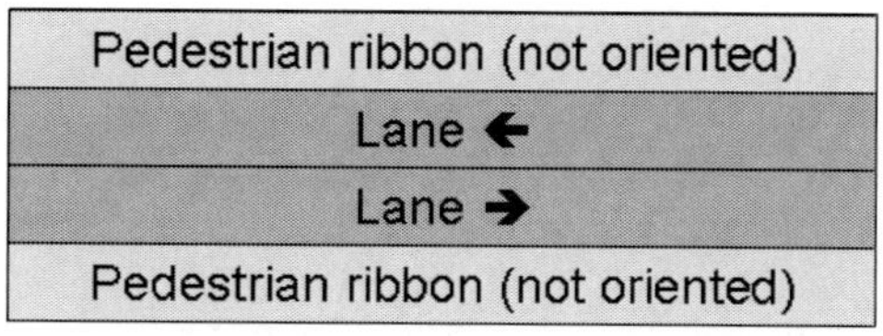

Figure 20. Ribbon orientation.

3.5.3. Chaining Ribbons

To model roads and rivers, usually polylines are used to describe the axis; but sometimes two polylines can be used to model river banks or the limits of the road.

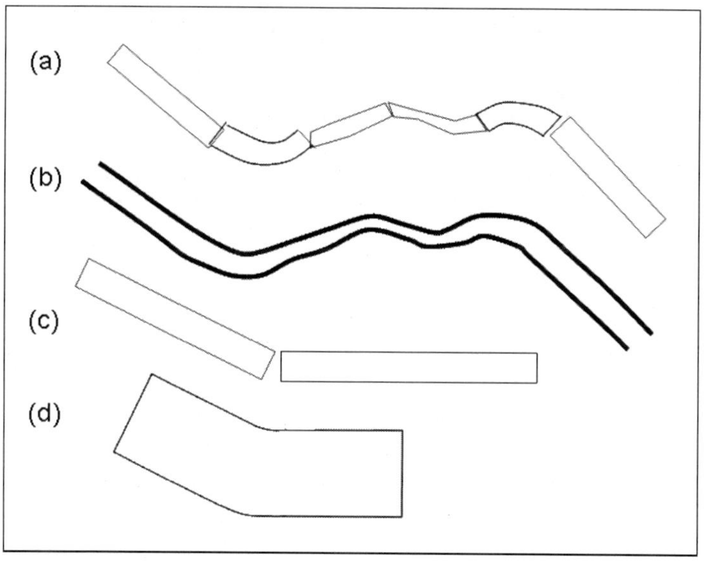

Figure 21. Chaining ribbons. (a) An example of different ribbons. (b) Chain of ribbons. (c) A case of two rectangular ribbons. (d) Additional curves to join the sides.

As a consequence those feature representations can be transformed into ribbons with different widths. For several other reasons, one can have a set of different ribbons that must be concatenated to form a chain of ribbons. Figure 21 gives an example (Figure 21a) of several ribbons transformed into a chain of ribbons (Figure 21b). In Figure 21c, a case is presented needing two additional curves to join the sides of two ribbons

3.6. Mutation of Topological Relations According to the Granularity of Interest

But according to the granularity of interest, topological relations can vary. For instance, it is common to claim that a road is going along the sea, so implying a TOUCHES relation between the road and the sea. But if we consider carefully, sometimes there are small beaches between the road and the sea (Figure 22).

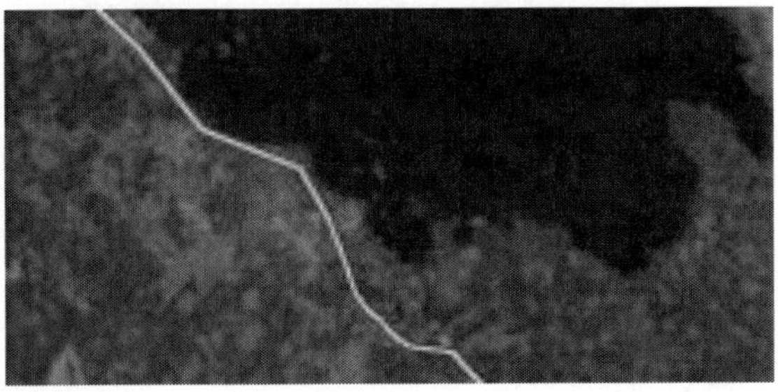

(a)

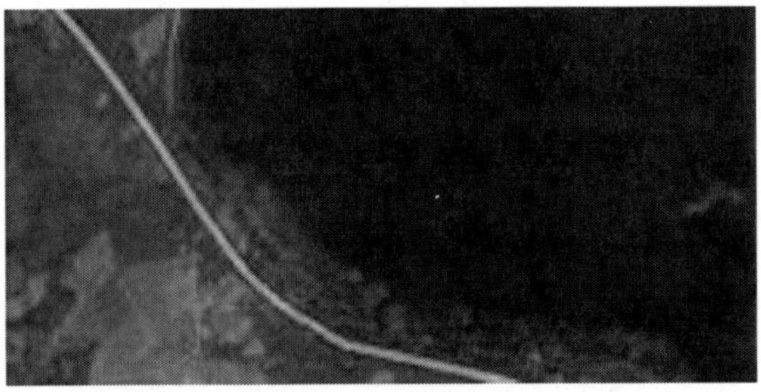

(b)

Figure 22. According to scale, the road TOUCHes or not the sea.

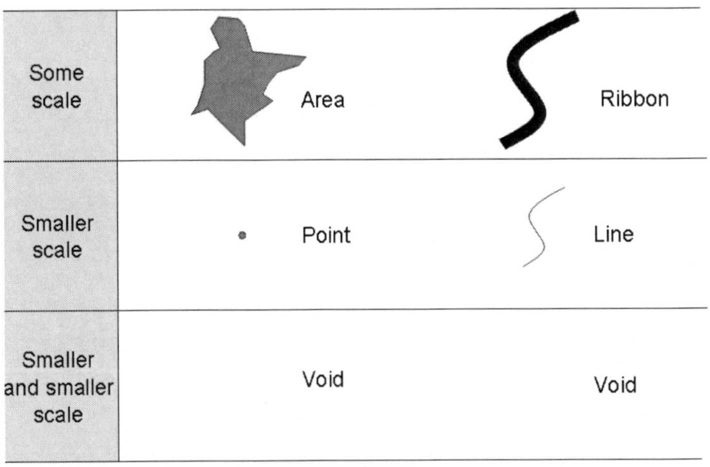

Figure 23. Mutation of geographic object representations.

From a cartographic point of view, the type of relation will vary: indeed at a scale of 1:1000, the relation is DISJOINT whereas at 1:100000, there is a TOUCHES.

More generally, the concept of granularity of interest will enlarge the concept of scale: it is clear that the interest for the same zone from a local politician and a nation-wide politician can be different.

So according to the granularity of interest, geographic objects can mutate according to two rules (see examples Figure 23). As scale diminishes, an area will mutate into a point and then will disappear and a ribbon will mutate into a line and then will disappear.

In the sequel to simplify the presentation, we will continue to use the thresholds for visual acuity instead of granularity of interest.

3.6.1. General Process

So, the complete process can be modeled as follows:

Step 0: original geographic features,

Step 1: as scale diminishes, small areas and ribbons will be generalized and possibly can coalesce,

Step 2: as scale continues to diminish, areas mutate into points and ribbons into lines,

Step 3: as scale continues to diminish, points and lines disappear.

Let us call this process "generalization-reduction-disappearance" (GRD process).

3.6.2. Visual Acuity Applied to Geographic Objects

It is well known that "Cartographic representation is linked to visual acuity". Thresholds must be defined. In classical cartography, the limit ranges from 1 mm to 0.1 mm. If one takes a road and a certain scale and if the transformation gives a width more that 1 mm, this road is an area, between 1 mm and 0.1mm, then a line and if less that 0.1mm the road disappears. The same reasoning is valid for cities or small countries such as Andorra, Liechtenstein, Monaco, etc. In these cases, the "holes" or small islands in Italy or in France disappear cartographically. With the thresholds ε_i, ε_{lp} previously defined, we can formally get (in which *2Dmap* is a function transforming a geographic object to some other scale possibly with generalization) the following:

a/ Disappearance of a geographic object (O) at scale σ:

$\forall O \in GeObject,\ \forall \sigma \in Scale \wedge O_\sigma = 2Dmap(O, \sigma) \wedge Area\ (O_\sigma) < (\varepsilon_{lp})^2 => O_\sigma = \varnothing.$

b/ Transformation of an area into a point (for instance the centroid of the concerned object, for instance taken as the center of the minimum bounding rectangle):

$\forall O \in GeObject,\ \forall \sigma \in Scale \wedge O_\sigma = 2Dmap(O, \sigma) \wedge\ (\varepsilon_i)^2 > Area\ (\ O_\sigma) > \ (\varepsilon_{lp})$

$\Rightarrow O_\sigma = Centroid(O).$

c/ Transformation of a ribbon *R* into a line (for instance its axis):

$\forall R \in Ribbon,\ \forall \sigma \in Scale \wedge R_\sigma = 2Dmap(R, \sigma) \wedge\ \varepsilon_i > Width(\ R_\sigma) > \varepsilon_{lp}$

$\Rightarrow R_\sigma = Axis(R).$

Therefore, one can say that any spatial relation varies according to scale. As previously told, one says that a road runs along a sea; but in reality, in some place, the road does not run really along the water of the sea due to beaches, buildings, etc. As previously said, at one scale, the road TOUCHES the sea, but at another scale at some places, this is a DISJOINT relation. Let consider two geographic objects O^1 and O^2 and $O_\sigma{}^1$ and $O_\sigma{}^2$ their cartographic representations, for instance the following assertion holds:

$\forall O^1, O^2 \in GeObject, \forall \sigma \in Scale \wedge O_\sigma{}^1{=}2Dmap(O^1, \sigma) \wedge O_\sigma{}^2{=}2Dmap(O^2, \sigma) \wedge Disjoint (O^1, O^2) \wedge Dist(O^1, O^2) < \varepsilon_2 \Rightarrow Touches(O_\sigma{}^1, O_\sigma{}^2).$

Similar assertions could be written when CONTAINS, OVERLAP relationships. In addition, two objects in the real world with a TOUCHES relation can coalesce into a single one.

As a consequence, in reasoning, what is true at one scale can be wrong at another scale. So, any automatic system must be robust enough to deal with this issue.

3.6.3. Example of Topological Mutation Due to Granularity of Interest: DISJOINT to TOUCHES

In this section, the Egenhofer's relations (Egenhofer, 1991) are treated mainly after the generalization, the object geometries are adapted to the perceptual limits imposed by the new (smaller) scale (Laurini, 2014). As example, let us analyze the "DISJOINT" relation which can mutate into the "TOUCHES" relation according the thresholds previously defined, the following assertion must apply (Figure 24):

$\forall O^1, O^2 \in GeObject \wedge \forall \sigma \in Scale \wedge O_\sigma{}^1{=}2Dmap(O^1) \wedge O_\sigma{}^2{=}2Dmap(O^2) \wedge Disjoint (O^1, O^2) \wedge Dist (O^1, O^2) < \varepsilon_2 \Rightarrow Meet (O_\sigma{}^1, O_\sigma{}^2).$

But a smaller object can disappear or be eliminated if its area is too small to be well visible. So in this case, the initial relation does not hold anymore.

$\forall O \in GeObject, \forall \sigma \in Scale \wedge O_\sigma = 2Dmap(O, \sigma) \wedge Area (O_\sigma) < (\varepsilon_1)^2 \Rightarrow O_\sigma = \varnothing.$

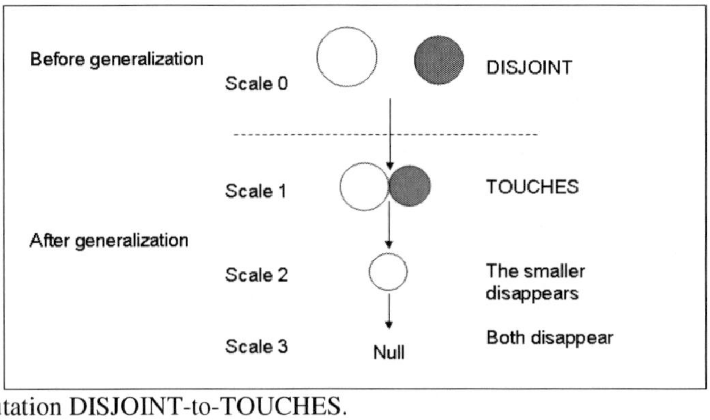

Figure 24. The mutation DISJOINT-to-TOUCHES.

4. Fundamentals of Geographic Knowledge

In addition to the importance of geometry and topology, geographic knowledge is also concerned by two types of structures, gazetteers and ontologies.

As ontologies are frequently used in artificial intelligence, in addition to conventional relations, they need to integrate spatial relations. But a second structure named gazetteer is concerned by place names, their organization and their location: indeed, several places can have the same names and several names can be assigned to places.

But geographic knowledge is linked to cartography and visualization. From several years new types of cartography are emerging under the general umbrella of geovisualization, especially with chorems. Let us examine those issues in details.

4.1. Geographic Ontologies

In general, an ontology specifies a vocabulary of concepts together with some indication of their meanings (Gruber 1993, Guarino 1998). As discussed in Smith and Mark (2003), the term 'ontology' is used nowadays by information scientists, in a non-philosophical sense to assist in the task of specifying and clarifying the concepts employed in given domains, above all by formalizing them within the framework of some formal theory with a well-understood logical (syntactic and semantic) structure. From a computational point of view, an ontology can be seen as a network of concepts linked essentially by the following relations:

- "*is a*" (females and males are subtypes or subclasses of human being),
- "*has a*" (a paper has one or several authors),
- "*part of*" (a finger is a part of a hand).

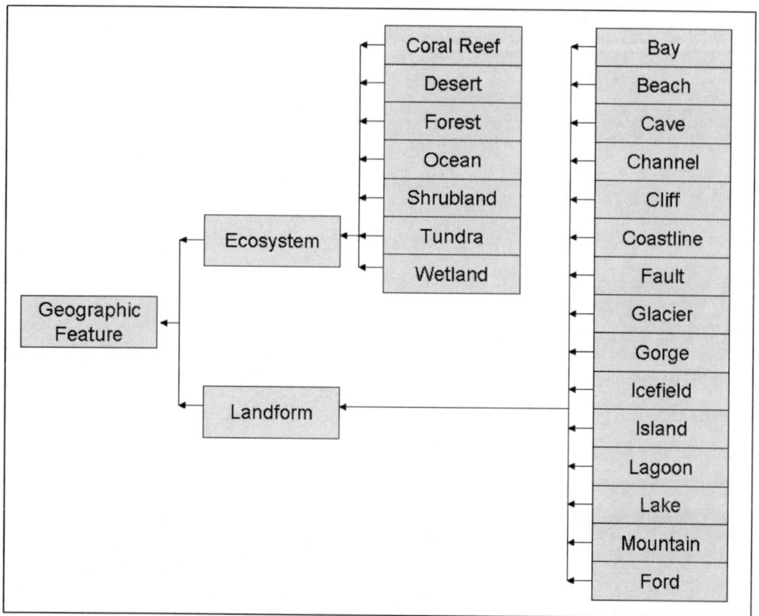

Figure 25. Example of the beginning of a geographic ontology only with *is-a* relations.

However, the specificity of geographic ontology does not lie only on geographic features (as illustrated in Figure 25) (Kavouras et al. (2005). But it lies overall on their geometry and on their spatial relationships (Laurini, 2012). Usually Egenhofer or RCC relations are fully integrated in the definitions of geographic features. See Figures 26 and 27 for such examples, the first for the planet, and the second for administrative subdivisions of a country.

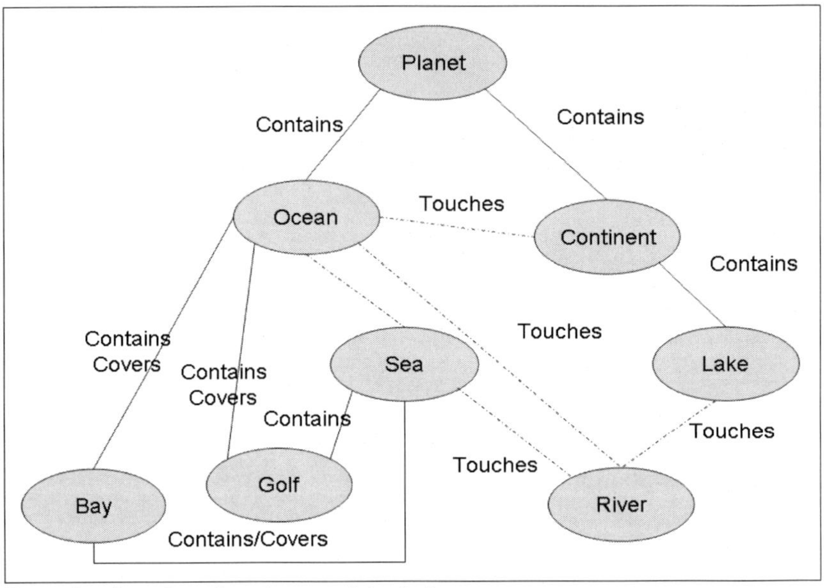

Figure 26. Example of ontology based on spatial relations.

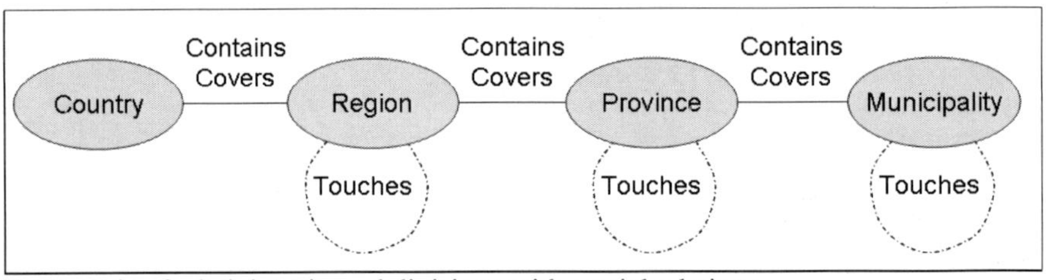

Figure 27. Example of administrative subdivisions with spatial relations.

4.2. About Geographic Names and Gazetteers

By definition, a gazetteer is a geographic dictionary or directory (Goodchild and Hill (2008), Keßler et al. 2009). But now, more and more gazetteers become complex databases. Since they more and more include other attributes of the named features, they tend to become some toponym ontologies (Smart et al., 2010, Hećimović et al., 2013, Laurini, 2015).

4.2.1. What under a Name?

Under a geographic name, various objects or features can exist. In the Earth, few points have names, maybe only the North and South Poles, and only a few lines such as Equator, Tropic of Cancer, Tropic of Capricorn, Greenwich Meridian, Polar Circle, etc. The majority of names are given to areas since even rivers are areas or maybe modeled as ribbons. As previously told, they must be considered as non-connected (with islands and holes) and they can be replaced by their centroids for some operations.

4.2.2. Generalities

Indeed, in addition to a pure list of placenames or toponyms, it is necessary to locate them with accuracy and to assign them some features or geographic objects. Moreover, a place can have different names in different languages and different periods of times. Let us first examine of few well-known examples:

- "Mississippi" can be the name of a river or of a state,
- The city is "Venice", Italy, is also known as "Venezia", "Venise", "Venedig" respectively in Italian, French and German.
- The local name of the Greek city of "Athens" is "Αθήνα" read [a'θina].
- "Istanbul" was known as "Byzantium" and "Constantinople" in the past.
- The today city of "Rome" is much bigger than in Romulus time.
- There are two Georgias, one in the United States and another one in Caucasia.
- The toponym "Milano" can correspond to the city of Milano or the province of Milano.
- Some cities have specific characteristics such as capital of a state; a river can have an estuary in a sea.
- The river "Danube" crosses several European countries; practically in each country it has a different name, "Donau" in Germany and Austria, "Dunaj" in Slovakia, "Duna" in Hungary), "Dunav" in Croatia and Serbia, "Dunav" and "Дунав" in Bulgaria, "Dunărea" in Romania and in Moldova, "Dunaj",and Дунай" in Ukraine. It is also called "Danubio" in Italian and Spanish, "Tonava" in Finnish and "Δούναβης" in Greek. Moreover, its name in feminine in German, and masculine in some other languages.
- Sometimes, names of places can be also names of something else; for instance "Washington" can also refer to George Washington or anybody with this firstname or lastname.
- Some placenames are formed of two or several words; for instance, "New Orleans", "Los Angeles", "Antigua and Barbuda", "Trinidad and Tobago", "Great Britain", "Northern Ireland", "Tierra del Fuego", "El Puente de Alcántara", etc.
- Some very long names can have simplification; the well-known Welsh town "Llanfairpwllgwyngyllgogerychwyrndrobwllllantysiliogogogoch" is often simplified into "Llanfair PG" or "Llanfairpwll".
- Some abbreviations can be common such as "L.A." for "Los Angeles".
- Peking became Beijing after a change of transcription to Roman alphabet; but the capital of China has not modified its name in Chinese.
- In some languages, grammatical gender is important so that placenames can be feminine or masculine; for instance in French, Italian and Spanish, names such as "Japan", "Brazil", "Portugal" are masculine whereas "Argentina", "Bolivia" and "Tunisia" are feminine; in addition as the great majority of toponyms is singular, some can be plural like "The Netherlands", "The Alps".

As consequence, there is a very complex many-to-many relationships between places and placenames (Figure 28).

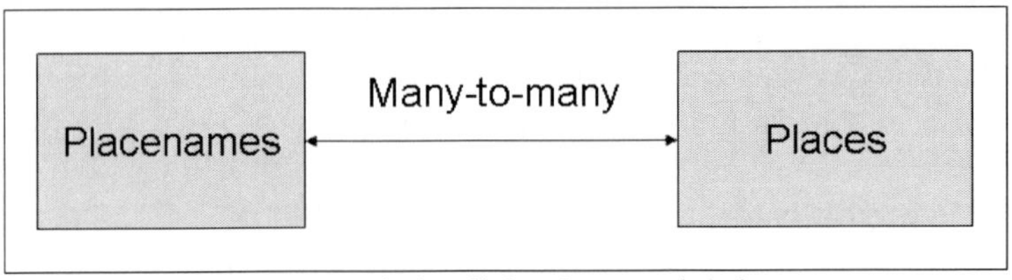

Figure 28. Very complex many-to-many relation links places and their names.

Among place names they are street names together with the number in the street (civic number); they are not so easy to handle. This is very important, not only for the automatic processing of postal addresses, but also for all applications connecting to emergency. The URISA association has organized many conferences on the topics (See www.urisa.org). The specificities of street names are as follows:

- some streets can have a few dozens of yards whereas other several miles;
- in some human settlements, streets have no names;
- sometimes there are variations about the way to write some street names; for instance "3rd Street", "Third Street", "Third St"; the words "avenues" and "boulevards" are simplified into "Ave", or "Blvd" or "Bd";
- in some countries, the equivalent of the words "street", "avenue", etc. are usually removed;
- in some places, streets can have several names; for instance in New York City, "Sixth Avenue" is also known as "Avenue of the Americas";
- etc.

As a main consequence, the name of a place cannot be a unique ID from a computing point of view.

In order to clarify, let us give a few definitions:

- *toponym* is the general name of a geographic feature or object;
- *endonym* is a local name in the official language of the country; there may be several toponyms in countries with different official languages (Brussel in Flemish, Bruxelles in French);
- *exonym* is a name in other languages than the official languages; for instance Brussels in English;
- *archeonym* is a name which existed in the past: for instance Byzantium for Istanbul;
- *hyperonym* and *hyponym:* names of places with subordination; hyponym is the opposite of hyperonym; for instance Europe is a hyperonym of France whereas France is a hyponym of Europe;
- *mereonym* is a name of a part of place without subordination; "Adriatic Sea" corresponds to a mereonym of the Mediterranean Sea;
- *hydronym* is a name of a waterbody; it can be also used for seas;
- *oronym* is a name for a hill or a mountain.

Figure 29 gives the essential elements of a gazetteer, the names, the features, the dates and everything regarding geometry and georeferencing according to Jakir et al. (2011).

To conclude this section, in an automatic system for searching geographic information in the web (known as GIR, Geographic Information Retrieval), a preliminary phase of disambiguation is necessary since the name can correspond to something which is not geographic.

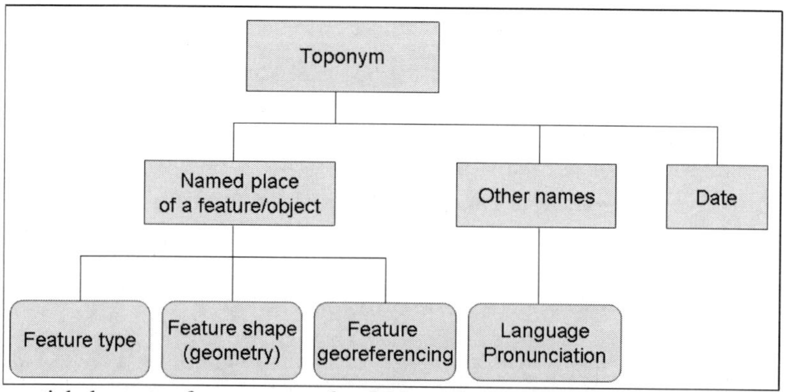

Figure 29. Essential elements of a toponym, after Jakir et al. (2011).

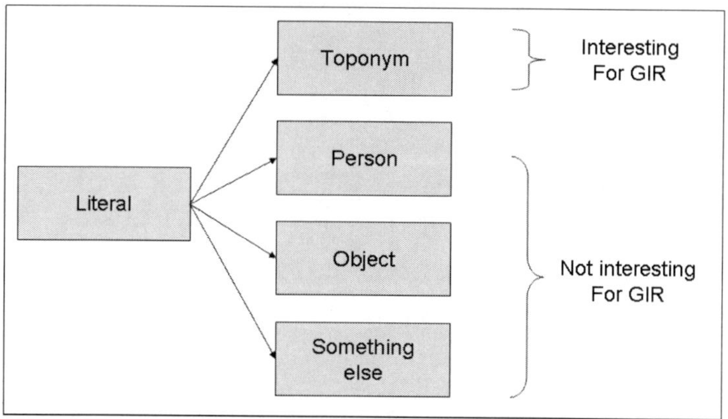

Figure 30. Disambiguation of literal to extract toponyms.

Let us define as a literal a string of characters (perhaps including blank spaces and hyphens): this literal may be a toponym, the name of a person (Washington) or something else (China and porcelain) (Figure 30).

4.2.3. Examples

Generally speaking, a gazetteer is designed for a specific activity, for instance to help post offices, to assist the history of a region. As a consequence, several gazetteers can have different structures. Let us examine a few examples.

4.2.3.1. Gazetteer as an Index for a Map (Street Directory)

The starting point is a map of a certain region with a precise objective and scale with a visual vocabulary presented in the legend. In this case, the map is usually split into a crossword-like grid in which squares are located by letters and numbers. For instance "River Street" goes from B3 to C7. The directory can have the following forms.

```
Location1 (street-name, beginning-location, ending-location)
```

In addition, an alternative could be with street-names with the names of the other streets which are the beginning and at the end.

```
Location2 (street-name, beginning-street-name, ending-street-
   name)
```

4.2.3.2. Gazetteer for a Local Post-Office

For the post-office, the gazetteer can have the previous forms, but in addition it can also include several important monuments, administrations, enterprises which can be stored:

```
Urban-feature (name, street-address)
```

4.2.3.3. Gazetteer for Hydrology

Here, there are only names of rivers, lakes, seas, etc. Important relations are for tributaries and possible estuaries with sea.

```
Hydronym (id, onto-type, geometry)
Endonym (id, hydronym)
Exonym (id, language, hydronym)
Tributary (id1, id2, location)
Estuary (id1, id2, location)
Mereonym (id1, id2)
```

4.2.3.4. Gazetteer for the History of a Place

Here, we essentially deal with ancient names. Anyway, let us start with the actual toponyms.

```
Placename (id, onto-type, geometry, beginning-date)
Archeonym (id, language, toponym, geometry, beginning-date,
ending-date)
Exonym (id, language, toponym) .
```

4.2.3.5. Gazetteer Covering Several Actual Countries, for Instance Europe

```
Placename (id, onto-type, geometry, beginning-date)
Exonym (id, language, toponym)
Hydronym (id, onto-type, geometry)
Endonym (id, hydronym)
Exonym (id, language, hydronym)
Mereonym (id1, id2).
```

4.3. Existing Systems

Concerning ontologies and gazetteers, several systems exist. Let us rapidly present two of them, GeoNames and GeoSPARQL.

4.3.1. GeoNames (http://www.geonames.org)

The GeoNames database contains over 10,000,000 geographical names corresponding to over 7,500,000 unique features. All features are categorized into one out of nine feature classes and further subcategorized into one out of 645 feature codes. Beyond names of places in various languages, data stored include latitude, longitude, elevation, population, administrative subdivisions and postal codes. Among spatial relationships in use in GeoNames, let us mention:

- `Children`, i.e., the list of administrative divisions (first relative sublevel);
- `Hierarchy`, i.e., the list of toponyms higher up in the hierarchy of a place name;
- `Neighbours`, i.e., the list of all for a country or administrative division;
- `Contains`, i.e., the list of all features within the feature;
- `Siblings`, i.e., the list of all siblings of a toponym at same level.

For instance, here is an excerpt of the description of Sicily:

```
<geoname>
   <toponymName>Sicilia</toponymName>
   <name>Sicily</name>
   <lat>37.75</lat><lng>14.25</lng>
   <geonameId>2523119</geonameId>
   <countryCode>IT</countryCode>
   <countryName>Italy</countryName>
   <numberOfChildren>9</numberOfChildren>
</geoname>
```

4.3.2. GeoSPARQL (http://geosparql.org/)

GeoSPARQL is a standard for representation and querying geospatially linked data for the Semantic Web from the Open Geospatial Consortium (OGC). It can be seen as an extension of SPARQL. The definition of a small ontology based on well-understood OGC standards is intended to provide a standardized exchange basis for geospatial RDF data which can support both quantitative and qualitative spatial reasoning and querying with the SPARQL (http://www.w3.org/2009/sparql/wiki/Main_Page) database query language.

But with SPARQL, some simple geographic queries, i.e., without geometric information and spatial relationships, can be launched. For instance: "What are all the country capitals in Africa?"

```
PREFIX abc: <http://example.com/exampleOntology#>
SELECT ?capital ?country
WHERE {
```

```
?x abc:cityname ?capital ;
abc:isCapitalOf ?y .
?y abc:countryname ?country ;
abc:isInContinent abc:Africa.
}
```

But with GeoSPARQL, not only geometric attributes (shapes) but also Egenhofer/RCC topological relations can be invoked.

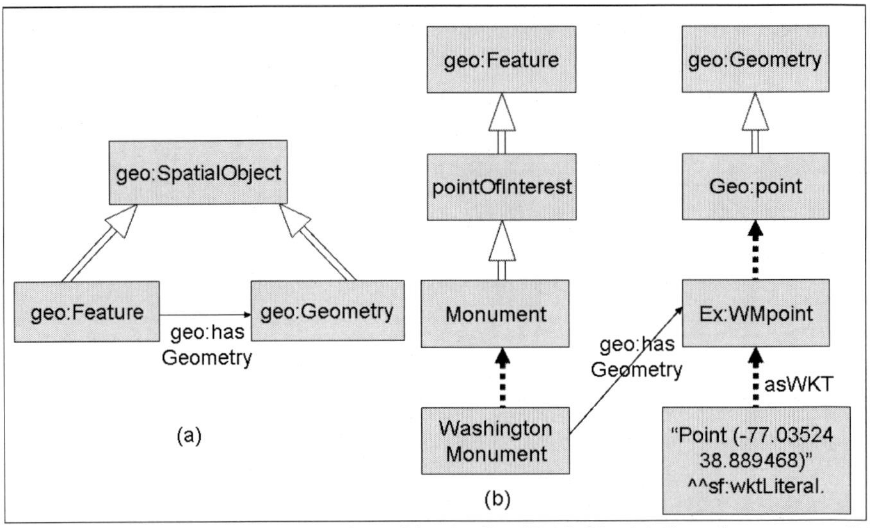

Figure 31. Example of describing geographic entities in GeoSPARQL. (a) Generic structure. (b) Example for a monument.

In addition, the following functions are integrated, distance, buffer, convex hull, intersection, union, difference, etc. The general structure and an example are given in Figure 31. To get the Washington monument, one has to write a small filter as a minimum bounding rectangle:

```
PREFIX geo: <http://www.opengis.net/ont/geosparql#>
PREFIX geof: <http://www.opengis.net/def/function/geosparql/>
PREFIX sf: <http://www.opengis.net/ont/sf#>
PREFIX ex: <http://example.org/PointOfInterest#>
SELECT ?a
WHERE {
?a geo:hasGeometry
?ageo .
?ageo geo:asWKT
?alit .
FILTER( geof:sfWithin(?alit, "Polygon((-77.089005 38.913574,-
77.029953 38.913574,-77.029953 38.886321,-77.089005 38.886321,-
77.089005 38.913574))"^^sf:wktLiteral)) }
```

For instance a query for getting the airports near London is as follows:

```
PREFIX co: <http://www.geonames.org/countries/#>
PREFIX xsd: <http://www.w3.org/2001/XMLSchema#>
PREFIX geo: <http://www.w3.org/2003/01/geo/wgs84_pos#>
SELECT ?link ?name ?lat ?lon
WHERE {
?link gs:within(51.139725 -0.895386 51.833232 0.645447) .
?link gn:name ?name .
?link gn:featureCode gn:S.AIRP .
?link geo:lat ?lat .
?link geo:long ?lon }
```

If somebody is looking for all land parcels with some type of commercial zoning that touch some arterial street, the query is the following:

```
SELECT ?parcel ?hwy
WHERE { ?parcel rdf:type :Commercial .
?parcel rdf:type ogc:GeometryObject .
?hwy rdf:type :Arterial_Street .
?hwy rdf:type ogc:GeometryObject .
?parcel ogc:touches ?hwy }
```

4.4. Geovisualization

Conventional cartography is usually based on Bertin semiology (Bertin 1967) who has established the fundamentals of graphics. Then several other tracks were followed, especially thanks to the facilities of data processing. For instance, a cartogram is a type of graphics that depicts attributes of geographic objects as the object's area. Because a cartogram does not show geographic space, but rather changes the size of objects depending on a certain attribute, a cartogram is not a true map, but it is a good representation of the phenomenon. An example can be illustrated by representing country areas according to their gross national products. It is argued that this kind of representations bring more knowledge than common representations.

After James J. Thomas and Kristin A. Cook (2005), visual analytics is the science of analytical reasoning facilitated by interactive visual interfaces. Applied to GIS, visual analytics is also known as geoanalytics and geovisualization. This is the way to transform data and especially digital data into drawings or maps so that anyone can access, understand and interact with to harvest rich insight from vast data sources. Visual analytics tools and techniques create an interactive view of data that reveals the patterns within it, enabling everyone to become researchers and analysts. It brings together information technology, information visualization, cognitive and perceptual sciences, interactive design, graphic design, and social sciences. For instance, cartograms are shown in the site http://www-personal.umich.edu/~mejn /cartograms/ in which all countries are presented in proportion of some phenomenon, i.e., their national gross products or the number of patients.

Remember that during millennia maps were both the visualization and the way to store geographic information. From half a century, progressively it was clear to distinguish between those two aspects. During a few decades, attention was paid on storing efficiently geographic data in databases. Now, it turns out to ameliorate visualization by trying to propose new tools which can facilitate geographic reasoning.

In other words, visual reasoning can be seen as a competitor to conventional spatial reasoning as it is known in artificial intelligence and computational geometry.

In this section, a few examples will be shown: Figure 32 for traffic flows whereas Figure 33 depicts pollution.

Figure 32. Novel representations: traffic flows in New-York City, Source http://www. nadiaamoroso.com with permission.

Figure 33. Novel representations: pollution level, Source http://www.nadiaamoroso. com with permission.

4.5. Chorems

For the representation of geographic knowledge, a visual solution could be based on chorems (Brunet 1980, DelFatto et al., 2007) which are schematic representations of territories.

An example is given Figure 34 representing Spain and its characteristics, a desert in the middle, farming and forests in the North-Western part, tourism saturation along the coast of the Mediterranean Sea and two big cities, Madrid and Barcelona.

Chorems are essentially used to schematize information about a territory, but the can also be used as an alternative access method to geographic databases.

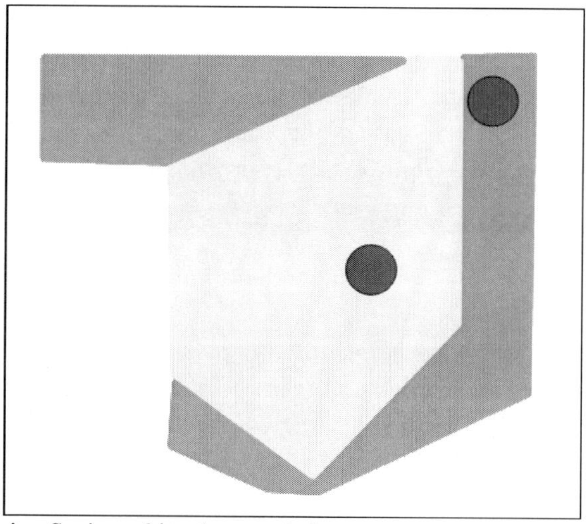

Figure 34. Chorem showing Spain and its characteristics.

5. GEOGRAPHIC RULES

Now that the key concepts are established, we can state some prolegomena as preliminary assertions constituting the underlying foundations of principles.

They are organized as follows (Laurini, 2014):

- the two first prolegomena state the origin of geographic data,
- the two next, particular cases of data transformation,
- the two next, updating of data,
- the five next ones, the structuring of objects and of geographic information,
- and the last one, the well-known Tobler's law. (Tobler, 1970).

5.1. Prolegomena

Prolegomenon #1 *(3D +T objects): "All existing objects are tridimensional and can have temporal evolution; lower dimensions (0D, 1D and 2D) are only used for modeling (in databases) and visualization (in cartography)*". Unlike geodetic objects which were created by man, all features are 3D, can move, can change their shape and can be destroyed.

Prolegomenon #2 *(Acquisition by measurements)*: "*All basic attributes (spatial or non-spatial) are obtained by means of measuring apparatuses having some limited accuracy*". Now more and more data come from sensors; more, citizens can be seen as sensors (Goodchild-Hill, 2008). In other terms, the word "apparatus" must be taken in a very wide sense, from sensors to census, etc.

In metadata, accuracy is perhaps one of the most important features, but too often real applications do not care enough about accuracy. One of the big practical difficulties is when different subsets of databases were acquired with various accuracies.

Prolegomenon #3 *(Continuous fields): "Since it is not possible to store the infinite number of value points in a continuous field, some sampling points will be used to generate the whole field by interpolation*". As a consequence, special data structures must be developed in conjunction with interpolating functions to estimate value anywhere in the field. See for instance Vckovski (1995), Gordillo (2001) or Kang et al. (2002) for more details.

Prolegomenon #4 *(Raster-vector and vector-raster transformations): "Procedures transforming vector to raster data and raster to vector data must be implemented with loosing less accuracy as possible*". Any geographic knowledge system must include those procedures.

Prolegomenon #5 *(From Popper's falsifiability principle (Popper, 1934)): "When a new apparatus delivers measures with higher accuracy, these measures supersede the previous ones"*. The practical consequence is that as a new generation of data comes, geographic data and knowledge basis must integrate those data and remove the previous data. But alas, due to the acquisition cost, a lot of actual systems are based on "obsolete" data.

Prolegomenon #6 *(Permanent updating): "Since objects are evolving either continuously (sea, continental drift) or event-based (removing building), updating should be done permanently respectively in real-time and as soon as possible*". Remember that "updating" in computing means three different things, (*i*) a characteristics of an object has varied (f.i. landuse in a parcel), (*ii*) the class of an object (so its description) has varied (a building formerly a residence is now for business), (*iii*) an error has been discovered in this object and then corrected (f.i. wrong coordinates or attributes). This prolegomenon implies that any procedure to check or increase data quality must be invoked.

Prolegomenon #7 *(Geographic metadata): "All geographic databases or repositories must be accompanied with metadata*". The necessity to accompany data by information regarding lineage and accuracy was first observed in the GIS domain. More precisely, now the International Standard ISO 19115 "Geographic Information - Metadata" from ISO/TC 211 provides information about the identification, the extent, the quality, the spatial and temporal schema, spatial reference, and distribution of digital geographic data. Practically, many geographic databases do not implement the whole standard, but only the more important aspects, because it is very time-consuming. Moreover metadata must be also updated when necessary.

Prolegomenon #8 *(Cartographic objects): "In cartography, it is common to eliminate objects, to displace or to simplify them*". This is due to ensure a maximal readability of maps.

Prolegomenon #9 *(One storing, several visualizations): "A good practice should be to store all geographic objects with the highest possible accuracy and to generate other shapes by means of generalization*". This can be seen as an extension of the well-known Douglas-Peucker's family of methods and algorithms for generalization (1973).

Prolegomenon #10 *(Place names and gazetteers): "Relationships between places and place names are many-to-many*". As previously told, Mississippi is the name of a river and the name of a state. The actual city of Rome, Italy, is larger than the same Rome in Romulus's time. The main consequence is that unique feature identifiers must be defined since "popular names" are not so easy to digitally manipulate.

Prolegomenon #11 *(Geographic ontologies): "All geographic object types are linked to concepts organized into a geographic ontology based on topological relations*". This comes from my own definition of geographic ontologies (Laurini, 2012). When necessary, raster information can be included into ontologies. For instance, roof textures can be used to identify a building, a wood texture for a wood, a corn field texture to a corn field, possibly with different level of maturity.

In the case of federating several several geographic databases, interoperability is often governed by ontologies. If ontologies of each database are different, a global ontology must be defined from the so-called local ontologies.

Prolegomenon #12 *(Tobler's law 1970): "Everything is related to everything else, but near things are more related than distant things*". This statement may be seen as a key-concept also for geographic data mining.

5.2. Principles

Now that prolegomena are stated, principles governing geographic knowledge may be listed in order to get robust reasoning and retrieval. The principles are organized as follows:

- The three first concerned the origin of geographic knowledge,
- The seven next ones, the transformation of geographic knowledge,
- The two last ones take the environment into account.

Principle #1 *(Origin of geographic knowledge): "Spatial knowledge is hidden in geometry whereas geographic knowledge comes in addition from non-spatial attributes*".

In other words, spatial knowledge is implicit and the question is whether to make it explicit. We can derive from coordinates that New-York city is west of Paris, and same kind of relations for all cities throughout the world. The good practice is to derive knowledge on-demand when necessary.

In addition, data coming sensors will support geographic knowledge whereas any indicator will be seen as composite knowledge derived from measures.

Some geographic knowledge can be extracted from data mining techniques.

Principle #2 *(Knowledge cleaning): "All geographic data, once captured, must be cleaned to remove errors and artifacts to get consistent knowledge*". This principle is directly connected with Prolegomenon #6 since all automatic acquisition system may include errors or anomalies.

For instance, any airborne laser beam to capture digital data for terrain or elevation can intercept a bird: in this case, the captured data will no more be the terrain altitude, but the bird altitude. Based on this principle, all procedures to increase geographic knowledge quality must be invoked.

However, in practical situations, geographic data or knowledge bases can still encompass some remaining (not yet discovered) errors, so implying often wrong results in treatment and reasoning. End-users must take care.

Principle #3 *(Knowledge enumeration): "It is not necessary to enumerate all possible chunks of geographic knowledge*". For instance, if one has *n* object, then *(-1)/2* North-South relationships can be also derived accordingly. Indeed, it is truly possible to derive them automatically when reasoning.

In other words, since any geographic knowledge repository is infinite (intensional), only implicit knowledge is stored, but other knowledge chunks can be derived when necessary.

Principle #4 *(From geoid to plane): "On small territories, a planar representation is sufficient whereas for big territories, Earth rotundity must be taken into consideration"*. But the question is "how to define a small or a big territory"? A solution can be to define a threshold, for instance a 100 km wide square. Let write O_σ, the planar map for any geographic object O at scale σ taking generalization into account: O_σ =2Dmap(O).

Principle #5 *(Visualization and visual acuity): "Cartographic representation is linked to visual acuity"*. Here again thresholds must be defined. In classical cartography, as previously said, the limit ranges from 1 mm to 0.1 mm. Let us suppose that one takes a road and a certain scale: if the transformation gives a width more that 1 mm, this road is an area, between 1 mm and 0.1mm a line, and less that 0.1mm the road disappears. The same reasoning is valid for cities or small countries such as Andorra, etc. In these cases, the "holes" in Italy or in France disappear cartographically. With the thresholds ε_i, ε_{lp} previously defined, we can formally get:

a/ $\forall O \in GeObject, \forall \sigma \in Scale \wedge O_\sigma = \text{2Dmap}(O) \wedge \text{Area}\ (O_\sigma) < (\varepsilon_{lp})^2 \Rightarrow O_\sigma = \varnothing$.

b/ $\forall O \in GeObject, \forall \sigma \in Scale \wedge O_\sigma = \text{2Dmap}(O) \wedge (\varepsilon_i)^2 > \text{Area}\ (O_\sigma) > (\varepsilon_{lp})^2 \Rightarrow O_\sigma = \text{Centroid}(O)$.

But this principle must be relaxed (Rule #1) when one has to map small objects.

For instance, let us consider an A4-format map showing Roman churches in France, those churches must stay whereas due to scale they should disappear.

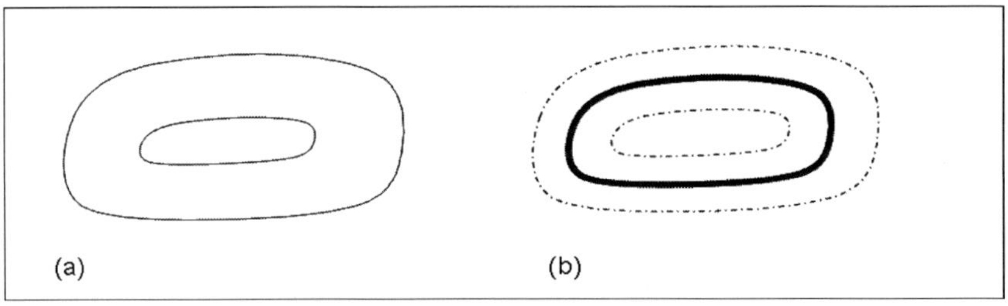

Figure 35. Crispification of a geographic object modeled by the egg-yolk representation. (a) the original model. (b) its reduction to a crisp object.

The other interesting case regards loose tessellations, i.e., "tessellations" with sliver polygons: when scale diminishes, those sliver polygons will vanish due to visual acuity, and so leading to a good-standing tessellation.

As previously explained, this principle can be reformulated taking the concept of granularity of interest into account.

Principle #6 *(Crispification): "At some scales every fuzzy object becomes crisp"*. If the egg-yolk representation is adopted to represent of geo-object, when the egg white distance is less than a threshold, the geo-object geometry can be taken for instance where the membership grade is 50%. Figure 35 illustrates this process. This process is similar to the reduction of a ribbon into a line.

In the case of the fuzzy set representation, the 50 % membership contour line can represent the boundary of the so-transformed polygon.

Principle #7 *(Relativity of spatial relations): "Spatial relation varies according to scale"*. Commonly, one says that a road runs along a lake. But in reality, in some place, the road does not run really along the water of the lake due to beaches, buildings, etc. At one scale, the road TOUCHes the lake, but at another scale at some places, this is a DISJOINT relation (Figure 20). Let consider two geographic objects O^1 and O^2 and their $O_\sigma^{\ 1}$ and $O_\sigma^{\ 2}$ their cartographic representations, for instance the following assertion holds:

$$\forall O^1, O^2 \in GeObject \wedge \sigma \in Scale \wedge O_\sigma^{\ 1} = 2Dmap(O^1, \sigma) \wedge$$
$$O_\sigma^{\ 2} = 2Dmap(O^2, \sigma) \wedge Disjoint\,(O^1, O^2) \wedge Dist\,(O^1, O^2) < \varepsilon_2$$
$$\Rightarrow Touches(O_\sigma^{\ 1}, O_\sigma^{\ 2}).$$

Similar assertions could be written when CONTAINS, OVERLAP relationships. In addition, two objects in the real world with a TOUCHES relation can coalesce into a single one.

As a consequence, in reasoning what is true at one scale, can be wrong at another scale. So, any automatic system must be robust enough to deal with this issue.

Principle #8 *(Transformation into graph): "Every set of ribbon or linear objects can be transformed into a graph"*. Indeed, reasoning with graphs is often easier that to reason with computational geometry. For instance this kind of transformation can be used for roads, rivers, metrolines, sewerages, etc.

Principle #9 *(From pictorial to geographic objects): "Any group of pixels having same characteristics located in a satellite image or in an aerial photo can be regrouped into a pictorial object; this pictorial object can be conferred a geographic type possibly using an ontology"*. Indeed as soon as a pictorial object is recognized, its type will be identified and it can be a part of a geographic object. For instance, a roof texture and an adjacent garden texture can reveal a parcel.

Principle #10 *(Visualization constraints): "The spatial relations between objects must hold after generalization"*. In Figure 36, an excerpt of the English Riviera coast along the Channel is showed. Suppose we generalize the shoreline by a single line: the city of Eastbourne will be in the middle of the sea whereas Plymouth and Bournemouth will stay in the mainland. In order to enforce the topological constraints, those harbors must move so that the COVER relations hold. Same reasoning is also valid for the rivers going to the sea. In the same spirit, some cities at the borders must stay in the proper country. See Geneva for example with the French border.

As a consequence of Prolegomena #5 and #6, when better or newer data supersede old data, topological constraints must hold on.

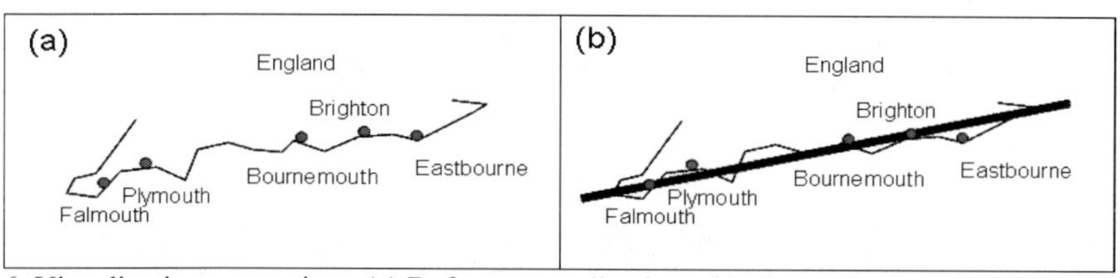

Figure 36. Visualization constraints. (a) Before generalization; (b) Generalization of the coastline, but harbors are badly located.

One of the difficulties about this principle is not to follow the constraints, but to ascertain that all visualization constraints are listed. In other words, how to prove that the list is exhaustive, irredundant and consistent? Here lies a technological barrier.

Principle #11 *(Influence of neighbors): "In geographic repositories, do not forget that objects at the vicinity (outside the jurisdiction) can have an influence*".

This is a consequence of Tobler's law (Prolegomenon #12); however the great majority of existing GIS do not follow this law. Taking again the example of Geneva, remember that a big part of its metropolitan area in located in the French Rhône-Alpes region; any automatic social-economic reasoning must take this characteristics into consideration. Therefore a kind of out-buffer zone must be defined. But the question is "where is the limit?" Similarly a threshold can be defined.

Principle #12 *(Cross-boundary interoperability): "Any geographic repository must provide key-information to ensure cross-boundary interoperability*". Once solved the sliver polygons problem located at the boundary, two cases are important, graph structures and terrains. Figure 37 illustrates a graph example in which two neighboring geographic repositories are present, obviously with geometric discrepancies (Laurini, 1998). Figure 37a shows two geographic repositories before integration and 37b the situation with a magnifying glass emphasizing the discrepancies at the boundary; Figure 37c shows the results of cartographic integration (maps look good; a successive step is not mention in the figure is object integration in which two objects (for instance, a road, a river) which were artificially cut into two pieces, fusion, i.e., same identifier.

Then Figure 37d shows the last step, graph integration: indeed before integration road graphs are not connected, but in order to allow graph reasoning, for instance minimum path algorithm across several repositories, graphs must be connected; in this case a node must be created in which a first edge belongs to the first repository, and the second edge to the second one.

In other words, before integration there was a set of non-connected ribbons and at the end the concerned ribbons are reduced to a unique ribbon, and so a unique graph is constructed.

Therefore, it is compulsory to provide necessary tools for both creating cross-boundary edges, and launching graph algorithms without blockage, not only for roads, but for any kind of networks as previously mentioned (water supply, telecommunications, etc.). In addition Rule #2 must be applied when scale is diminishing.

In the case of disconnected terrains, the case is a little bit more complex for two reasons. First elevations can be defined differently essentially because the reference points (mean sea level) are different (for instance 2.34m between Belgium and The Netherlands). And secondly, the mathematical shape of the geoid can differ. Once those discrepancies are overcome, the integration of terrains can be launched. In Laurini (1998), a solution based on triangles was proposed.

Do not forget that by applying Principle#11, already a buffer zone is integrated in our geographic knowledge base, and some discrepancies can occur.

This principle drives the design of consistent distributed geographic knowledge base systems.

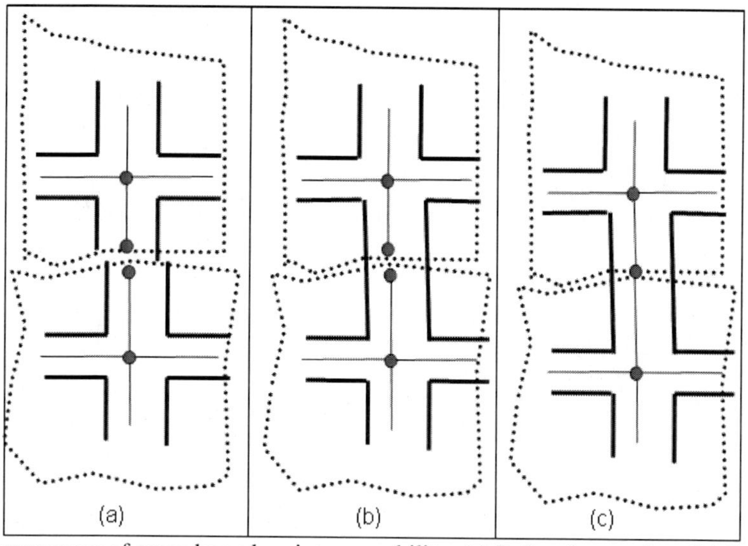

Figure 37. Consequences of cross-boundary interoperability. (a) Before integration. (b) Cartographic integration. (c) Graph-reasoning integration.

6. Encoding Geographic Knowledge

In addition to conventional categories such as facts, concepts, processes and rules, geographic knowledge engineering need not only to redefine them but also to include new items. First let us examine the different types of geographic knowledge and then the different ways to represent knowledge chunks.

6.1. Types of Geographic Knowledge

The ChorML project (Coimbra, 2008) mentions the following, geographic facts, cluster of areas, flows (persons, goods, etc.), and co-location rules. But we need to add gradients, external information and topological constraints.

6.1.1. Geographic Facts

The notion of geographic facts must be revisited. In some cases, facts are simple to define. For instance a place must be mentioned either by a place name or identifier or by means of its coordinates; for instance "The Mont Blanc summit is located in North 45°49'59 and East 6°51'53 and its elevation is 4807m". But when saying that there are 60 million of inhabitants in France, there is no problem. But when one says that France is located at the South of Belgium, it is a little more awkward to encode because some points of Belgium are located at the South of some French places. A solution seems to claim that the majority of Belgium points are located at the North of French points; as previously said, a solution can be based on centroids.

6.1.2. Clusters of Area

In some situation, it could be interesting to regroup areas (polygonal zones) into a single cluster according to some criteria (See Figure 38). This cluster will constitute a new tessellation perhaps with disconnected pieces or with holes.

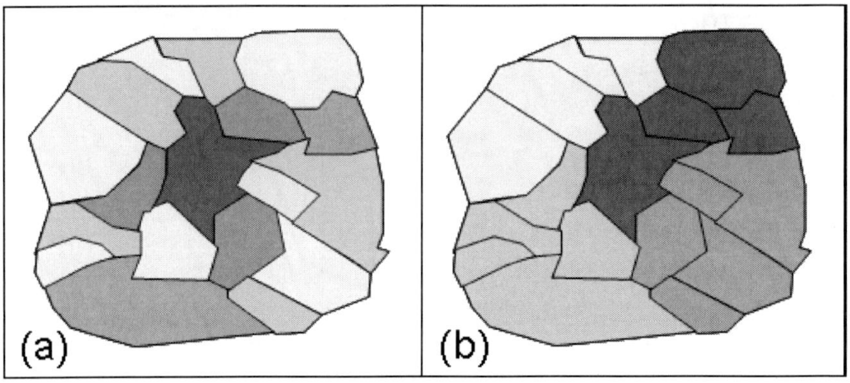

Figure 38. Example of clustering. (a) Initial configuration. (b) One clustering solution in four clusters.

For instance in UK:

```
UK= CLUSTER (England, Scotland, Wales, NorthernIreland).
```

6.1.3. Flows

Generally two areas (seen as origin and destination) can be linked by flows of people or goods; flows can be unidirectional, bidirectional; if origin is multiple or unknown, the flow is converging (for instance speaking of immigration) then the destination zone is called sink, elsewhere if destination is multiple or unknown, the flow is diverging (the origin node is a source); flows are defined from areas which can be reduced as points at some scales. See Figure 39.

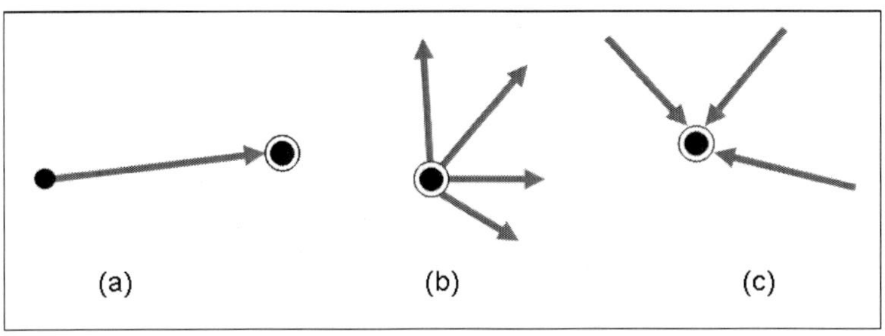

Figure 39. Examples of flows, (a) unidirectional, (b) diverging, (c) converging.

6.1.4. Co-Location Rules

One of the scopes of geographic data mining (Mennis-Guo, 2009) is to look for co-location rules. When two sets of features are concerned; for instance "near a big city, there is an airport". Figure 40 shows an example of co-locations.

6.1.5. Gradients

When a geographer reads "the more of this, the more of that", there is a high probability that some continuous fields will be concerned. For instance, let us examine the following assertion, "in a beach resort, the nearer to the beach, the higher the price of houses". Behind this assertion, one can discover the continuous field of house prices, or more exactly a smoothed continuous field.

Since it is not easy to describe knowledge neither with functions nor with derivatives, a solution can be to consider two similar houses *H1* and *H2*, each at the distances *d1* and *d2* from the beach. Suppose *d1* is smaller than *d2*, one can write:

```
When d1 < d2 Then price (H1) > price (H2).
```

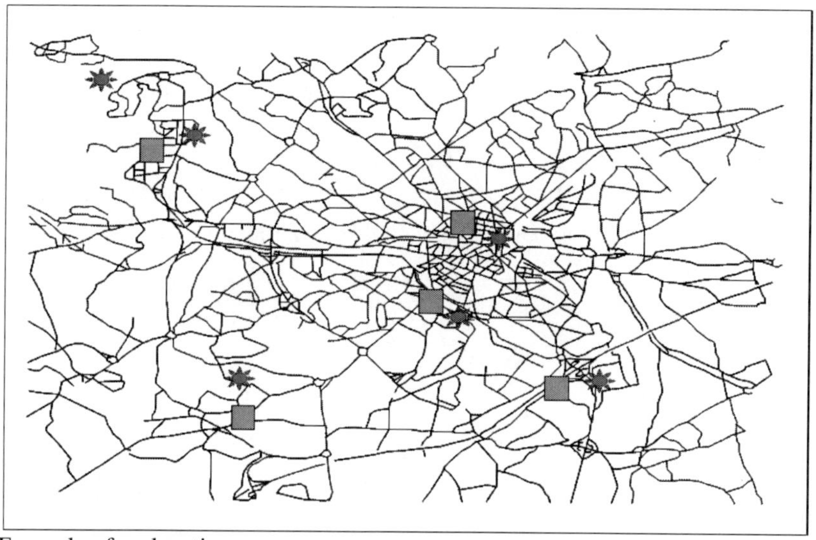

Figure 40. Example of co-locations.

6.1.6. External Information and Knowledge

As stated in Principle #11, information regarding the vicinity is important. By external information, we mean everything which is outside the concerned territory but which can be of interest for geographic reasoning. An example is given Figure 41 showing external information for Spain in which two categories are mentioned:

- land borders for France, Portugal, Gibraltar and Morocco (considering Ceuta and Melilla),
- and sea borders for the Atlantic Ocean and the Mediterranean Sea.

6.1.7. Topological Constraints

Some examples were already given in Principle #10; these constraints must be used not only for visualization but also for reasoning and retrieval. Figure 42 gives a visual example of topological constraints in France; due to generalization, some cities can be badly located, for instance the French city of Marseilles and the Swiss city of Geneva.

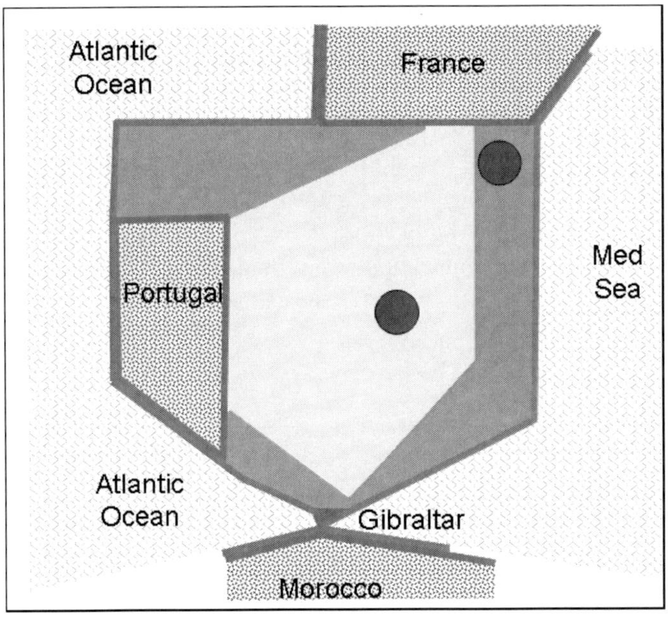

Figure 41. Spain and its external information to support some reasoning.

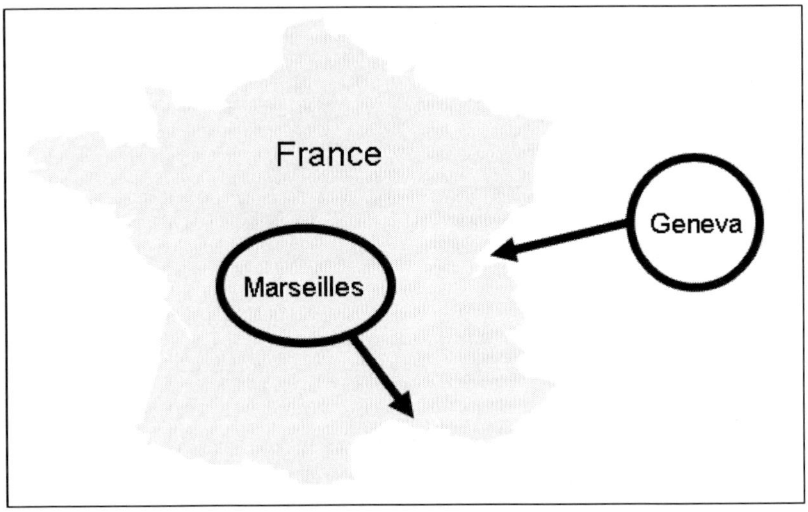

Figure 42. Example of visual representation of constraint stating that the city of Marseilles must be always inside (TOUCHES relation) the French territory, and Geneva outside (~COVERS).

6.2. Representing Geographic Knowledge

Presently, geographic knowledge can be represented by four different methods, natural language (but which is outside the scope of this chapter), logics, XML-encoding and visual representation. Let us examine them rapidly.

6.2.1. Natural Language

Historically speaking, the objective of conventional geography was to exhibit geographic knowledge with natural language; but the main drawback is that this mode of representation is not very machine-treatable. Let us take an example "*when there is a lake and a road going to the lake, then there is a restaurant*".

6.2.2. Logics

Geographic knowledge can be expressed by logic under the condition to include spatial relations and spatial operators. The previous statement can be encoded:

$$\forall l \in Lake \wedge \forall s \in Street \wedge Touches\ (l, s) \Rightarrow \forall\ \exists r \in Restaurants$$
$$\wedge\ (Dist\ (r,l) < 100 \wedge (Dist\ (r,s) < 100.$$

Practically, everything can be encoded provided that the corresponding spatial relations can be used. Do not avoid that spatial relations sometimes include sophisticated computational geometry algorithms.

6.2.3. XML-Encoding

XML can be the basis of geographic knowledge: for instance SpatialML (Mani et al. 2010) is a markup language for representing spatial expressions in natural language documents; its goal is to allow for better integration of text collections with resources such as databases that provide spatial information about a domain. Here is an example for the phrase "a building 5 miles east of Fengshan":

```
    a <PLACE id="1" type="FAC" form="NOM">building</PLACE>
    <SIGNAL id="2">5 miles</SIGNAL>
    <SIGNAL id="3">east</SIGNAL> of
    <PLACE id="4" type="PPL" country="TW" form="NAM"
latLong="22∘37'N 120∘21'E">Fengshan</PLACE>
    <PATH id="5" source="4" destination="1" distance="5:mi"
direction="E" signals="2 3"/>
```

The used spatial relations based on the RCC model are given in Table 1

Table 1. Spatial relations in SpatialML (Mani et al. 2010)

Spatial relations	Example
IN (tangential and non-tangential proper parts)	[Paris], [Texas]
EC (extended connection)	the border between [Lebanon] and [Israel]
NR (near)	visited [Belmont], near [San Mateo]
DC (discrete connection)	the [well] outside the [house]
PO (partial overlap)	[Russia] and [Asia]
EQ (equality)	[Rochester] and [382044N, 0874941W]

6.2.4. Visual Representations

Another possible track is a visual language since geography and cartography are essentially visual. Let us very rapidly present a few visual concepts. But first let us detail contexts of interpretation.

6.2.4.1. Contexts of Interpretation

In fact, by considering drawings, four types of interpretation spaces are possible, identified by four interpretational icons (Figure 43):

- *Cartographic space* which corresponds to conventional cartography with an arrow to North and a scale; the horizontal axis represents eastings; this context is identified by the North arrow icon; according to scale, it can be based on planar projections or spherical; it has two alternatives, the planar one (iconized by a square), the global one (circle)
- *Topological space* in which only cardinal directions have no importance, but the importance is given to the respective positioning of geographic objects; the horizontal and vertical axes have no meaning; this context is identified by an "overlap relation";
- *Time line* in which the horizontal axis represents time; this context is identified by a clock icon; remind that this interpretation context is outside the scope of this chapter
- *Chorematic space* represented by a hexagon (indeed, as example France is often schematized as a hexagon).

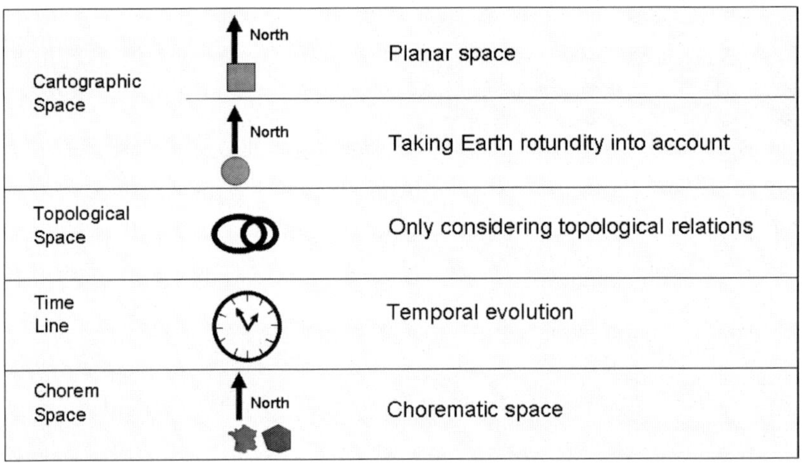

Figure 43. The contexts of interpretation, cartographic space, topological space, time line and chorematic space.

6.2.4.2. Examples

In those examples, only three elements will be introduced, presentation of facts, presentation of a query and presentation of a co-location rules. Some other examples can be found in (Laurini, 2014). But first let us give some pieces of visual vocabulary in Figure 44 in which in the first row some entity icons are presented whereas in the second row there are emblems of two cities and a flag.

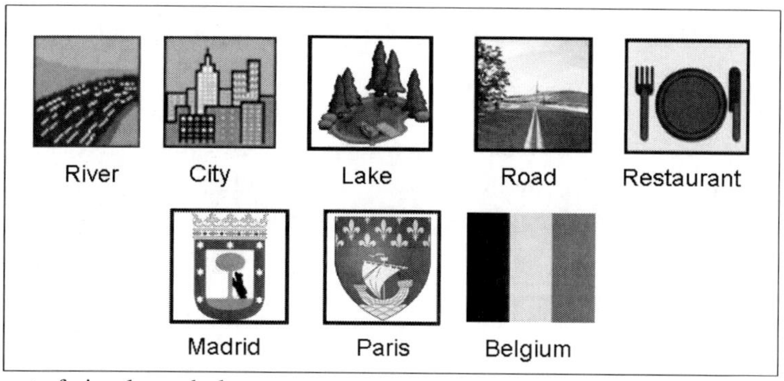

Figure 44. Excerpt of visual vocabulary.

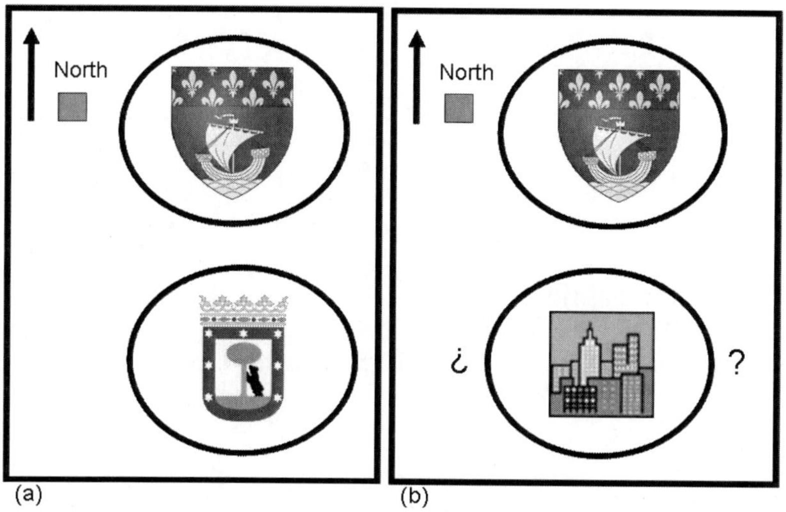

Figure 45. Example of visual representation in the cartographic space. (a) Fact stating that London is north of Madrid. (b) Query asking for cities located south of London.

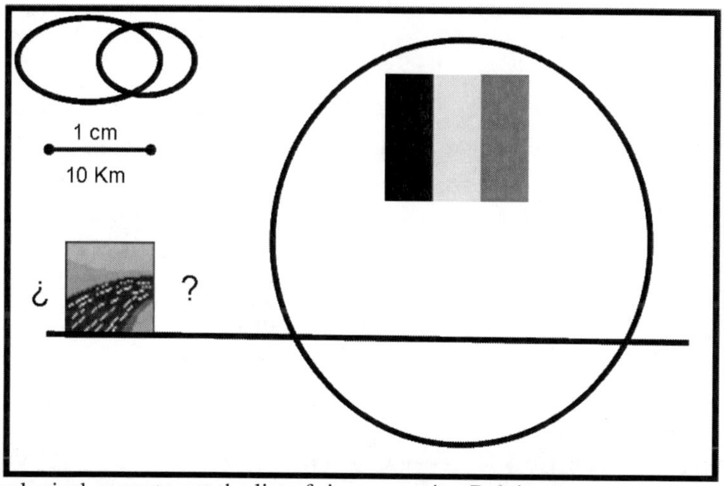

Figure 46. A topological query to get the list of rivers crossing Belgium.

7. Discovering Geographic Knowledge

As stated in Principle #1, geographic knowledge comes from data, not only from vector databases, but also from other various sources such as data mining, Internet, existing maps which are scanned, aerial photos, satellite images, sensors and people. The role of this section is not to detail all those aspects, but only to give some important issues.

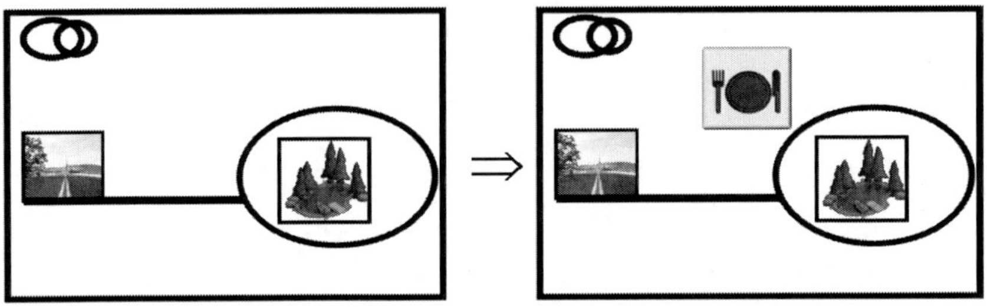

Figure 47. Example of visual representation of co-location rule "*Lake, Road and Restaurant*" in a topological space.

7.1. Geographic Data Mining

In information technology, the scope of data mining is to analyze database contents so to find frequent item sets. In other words, this is to extract unknown knowledge from data.

The prototypic example is taken from a relational database in which it can be shown that if for instance, *A* and *B* have certain value then *C* has a precise value according to two indicators, confidence and support. Data mining can be used for anomaly detection, associative rules modeling, clustering, classification and regression.

In our domain, (Mennis-Guo, 2009) data mining can be used for instance for public health services searching for explanations of disease clustering, for environmental agencies assessing the impact of changing land-use patterns on climate change, for police analyzing criminality, etc.

But the main application is called co-location rule discovery in which two neighboring features are usually linked, for example in a lot of places, the town hall is located in or near the main square.

An interesting direction is the use of sensors. More and more sensors for temperature, noise, etc. are placed in cities. Those sensors send regularly measures to a database against which data mining queries can be addressed in real time against logs. For instance, imagine some sensors located along a river. By spatial data mining, flood or pollution can be rapidly detected so that local decision-makers can get immediately informed.

7.2. Geographic Information Retrieval in Internet

During decades, the key-GIS problem was to search information in geographic databases, rapidly and efficiently. Now the main query is to be launched not against one or several databases, but against the whole Internet. Suppose somebody wants to retrieve some geographic information about Prussia, a country which does not exist anymore. In Internet, various information pieces can be retrieved in various languages, predominantly in German in this case. In addition to textual information, maps and paintings can be retrieved.

This is the role of GIR (Geographic Information Retrieval) to develop methodology able not only to retrieve this kind of information based essentially on gazetteers and ontologies, but also to synthesize correctly information coming from different media.

7.3. Knowledge from Scanned Maps

In libraries, there are a lot of historical maps which were made for different purposes. Generally, they are accompanied by a legend describing the visual language which is used for the map. Sometimes, there are also dates and other information which can be considered as metadata.

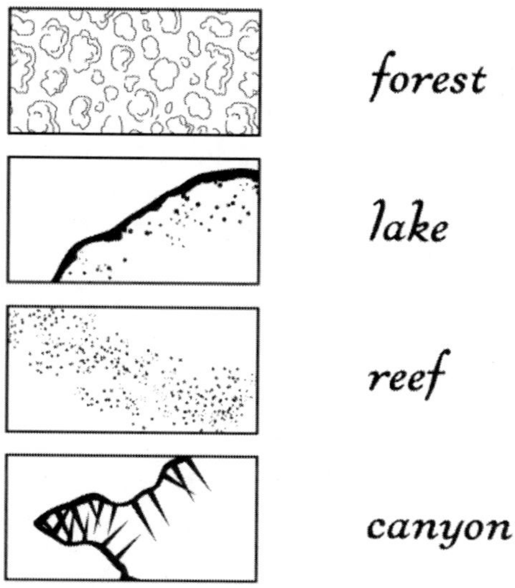

Figure 48. Example of symbols in an old map. Source: http://a-patel0710-dc.blogspot.fr/2009/12/map-legends-compass.html.

The first step is the analysis of this legend in order to extract patterns in the legend such as illustrated in Figure 48. Based on this vocabulary, the results can be easily encoded to be processed.

In other words, this is a kind of image processing problem driven by well-defined textures. So, several features can be recognized, for instance cities and their sizes, rivers and their beds, roads, etc. For that task, historical gazetteers would be a key-element. As feedbacks, those gazetteers can be enriched by old placenames which were not already included.

7.4. Damaged Map Recovery

Alas, often the old maps did not have resisted the wear of time, they are damaged and they need some recovery. Often, badly-made restorations have also deteriorated the quality of information (Figure 49). To recover those maps, the first preliminary steps can be as follows:

- scanning the maps with high density of pixels,
- determining the type of Earth projection,
- choosing four points for which we know exactly longitudes and latitudes,
- establishing the formula for rubber-sheeting so that latitude lines be parallel to the x-axis,
- applying rubber sheeting to all pixels
- possibly filling some gaps

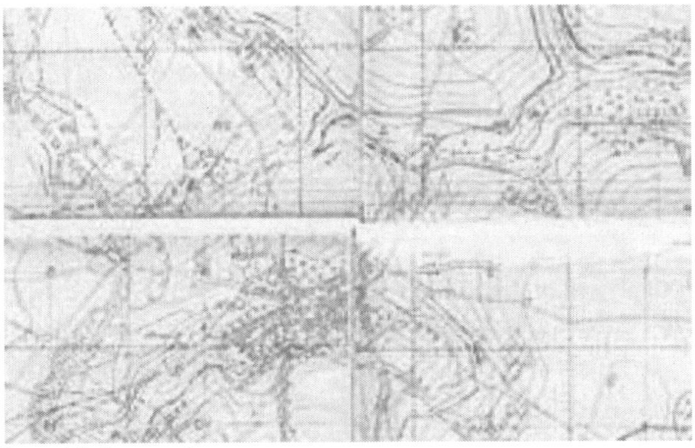

Figure 49. Example of an old damaged map.

In addition, sometimes maps were creased, torn and badly glued with cellotape: the roads, rivers, etc. are no more aligned. In this case, a special algorithm must be launched to join all features which were torn or damaged.

After those initial steps, the recognition of features can be launched based on the visual vocabulary.

7.5. Cartography from Textual Information

Suppose on radio you are hearing weather forecast for the whole country: you try to imagine what could be the meteorological conditions in your city. By doing that you are mentally constructing a map from text. Cartography of textual information is based on:

- existing basic maps,
- gazetteers,
- and existing symbology for weather phenomena (rain, snow, temperature, wind, etc.).

In GIR, this is common to try to transform a text either into a map or into some textual knowledge representations.

7.6. From Experts and from Citizens

In the 80-90ies, the buzzword "expert systems" was mainstream meaning that some so-called experts can deliver rules of their disciplines. But in reality, those experts had difficulties to express their knowledge as IF-THEN rules. Moreover, it was really difficult to manage an important number of rules especially for checking inconsistencies and completeness.

More recently, citizens were seen as possible sensors, i.e., as providers of geographic information (Goodchild, 2008). With the creation of VGIS (Volunteered GIS), any citizen can bring fresh information and novel knowledge chunks. But this information must often be cross-checked before being stored. Another interesting track is provided by crowdsourcing (Papadapolou-Giaoutzi, 2014) which is a new way to acquire geographic knowledge. Indeed crowdsourcing is mainly based on the idea of an open-call publication of a problem, requesting the response of the crowd for reaching the most appropriate solution.

8. Territorial Business Intelligence

But the main application of geographic reasoning is targeted to decision-makers for territorial intelligence or more exactly for all those who have some territory to plan and manage. Essentially those decision-makers involve politicians, urban and environmental managers. But also companies can be interested in geomarketing needs like demarcating best sales territories. Territorial intelligence can have various facets such as:

- Site selection for commercial or industrial establishments,
- Urban area housing permit and re-zoning decisions,
- Path-finding,
- Emergency vehicle dispatching,
- Delivery truck routing and scheduling,
- Hydrology research like modeling chemical discharges,
- Territorial waters delineation,
- Understanding climatological processes,
- Hazard and disaster prevention, risk management,
- Pollution fighting,
- Disease distribution studies,
- Inferring the geometric shape of strata from borings,
- Proximity to social services design,
- Crime prediction and prevention,
- Positioning of antennas for mobile phones,
- Positioning of sensors and video-cameras,
- Etc.

In this section, not all facets will be presented but only some very small applications in territorial intelligence.

8.1. Urban Planning

The design of the city of the future is a huge challenge. Urban planners are trying to do their best from centuries and new tools in information technology (Laurini, 2002) are key-elements not only to plan a city, but also as cornerstone of smart cities. In this chapter, only a few examples will be presented as rules.

In strategic urban planning, let us take some examples:

Rule 1: `IF a zone is a marshland or floodable`
`THEN prohibit construction.`
Rule 2: `IF there is unemployment`
`THEN raise up enterprise creation`
`AND create industrial areas.`
Rule 3: `IF a parcel is closed to an airport`
`THEN limit building height.`
Rule 4: `IF a parcel is near to a fireman station`
`THEN prohibit hospital construction.`
Rule 5: `IF a building has a good architecture`
`AND IF it is more than 100 year old`
`AND IF the building state is mediocre`
`AND IF the owner does agree`
`THEN suggest restoration.`
Rule 6: `IF a building falls into ruins`
`AND IF nobody dwells in it`
`THEN demolish it.`
Rule 7: `IF a building has a poor architecture`
`AND IF inner rooms are degrading`
`AND IF money is raised`
`THEN suggest rehabilitation..`

8.2. Districting for Elections

Among the many facets of geographic reasoning, districting is an important real world task. We use the term zoning for the division of a continuous space of land into a tessellation, and the term districting to refer to any regrouping of basic zones into another tessellation. Sometimes the word clustering is used. Generally speaking, districting is undertaken for a special purpose, according to certain rules and criteria to be optimized.

Drawing boundaries is an element common to the situations of a country modifying its electoral precincts, or a municipality creating new school regions. Among the different instances, we examine only the case of electoral districting.

In some countries like the USA, boundaries are redrawn every so often in order to match more closely population distributions (Laurini-Thompson, 1993).

We set out now the nature of a spatial reasoning approach to the task of districting an hypothetical state with three hundred elementary zones into ten electoral districts in order to elect ten representatives. For each zone we have data for the number of registered voters, the number of votes cast in prior elections for each party, and the geometric description (Figure 49). We utilize a process beginning with some seed zones, adding neighbors to form the districts and stopping the process when some conditions are met. Assuming that the protection of incumbents is important (to reduce their competition one against another), then we will initiate the process from the zones of incumbent representatives, or a spatially random selection if there is no incumbent.

Starting from this basis, a spatial reasoning mechanism can be invoked to create different sets of districts. These alternative plans will be evaluated against three kinds of criterion. First of all, we employ a *population fairness* criterion. For this element we state that the population of all districts should be approximately the same, possibly within a range of 50,000 plus or minus 5 per cent. Secondly, we require district shapes not to be suspiciously strange. By *shapefairness* we mean that the districts shall not have holes or isolated pieces, and no long tentacles. Thirdly, we require *political fairness*, meaning that no political party is drastically over- or under-represented.

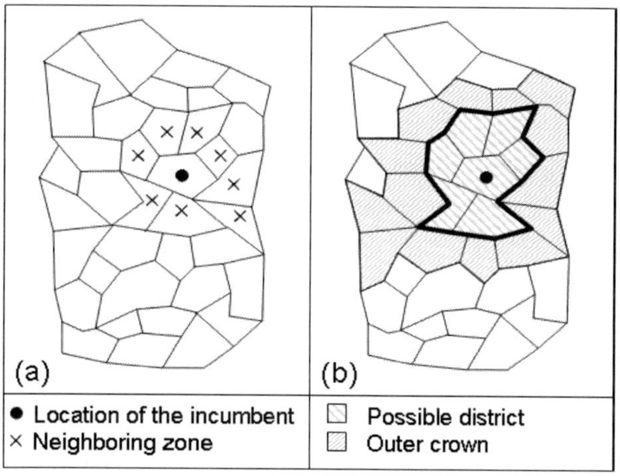

Figure 50. An example for illustrating the districting reasoning procedure. (a) Map emphasizing a seed zone and its neighbors, (b) Map presenting the inner crown zones and the outer crown zones of a possible district.

The population fairness criterion, for one example, can be based on the standard deviation of the number of voters per district.

For the criterion of shape fairness we can optimize any index which favors the shape of a circle. Among several, we use a simple measure comparing the ratio of the squared perimeter to area, which is at a minimum for a circle.

Regarding the political fairness criterion, one possibility is to aim for a result in which for each political party the ratio of elected representatives to the total number will be approximately the same as the proportion of voters by party preference. So we can define REPR(d, p) as an integer variable, having the value of 1 when the result is that the district gets a representative of the party p, and 0 in the other case. The political fairness criterion may be measured by the difference (or ratio) between the percentage of people voting for each party and the percentage of elected representatives for each party.

That is, with reference to Figure 50, we recognize an inner crown (Figure 50b), a set of zones bordering a currently active grouping as legitimate candidates to be added. There also exists a set of zones bordering a completed district, called here the outer crown. Such zones are candidates for swapping with one or more inner crown zones as adjustments are made to a district to make its population total closer to the desired number. While the map shows the possibility of swapping neighbors in the inner and outer crowns, the process can be set up to allow swapping of non-adjacent zones. For optimizing the political fairness criterion, we must determine globally the state of under- or over-representation for one or more political parties.

Thus, when a solution is reached, it corresponds to a new plan, which can then be compared with alternatives in order to make a selection.

8.3. Crime Analysis and Prevention

In several cities, criminality is a main problem. Police usually records criminality events and statistics tends to show that repetitions of those events. So both criminality analysis and prevention play an important role in those cities.

Analysis is not only based on mapping on recent crimes (see Figure 51), but overall on the discovery of causes leading to an increase of criminality. Geographic data mining can help a lot.

Prevention can have to facets. In one hand people can secure their homes and shops and create some community watch groups. In the other hand police organize patrols and police beats which can be more or less frequent.

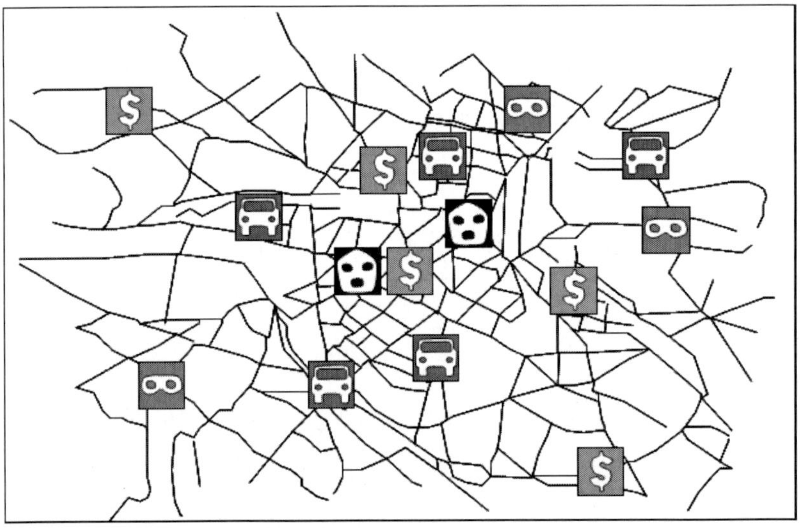

Figure 51. Example of a map for crime analysis.

The organization of those beats can be based on geographic knowledge (location of recent crimes, new alerts, etc.), time knowledge (night/day) and other knowledge essentially based on the availability of police manpower.

CONCLUSION AND PERSPECTIVES

Our objective was to give not only the fundamentals of geographic knowledge engineering, but also to show that it stands at the crossroads of several disciplines including computational geometry, topology, social sciences, cognitive sciences and so on.

Territorial intelligence must mix knowledge from people and automatic reasoning in order to plan the city of the future.

Good tools to tackle this kind of knowledge must not only model reality with a nice precision but overall be robust against measuring errors and scaling effects.

By the theory of ribbons, a kind of bridge has been done between lines and areas allowing a more efficient concept for modeling roads and rivers. Moreover, this concept could be of interest for a sort of grammar for urban features.

Thanks to twelve prolegomena and twelve principles, the fundamentals of geographic knowledge engineering have been proposed to build the foundations of a general framework robust to errors and scaling.

Several applications were rapidly presented in order to show the panorama of possibilities for geographic knowledge engineering.

But for designing a software product able to deal efficiently with automatic geographic reasoning, this is a long way to go. Anyhow, the following issues must be clarified:

- How to introduce easily computational geometry and spatial analysis in such a framework?
- How to organize a geographic knowledge base in order to guarantee rapid access to geographic information? Will spatial indexing (for instance based on *r*-trees) be useful to reach efficiency?
- What kind of intelligence for smart cities and how to integrate human intelligence and artificial intelligence?
- How to fusion knowledge from experts, knowledge from citizens and knowledge issued from geographic data mining?
- Will geographic reasoning increase or diminish citizen empowerment in a context of territorial intelligence?
- How to introduce criteria such as for sustainable development?
- How to introduce visual representations and visual interfaces?
- How to combine geographic automatic reasoning and visual reasoning from geovisualization?
- How to integrate such consideration in cloud computing?
- How to ensure interoperability of geographic knowledge base?
- Etc.

To conclude this chapter, let me thanks Dr. Françoise Milleret-Raffort for her help in discussing various aspects of this research.

References

Allen J.F. (1983) Maintaining knowledge about temporal intervals. In: Communications of the ACM. 26 November 1983. ACM Press. pp. 832–843, ISSN 0001-0782.

Bertin J. (1967) Sémiologie Graphique. Les diagrammes, les réseaux, les cartes. Paris: Gauthier-Villars. (Translation 1983. Semiology of Graphics by William J. Berg).

Brunet R. (1980) La composition des modèles dans l'analyse spatiale, in L'Espace géographique, n° 4, 1980.

Clementini E., Di Felice P. & van Oosterom P. (1993). A small set of formal topological relationships suitable for end-user interaction. In Abel, David & Ooi, Beng Chin. Advances in Spatial Databases: Third International Symposium, SSD '93 Singapore, June 23–25, 1993 Proceedings. *Lecture Notes in Computer Science*. 692/1993. Springer. pp. 277–295.

Cohn A. & N. Gotts. (1996) The "Egg-Yolk" Representation of Regions with Indeterminate Boundaries. In: P. Burrough and A. Frank (Eds.) *Geographic Objects with Indeterminate Boundaries*, pp. 171-187. Taylor & Francis.

Coimbra A. (2008). ChorML: XML Extension for Modeling Visual Summaries of Geographic Databases Based on Chorems, Master Dissertation, INSA-Lyon.

Del Fatto V., Laurini R., Lopez K., Loreto R., Milleret-Raffort F., Sebillo M., Sol-Martinez D. & Vitiello G. (2007) Potentialities of Chorems as Visual Summaries of Spatial Databases Contents, VISUAL 2007, 9th Int'l Conf. on Visual Information Systems, Shanghai, China, 28-29 June 2007. Edited by Qiu, G., Leung, C., Xue, X.-Y. & Laurini, R., Springer Verlag LNCS, Volume 4781 *Advances in Visual Information Systems*, pp. 537-548.

Douglas, D.H. & Peucker, T.K. (1973) Algorithms for the reduction of the number of points required to represent a digitised line or its caricature, *The Canadian Cartographer* 10 (2) pp. 112-122.

Egenhofer M. & R.D.Franzosa R.D. (1991) Point-set topological spatial relations", *International Journal of GIS*, vol.5, no.2, pp. 161-174.

Egenhofer M. (1994) Deriving the Composition of Binary Topological Relations. *Journal of Visual Languages and Computing* 5(2), pp. 133-149.

Goodchild, M.F. (2007). Citizens as sensors: the world of volunteered geography. *GeoJournal,* 69 (4) pp. 211–221.

Goodchild M. F. & Hill L. L. (2008). Introduction to digital gazetteer research. *Int'l Jour. of Geographical Information Science,* 22(10), pp. 1039-1044.

Gordillo S. (2001) Modélisation et manipulation de phénomènes continus spatio-temporels. PhD dissertation, October 12, 2001. Université Claude Bernard Lyon I.

Gruber T. R. (1993) A translation approach to portable ontologies. *Knowledge Acquisition,* 5(2) pp. 199-220.

Guarino, N. (1998). Formal Ontology and Information Systems. In N. Guarino (Ed.), Formal Ontology in Information Systems (pp. 3-15). Amsterdam, Netherlands: IOS Press.

Hećimović Z. & Ciceli T. (2013) Spatial Intelligence and Toponyms, Proceedings of the 26th International Cartographic Conference, Dresden, Germany, 25–30 August 2013, Edited by Manfred F. Buchroithner, ISBN: 978-1-907075-06-3..

Jakir Ž, Hećimović Ž; & Štefan Z. (2011) Place Names Ontologies. In Ruas A (Ed.) Advances in Cartography. Lecture Notes in Geoinformation and Cartography, Springer Heidelberg, pp. 331-349.

Kang M.A., Faloutsos C. Laurini R. & Servigne S. (2002) Indexing Values in Continuous Field Databases. In Proceedings of the International Conference on Extending Database Technology (EDBT 2002), March 2002, Prague. ISBN: 3-540-4332

Kavouras M., Kokla M. & Tomai E. (2005) Comparing categories among geographic ontologies, Computers & Geosciences (2005) Volume: 31, Issue: 2, Pages: 145-154 ISSN: 00983004.

Keßler C., Janowicz K. & Bishr M. (2009) An agenda for the next generation gazetteer: geographic information contribution and retrieval. Proceedings of the 17th ACM SIGSPATIAL International *Conference on Advances in Geographic Information Systems*, pp. 91-100, ACM New York, ISBN: 978-1-60558-649-6.

Laurini R. (1998) Spatial Multidabase Topological Continuity and Indexing: a Step towards Seamless GIS Data Interoperability. *International Journal of Geographical Information Sciences.* Vol. 12, 4, June 1998, pp. 373-402.

Laurini R. (2012) Importance of spatial relationships for geographic ontologies. In Planning Support Tools: Policy Analysis, Implementation and Evaluation Proceedings of the Seventh Int'al Conf. on Informatics and Urban and Regional Planning INPUT 2012 (Editors: M. Campagna, A. De Montis, F. Isola, S. Lai, C. Pira & C. Zoppi) (ISBN code: 9788856875973), pp. 122-134.

Laurini R. (2014) A conceptual framework for geographic knowledge engineering, *Journal of Visual Languages and Computing* 25 (2014) pp. 2–19.

Laurini R. (2015) "Geographic Ontologies, Gazetteers and Multilinguism", *Journal Future Internet* 7 (2015) pp. 1–23; doi:10.3390/fi7010001.

Laurini R. & Milleret-Raffort F. (1989) L'ingénierie des connaissances spatiales. Paris, Hermès, Collection Technologies de pointe, n° 30, 64 p.

Laurini R. & Thompson D. (1993) Fundamentals of Spatial Information Systems. Academic Press, (A.P.I.C. Series, No 37), March 1993.

Lee S.-Y. & Hsu F.-J., (1990) 2D C-string: A new Spatial Knowledge Representation for Image Database Systems, *Pattern Recognition*, vol. 23, no 10, pp. 1077-1087.

Lee S.-Y. & Hsu F.-J., (1992) Spatial Reasoning and Similarity Retrieval of Images Using 2D C-string Knowledge Representation, *Pattern Recognition*, Vol. 25, No 3, pp. 305-318.

Mani I., Doran C., Harris D., HitzemanJ., Quimby R., Richer J., Wellner B., Mardis S. & Clancy S. (2010) SpatialML: Annotation Scheme, Resources and Evaluation. The MITRE Corporation 202 Burlington Road Bedford, MA 01730, USA. http://www.mitre.org /work /tech_papers/tech_ papers_09/09_3827/09_3827.pdf.

Mennis J. & Guo D. (2009) Spatial data mining and geographic knowledge discovery – An introduction, *Computers, Environment and Urban Systems*, Volume 33 (6), November 2009, pp. 403-408.

Papadopoulou C.A. and Maria Giaoutzi M. (2014) Crowdsourcing as a Tool for Knowledge Acquisition in Spatial Planning. *Future Internet* 2014, 6, 109-125; doi:10.3390/fi6010109.

Popper K. (1934) The Logic of Scientific Discovery, (Logik der Forschung, English trans. 1959), ISBN 0-415-27844-9.

Preparata F. & Shamos M. (1985) *Computational geometry: an introduction*. Springer-Verlag 1985, ISBN: 0-387-96131-3.

Randell D.A., Zhan C. & Cohn A.G. (1992) A Spatial Logic based on Regions and Connection, In Proceedings 3rd Int'l *Conf. on Knowledge Representation and Reasoning,* Cambridge, MA (Morgan Kaufmann), pp. 165-176.

Smart, P.D., Jones C.B. & Twaroch F.A. (2010) Multi-Source Toponym Data Integration and Mediation for a Meta-Gazetteer Service, In Proceedings of GIScience 2010, Zurich, Switzerland, Lecture Notes In Computer Science 6292, pp. 234-248.

Smith B. & Mark D. Do Mountains Exist? Towards an Ontology of Landforms. *Environment and Planning B*, 2003, 30(3), pp. 411-427.

Thomas J.J. & Cook K. A. (2005) Illuminating the Path: The R&D Agenda for Visual Analytics. US National Visualization and Analytics Centre, 2005.

Tobler W. (1970) A Computer Movie Simulating Urban Growth in the Detroit Region. *Economic Geography*, 46(2) pp. 234-240.

Vckovski A. (1995) Representation of Continuous Fields, *Proceedings of 12th AutoCarto,* Vol.4, pp. 127-136, 1995.

Zadeh L. (1995) Fuzzy Sets, *Information and Control*, vol. 8, pp. 338-353.

TECHNICAL GLOSSARY ON KE

Chorem: a schematic representation of a territory. For geographers, this is a sort of simplified map of a territory emphasizing only important characteristics. For computer scientists, a chorem is a possible visual representation of geographic knowledge.

Gazetteer: originally a dictionary or a list of toponyms or place names. Now a gazetteer can be defined as a database integrating not only different names of the same place but also locations and variations upon time and in different languages.

Generalization: in cartography, a procedure for simplifying polylines, i.e., reducing the number of points. For instance, consider a country with two geometric representations, first with 1000 points and the second with 100 points. The latter one is called a generalization of the former one.

Geographic features: features in the real word; they can be natural or manmade.

Geographic knowledge: knowledge relative to places on the Earth usually taking Earth rotundity into account.

Geographic objects: computer representation of geographic features.

Geographic ontologies: two definitions exist; (*i*) an ontology of geographic terms; (*ii*) an ontology of geographic terms with spatial relations.

Ribbon: various mathematical definitions were provided but none are totally satisfactory. In a non-mathematically correct way but very easy to understand, a ribbon can be considered as a line with a width.

Spatial knowledge: knowledge implying spatial relations often in a Cartesian plan.

Spatial relations: geometric relations between two or several objects such as topological relations, distance relations and projective relations.

Territorial intelligence: like business intelligence but applied to the management of geographic units, countries, regions, cities, etc.

Tessellation: a tiling of a surface. The tiles can be regular or irregular.

Some Feedback Questions to the Reader

Q1 – Starting from Figure 1 write its description with ribbons relations.

Figure 1. Banks of the Rhone River.

Q2 – Explicit the main characteristics of the city you live in and design manually its chorem.

Q3 – When making a generalization of the borders of your country, give the list of topological constraints; for instance you must enforce constraints so that harbors always stay in land near the sea.

Q4 – Design a visual query for getting the English cities located west of London, UK.

Q5 – Give a minimum of 10 placenames of your neighborhood to constitute a gazetteer.

Q6 – Look for the description of your city in GeoNames. Is it correct?

Q7 – Encode the following chunks of geographic knowledge "*Near big cities, there is an airport*", "*The majority of big Canadian cities are located in the South of the country*", "*In all city, land prices diminish with the distance of the central business district*"

About the Author

DR. ROBERT LAURINI is presently Professor Emeritus at INSA-Lyon, University of Lyon, France. He submitted two doctorates, an engineering doctorate in 1973, and a State doctorate in 1980 both in computing. He is a pioneer and a worldly-known specialist in geographic information systems. He speaks French, English, Italian and Spanish. He held positions at the University of Cambridge, UK, at the University of Maryland College Park, USA and at the IUAV University of Venice. He was more than 20 times invited professor in Argentina and Mexico. He has recently created "Academics Without Borders" which is a network of university consultants for assisting higher education institutions in developed countries. He is also Fellow of the Knowledge Systems Institute of Chicago. He wrote more than 200 papers and 7 books, the more important being “Information Systems for Urban Planning: A Hypermedia Cooperative Approach” in 2001 and “Fundamentals of Spatial Information Systems” with Derek Thompson, in 1993.

In: Knowledge Engineering
Editor: Alfonso Perez Gama
ISBN: 978-1-63463-909-5

Chapter 2

KNOWLEDGE MANAGEMENT OF CONTROLLED VOCABULARIES IN HEALTHCARE AND THE SEMANTIC INTEROPERABILITY CHALLENGE

Timothy Wayne Cook[1], Joyce Rocha de Matos Nogueira[2] and Luciana Tricai Cavalini[3]*

[1]National Institute of Science and Technology –
Medicine Assisted by Scientific Computing, Brazil
[2]MLHIM Technological Development Unit,
Rio de Janeiro State University, Brazil
[3]Department of Health Information Technology,
Rio de Janeiro State University, Brazil

ABSTRACT

The complexity of healthcare information is caused by the dynamic nature of healthcare systems and how biomedical science in general evolves. This brings challenges to the achievement of semantic interoperability and the maintenance of healthcare information systems. Changes in the software code must be performed much more frequently in healthcare applications than in software applied to other sectors of the economy; this scenario necessarily increases the price of the final product, when the conventional annual or semi-annual updates are deployed.

The enormous amount of concepts in biomedical sciences (something in excess of 2,000,000 terms) and the difficulty of reaching consensus among experts about the representation of medical knowledge, results in extreme variability of the system requirements. This is true even within the same level of complexity of care. Some of the reasons for this extremely complexity lay on the fact that the route of each patient through various healthcare settings is not consistent with every other patient, and the outcomes of any individual encounter may affect the outcome of the following. This

* Corresponding Author: Luciana Tricai Cavalini, lutricav@lampada.uerj.br.

makes the acquisition of semantic interoperability between the various information systems a basic necessity for the health informatics field.

One of the most common solutions proposed in the scientific literature for handling the complexity of healthcare information systems, and in particular for obtaining semantic interoperability among healthcare applications, is the adoption of controlled vocabularies, primarily terminologies and ontologies. Controlled vocabularies play an essential role in the standardization of medical knowledge representation models. Many projects have demonstrated success and longevity in this direction.

Controlled vocabularies are considered essential for achieving semantic interoperability, given the features related to the standardization of the knowledge representation models in biomedicine. However, the isolated adoption of terminologies, classifications or ontologies has not been enough to acquire the desired ability to communicate semantically valid extracts of information between independently developed, distributed applications.

This Chapter has the objective to examine the development and governance of controlled vocabularies, interoperability standards and specifications and the key relationships between them. The main global projects on controlled vocabularies, standards and specifications currently available in the healthcare domain are described in depth, with focus on their specific contributions and the correspondent technological and sociopolitical challenges for the solution of the semantic interoperability and software maintenance in healthcare.

1. INTRODUCTION

The adoption of Information Technologies (IT) has been proposed as the path to overcome the contemporary challenges of healthcare systems at the national and local levels [1]. It has been promised that healthcare IT will; improve the quality of care, increase patient safety, improve treatment adherence, improve user satisfaction, free healthcare providers from unnecessary workload, organize workflows and reduce costs for final users, improve decision making by hospital managers and policy makers [2-7]. However, there is little evidence that many of those outcomes have been reached by the computerized medical systems that have been implemented over the last half of the century [8].

There is no consensus about why there is such a gap between the evident evolution of other sectors of the economy achieved by IT adoption and the reality observed in healthcare [9]. Biological processes have a different nature from human engineered, industrial processes. Biological processes have a different architecture and therefore a new design approach should be used on biomedical software applications [10]. It is unlikely that the currently available healthcare IT products meet the requirements for modelling biological systems in general and healthcare in particular [11].

The complexity of healthcare information is derived from the dynamic nature of healthcare systems and how biomedical science evolves. This creates challenges for the achievement of semantic interoperability and the maintenance of healthcare information systems [12]. An additional challenge is the approach used by healthcare domain experts to interpret and express healthcare concepts. These expressions can vary based on culture, geographical location and educational background [13].

The current adoption scenario of IT in healthcare is quite low, almost all of it centralized in developed countries [14] where distributed, independently developed applications are deployed in healthcare facilities, locking fragments of the patient's health information into isolated, incommunicable silos [15].

Due to the evolving science around biological systems, changes in the software code must be performed much more frequently in healthcare applications than in software applied to human engineered domains. In turn, this scenario increases the price of the final product, when the conventional annual or semi-annual updates are deployed [16].

The variation in expression and interpretation of concepts creates an environment where the software is not easily deployed in multiple locations as is the case with other 'industrialized applications', such as a word processing or even a complex customer resource management application. The evidence for this is seen as user dissatisfaction, typically expressed in surveys as complaints about inadequate work-flow or user interface design, although this same application could be better rated in one or a few particular installations [17].

This brings us to a point of where every healthcare IT installation appears to be unique in order to satisfy the needs of the sub-domain and the user specific workflow. This naturally creates interoperability issues between these applications [18].

The enormous amount of concepts in biomedical sciences (something in excess of 2,000,000 terms) and the difficulty of reaching consensus among experts about the representation of medical knowledge, results in extreme variability of the system requirements, which is true even within the same level of complexity of care. Some of the reasons for this extreme complexity lay in the fact that the route of each patient through various healthcare settings is not consistent with every other patient, and the outcomes of any individual encounter may affect the outcome of the following. This makes the acquisition of semantic interoperability between the various information systems a basic necessity for the health informatics field [19].

One of the most common solutions proposed in the scientific literature for handling the complexity of healthcare information systems, and in particular for obtaining semantic interoperability among healthcare applications, is the adoption of controlled vocabularies, primarily terminologies, classifications and ontologies [20]. Controlled vocabularies play an essential role in the standardization of medical knowledge representation models. Many projects have demonstrated some success with this approach [21]. A major example is the Unified Medical Language System® (UMLS®), a set of controlled vocabularies in medicine (the Metathesaurus) managed by a software suite that includes the Semantic Network, connecting semantic types (the broader categories of medical terms) through relations between the vocabularies, also including Lexical Tools for natural language processing [22].

Controlled vocabularies are considered essential for achieving semantic interoperability, given the features related to the standardization of the knowledge representation models in biomedicine [23]. However, the isolated adoption of terminologies, classifications or ontologies has not been effective in delivering the desired ability to communicate semantically valid extracts of information between independently developed, distributed applications [24]. To effectively communicate, both *structure* and *semantics* must be decidable between the communicating parties.

The most widespread healthcare *information exchange* standard, Health Level Seven (HL7™), has adopted in its version 3, the TermInfo project and the specification of a Common Terminology Service (CTS) [25]. While HL7 is not a controlled vocabulary it is important for the reader to see the connection between defining concepts and the ability to exchange them in a useful manner.

The TermInfo project [26] began in 2004 with a Draft Standards for Trial Use (DSTU) first issued in September 2007. This project has also been supported by the International Health Terminology Standards Development Organisation (IHTSDO), the developers of the Systematized Nomenclature of Medicine – Clinical Terms (SNOMED-CT™). The 2007 TermInfo DSTU expired in May 2009. There is a plan to issue a new DSTU in January 2014.

The CTS project [25] began in 2005 and is both a DSTU and an implementation of a subset of a terminology service. There was a CTS DSTU issued in October 2009 and it expired in October 2011. There are no comments available on the public wiki regarding any status update. However, there is ongoing work at least on the implementation in efforts to work with the Service Functional Model Group at HL7. The exact relationship between the TermInfo project and the CTS project is currently unclear.

Uptake of these projects has not been followed by enough reports on the successful exchange of semantically coherent extracts of information between different applications; the few reports of successful implementation were in extremely controlled situations. This has not led to any significant following for situations that are typically found in the reality of the healthcare systems [27].

This Chapter has the objective to examine the development and governance of controlled vocabularies, interoperability standards and specifications and the key relationships between them. The main global projects on controlled vocabularies, standards and specifications currently available in the healthcare domain are described, with focus on their specific contributions and the correspondent technological and socio-political issues for the solution to the challenges of semantic interoperability and software maintenance in healthcare. As a conclusion, a solution to produce knowledge models using controlled vocabularies with semantic interoperability, based on multilevel model-driven software development, is presented, as well as a use case about the current state of knowledge modeling in nursing sciences, in which controlled vocabularies are prevalent and play a major role.

1.1. Questions

1. What are the main challenges to the wider implementation of healthcare Information Technology (IT) worldwide?
2. What is one of the most common approaches to dealing with the complexity and dynamics of knowledge representation in healthcare?
3. Perform a web search on the healthcare controlled vocabularies projects listed in this Chapter and try to identify convergences and divergences between them.

Controlled Vocabularies

The three major controlled vocabularies, the International Statistical Classification of Diseases and Related Health Problems, known as International Classification of Diseases (ICD), the SNOMED-CT and the Logical Observation Identifiers Names and Codes (LOINC) are presented in detail in the section below, as well as an overview of the application of ontologies in healthcare knowledge representation.

1.2. International Classification of Diseases (ICD)

The earliest recorded attempts to classify diseases in a systematic manner is attributed to François Bossier de Lacroix (1706-1777) published under the title *Nosologia methodica*. Throughout the 18th and 19th centuries there were several attempts to organize the reporting of health and death statistics. The first International Statistical Congress, held in Brussels in 1853, requested William Farr and Marc d'Espine, of Geneva, to prepare an internationally applicable, uniform classification of causes of death. They each prepared documents that were based on quite different approaches. Through an evolutionary process of the organization as well as the vocabularies, the International List of Causes of Death was adopted by delegates from 26 countries in 1900, with a plan to update the list every 10 years. Over the early 20th century this list was updated and merged with other lists and emerged in the latter half of the century under the auspices of the World Health Organization (WHO) as the International Classification of Diseases (ICD) [28]. ICD is now in its 10th Revision, released in 1990. The latest version was published in 2010. Revision 11 is now in a beta phase and is expected to be released in 2015 [29].

All WHO Member States use the ICD and it has been translated into 43 languages. Most countries (117) use the system to report mortality data, a primary indicator of health status. Therefore the primary intent of ICD is to enable the ability to aggregate data for analysis on a global scale [30].

The ICD is essentially a nested hierarchical listing of coded terms. The codes allow for concise representation of specific concepts agreed upon by consensus of a group of international experts. This structure is very useful for computerization of healthcare data stored in SQL databases [31]. The negative aspect of this structure is that it does not easily expand and encompass new concepts, which results in several issues related to the validity and reliability of diagnostic information recorded according to the ICD terms [32].

1.3. Systematized Nomenclature of Medicine – Clinical Terms (SNOMED-CT)

The SNOMED-CT is a comprehensive vocabulary that covers almost every aspect of clinical care, ranging from anatomy to diagnoses to observations and procedures. It is effectively a merge of the Systematized Nomenclature of Pathology (SNOP) from the College of American Pathologists (CAP) and the Read Codes (renamed Read Terms then renamed to Clinical Terms) used by the National Health Service (NHS) in England. The original project was a cooperation between the ACP and the NHS to develop a common vocabulary. The International Health Terminology Standards Development Organization (IHTSDO) was formed in 2007 and purchased the rights to SNOMED-CT. SNOMED-CT is updated continuously and new releases are published twice each year [33].

The vocabulary is organized [34] as an acyclic graph consisting of ***is-a*** relationships, based on a root concept, "*SNOMED CT Concept*". This root concept is the immediate parent of all top-level concepts and is the only SNOMED-CT concept without a parent. The Table 1 presents a list of all top level concepts, and Figure 1 The diagram below depicts a summarized view of relationship styles in a concept definition in SNOMED-CT.

Table 1. List of the top level concepts in SNOMED-CT

Clinical finding	Procedure
Observable entity	Body structure
Organism	Substance
Pharmaceutical / biologic product	Specimen
Special concept	SNOMED CT Model Component
Physical force	Event
Environment or geographical location	Social context
Situation with explicit context	Staging and scales
Physical object	Qualifier value
Record artifact	

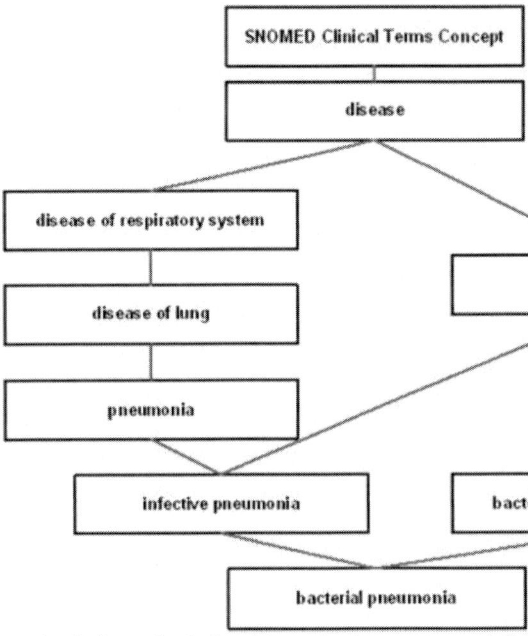

Figure 1. Summarized view of relationship styles in a concept definition in SNOMED-CT.

A SNOMED-CT expression [35] is a combination of one or more unique identifiers, delimiters and optionally human readable text. Expressions come in two types; *pre-coordinated* and *post-coordinated.*

Pre-coordinated expressions are defined as those expressions that exist in SNOMED-CT as a complete entity. An example of a pre-coordinated expression is;

31978002 |fracture of tibia |

Post-coordinated expressions contain two or more concepts from SNOMED-CT. Post-coordination is an essential function for developing useful implementations of healthcare applications that use SNOMED-CT to enhance the semantic interoperability of the captured information.

Pre-coordinated expressions in SNOMED-CT can be also be defined as a post-coordinated expression using its supertypes. From an example in the Starter Guide:

174041007 |laparoscopic emergency appendectomy|

can also be defined as

80146002 |appendectomy|: 260870009 |priority|= 25876001 |emergency|, 425391005 |using access device|= 86174004 |laparoscope|

since the former is a complete and computable subtype of the latter.

Post-coordination allows for implementations to create complex clinical statements that are fully coded in SNOMED-CT. These complex compositions can then be used by any other application with to calculate the semantics inferred at the time the information was recorded.

A note of caution needs to be issued though. It is well known that there are tradeoffs when storing complex hierarchical data in SQL databases. There is a tendency in implementations to create post-coordinated expressions and assign them an ID at the national level, analogous to the International Classification of Diseases – Clinical Modification (ICD-CM) codes. If these nationally assigned IDs are used in implementations and those implementations do not have computational access to the SNOMED-CT components from which they are created, this is a point where global interoperability ceases. If an implementation creates messages that use national subset IDs and those messages or record summaries are transferred to some place without access to that national subset, the core purpose of SNOMED-CT is defeated.

If IHTSDO wants SNOMED-CT to be the global interoperability vocabulary, they should cease encouraging national subsets. On the other hand, close to user, post-coordinated expressions should be created at the implementation level. All outgoing messages and record summaries should use complete pre-coordinated expressions that can be validated against the International Release.

One study purported to be on the reliability of SNOMED-CT actually is not about the reliability of it as a vocabulary; it is much more of a comment on the inconsistent naming and coding of things by healthcare providers [36]. First, at the level of how codes and definitions are added to the vocabulary and then to how healthcare providers and coders choose codes within the constraints of the vocabulary. An interesting metric would have been to also record the option for a coder to say when no appropriate match was found. The real problem is fundamental to medical education and global cultural differences. Since medical education will never be consistent in every medical college [37], there will always be discrepancies in the view on how a term should be coded from a controlled vocabulary; and even to what the content of the vocabulary should be.

Clearly, there needs to be a solution that provides the healthcare provider with the ability to share the complete semantics, as they intended when something is recorded. This is the case behind free text descriptions. The issue is then, reliability in computing this information for clinical decision support and public health aggregate analysis [38].

1.4. Logical Observation Identifiers, Names and Codes (LOINC)

In contrast to SNOMED-CT, LOINC [39] is a freely available vocabulary that can be downloaded from http://loinc.org/ and used worldwide, royalty free. LOINC is sponsored by the medical research organization Regenstrief Institute, associated with Indiana University. The scope of LOINC is all of laboratory medicine but it also includes a set of clinical observations.

LOINC is used in 157 countries for coding clinical and laboratory concepts. Regenstrief also provides an interface tool for LOINC known as Regenstrief LOINC Mapping Assistant (RELMA). It is a MS Windows only, aid to mapping LOINC codes to local codes as well as a search engine for LOINC. There is also an online search engine for LOINC at http://search.loinc.org. LOINC is distributed as a JET database file and as a Comma Separated Values (CSV) file, and the Release 2.46 is composed of 73,116 entries of 48 columns, listed on Table 2 [40].

Though the goal of semantic interoperability for clinical and laboratory observations is stated, it is observed from the column names that aspects of other purpose specific domains have crept into the format. Specifically; 'SURVEY_QUEST_TEXT' and 'SURVEY_QUEST_SRC' are concerned with surveys and not with clinical observations. Thus, the format of LOINC needs to be revisited in order to create a cleaner vocabulary for general use.

The other LOINC resources are; a map from one LOINC code to another when a code has been deprecated and should be replaced by the newer code and a list of contributing organizations and additional restrictions on code use, linked to the codes by the copyright ID found in LOINC.

Table 2. List of the LOINC components

LOINC_NUM	COMPONENT	PROPERTY
TIME_ASPCT	SYSTEM	SCALE_TYP
METHOD_TYP	CLASS	SOURCE
DATE_LAST_CHANGED	CHNG_TYPE	COMMENTS
STATUS	CONSUMER_NAME	MOLAR_MASS
CLASSTYPE	FORMULA	SPECIES
EXMPL_ANSWERS	ACSSYM	BASE_NAME
NAACCR_ID	CODE_TABLE	SURVEY_QUEST_TEXT
SURVEY_QUEST_SRC	UNITSREQUIRED	SUBMITTED_UNITS
RELATEDNAMES2	SHORTNAME	ORDER_OBS
CDISC_COMMON_TESTS	HL7_FIELD_SUBFIELD_ID	EXTERNAL_COPYRIGHT_NOTICE
EXAMPLE_UNITS	LONG_COMMON_NAME	HL7_V2_DATATYPE
HL7_V3_DATATYPE	CURATED_RANGE_AND_UNITS	DOCUMENT_SECTION
EXAMPLE_UCUM_UNITS	EXAMPLE_SI_UCUM_UNITS	STATUS_REASON
STATUS_TEXT	CHANGE_REASON_PUBLIC	COMMON_TEST_RANK
COMMON_ORDER_RANK	COMMON_SI_TEST_RANK	HL7_ATTACHMENT_STRUCTURE

The only governance statement regarding the uniqueness of the codes is found in the usage guidelines [39], where users are instructed to place an 'X' as the leading character when they insert their own codes into the table. Although the LOINC documentation discusses the use of 'classes' of codes, these are used only as aggregating classifiers in the code set, the LOINC database structure is a flat table.

Though LOINC is widely used it may become more part of the problem than the solution if the governance and clarity of vision are not addressed.

2. Ontologies

Ontology [41] is an emerging methodology used to fully describe concepts in context. In healthcare information management, ontologies have the potential to be connected to resolving the semantic context of concepts [42]. The most prominent place to explore the use of ontologies for healthcare is on Bioportal (http://bioportal.bioontology.org/), which is home to more than 350 ontologies and the mappings between them.

Many controlled vocabularies have been converted to an OWL (web ontology language) representation and added to the Bioportal, including the three controlled vocabularies discussed above, including several versions and the US customization of ICD [43]. A prominent feature of Bioportal includes the fact that a Permanent Universal Resource Locater (PURL) is linked for every concept. For example, Miliary Tuberculosis in ICD10 is assigned to the PURL http://purl.bioontology.org/ontology/ICD10/A19. A "Mappings" tab is also available, to show the mappings that have been created to other ontologies, reaching to 18 other controlled vocabularies. Bioportal can be regarded as a very powerful tool for establishing the semantics of a biomedical concept. However, it is important to notice that some of the vocabularies found on Bioportal, such as SNOMED-CT, are covered by intellectual property restrictions and even though they are reachable via Bioportal, they may not be legal to be used in knowledge modelling for real biomedical applications. Thus, it is incumbent upon the knowledge modeler to determine the appropriateness of any links from this site.

2.1. Questions

1. List the major advantages and disadvantages of each one of the following controlled vocabularies (if necessary, perform a web search on their official websites for completeness):
   a) International Classification of Diseases (ICD)
   b) Systematized Nomenclature of Medicine – Clinical Terms (SNOMED-CT)
   c) Logical Observation Identifiers, Names and Codes (LOINC)

2. Perform a web search on the Bioportal for the terms "blood pressure", "cough" and "penicillin" and:
   d) check if there are related terms on the 3 controlled vocabularies covered by this Chapter
   e) verify if there are other controlled vocabularies representing these concepts.

f) Do the terms coming from different controlled vocabularies represent exactly the same concept? Elaborate.

3. Use Case: Knowledge Representation and Controlled Vocabularies in Nursing Sciences

The evolution of knowledge representation models in nursing informatics is remarkable, given the well-established developments of several reference terminologies for nursing concepts, including collaboration with the development efforts of more general terminology for the entire spectrum of healthcare. A standardized terminology should guarantee that a term is used with the same meaning for different users; thus, the establishment of a common language for nursing practice would allow the comparison of databases across clinical different populations and settings over time [44].

Regarding the construction of nursing controlled vocabularies, there are several international development initiatives being conducted with the purpose of creating a common vocabulary for nursing practice. However, these initiatives are disjointed, since there are different terminologies used by different application developers. Thus, despite the fact that the different nursing terminologies provide a richness of representation terms of nursing phenomena and related domains of practice, there is currently no practical means of translation (i.e., mapping) of such terminologies in order to aggregate and compare data recorded according to different terminologies [45, 46].

The most widely adopted nursing controlled vocabularies are; the International Classification for Nursing Practice (ICNP), the North American Nursing Diagnosis Association terminology (NANDA), the Nursing Interventions Classification System (NIC), the Nursing Outcomes Classification (NOC), the Clinical Care Classification (CCC), the Omaha System, the Patient Care Data Set (PCDS) and the Perioperative Nursing Data Set (PNDS).

The International Classification for Nursing Practice (ICNP) has been developed by the initiative of the International Council of Nurses (ICN). It is defined as a classification of nursing phenomena, actions and results, having two versions released since its beta release in 1999 [47].

Established in 1982, the North American Nursing Diagnosis Association (NANDA) terminology initially classified nursing diagnoses according to Taxonomy I, which was structured in nine categories from the Human Response Patterns conceptual model. From this structure, further modifications were made, adding some areas and renaming others. Finally, in 2000, the NANDA Taxonomy II was defined, which currently contains 13 domains, 47 classes and 201 diagnoses [48].

The Nursing Interventions Classification System (NIC) was developed by researchers at the University of Iowa, having been launched in 1992 and now it is in its fifth edition. The first edition had 336 interventions, and the fourth had 514, with more than 12,000 actions and activities. Currently, the NIC has seven domains and 30 classes. Since the third edition, the essential interventions comprise a total of 43 specialties [49].

Launched in 1991, the Nursing Outcomes Classification (NOC) has also been created by researchers at the University of Iowa. The first publication of the NOC, in 1997, contained

190 results. The second edition (2000) included 260 results, and the third publication (2004) was expanded to 330 results. The fourth edition (2008), includes 385 results grouped into 31 classes and seven domains. NOC includes Nursing Results (RE) describing the status, behaviors, reactions and feelings of the patient in response to the care provided [50].

The Clinical Care Classification System (CCC) was originally created at Georgetown University in 1991 to document nursing care, both domiciliary (home care) and outpatients. It contains 176 concepts of nursing diagnoses and 198 concepts of nursing interventions. The diagnoses have three modifiers (Enhanced, Stabilized, or Deteriorated) to document both the current and the expected results. Nursing interventions are also expansible by using four modifiers, in order to document the type of action for each nursing intervention [51].

The Omaha System was developed by the Division of Nursing at Omaha, Nebraska (USA) between 1975 and 1986, funded by the United States Department of Health and Human Services. It consists of terms related to Issues, Interventions and Outcomes. The classification problems scheme (n = 44) is composed of four domains (environmental, psychosocial, physiological and health-related behaviors). The problems are then described by the organization of the two sets of modifiers: (a) type of problem (actual or potential health promotion) and (b) type of customer (individual, family or community) [52].

The Patient Care Data Set (PCDS) was originally developed at the Virginia University and has been reviewed by researchers at the Vanderbilt University Medical Center. The PCDS Version 4.0 (1998) contains a data dictionary and terms of representation of values and codes for specific patient Problems (363 terms), Targets Care (311 terms) and Orders for Patient Care (1,357 terms) [53].

The Perioperative Nursing Data Set (PNDS) is a nursing controlled vocabulary that provides a universal language for recording problems and perioperative treatments, containing four domains: (a) safety, (b) physiological response to surgery, (c) behavioral response of the patient and the family to surgery and (d) the healthcare system. Each domain is accompanied by the desired outcomes of nursing interventions and nursing diagnoses [54].

These efforts in knowledge modeling are important to ensure that nursing concepts are accurately represented in computerized systems, in a way that facilitates local, national, regional and international use of the information. However, with the expansion of the nursing informatics field, it can be noticed that the nursing controlled vocabularies have followed the same path of confusion that already occurs between other healthcare vocabularies; which is not desired. Some authors postulate that the solution would create a health information ecosystem sharing a common language, a universal model, where all the controlled vocabularies used in the area were easily linked in a single operational model [55], which is a pre-intuition of the fundamentals of multilevel model-driven software development described below.

Therefore, it is important to emphasize that the simple introduction of controlled vocabularies in nursing information systems is no guarantee for effective interoperability. Moreover, the widespread adoption of different nursing controlled vocabularies in independently developed, distributed systems reduces the probability of data sharing [56]. Since there is no consensus on the adoption of one or other of the existing nursing controlled vocabularies, there is a need to analyze each of them individually, but model them uniformly (as presented in the next section), in order to allow those initiatives to accomplish their primary mission of providing semantic interoperability.

3.1. Questions

About the nursing terminologies mentioned in this Chapter:

1. Do they overlap in terms of concept coverage?
2. Are they complimentary in terms of concept coverage?
3. Perform a web search to identify terminology harmonization projects that include them.

4. Implementing Controlled Vocabularies

In the previous sections of this Chapter we have introduced some of the major, out of hundreds, controlled vocabularies used in healthcare, as well as a major resource for exploring ontologies and semantic mappings between them. The remaining challenge is to implement those resources in healthcare real-world applications, in order to improve the information produced and shared [57]. These vocabularies can provide semantic reference points for concepts, but the computability must be consistent across various systems as well.

As discussed before, using a controlled vocabulary is not enough to provide interoperability, since their function is to provide the semantics of the concepts [27]. Thus, in order to achieve semantic interoperability, the information structure and syntax must also be exchangeable in order for the receiver to use the information in a computable manner.

The great majority of existing healthcare applications that use controlled vocabularies (many do not use them or at best use local codes), do so in support of messages for billing; some also use codes for exchange of clinical summaries [58]. In this way, the predetermined message format tells the sender of the message to select content from their system to send to the receiver of the message, which is unaware of the semantic context in which the original data was captured. For example, in most cases, a blood pressure reading will be sent for systolic and diastolic values and usually the unit of measure of millimeters of mercury (mmHg). Usually it is not possible for the receiver to get any additional information about the patient state, equipment or environment during the measurement period; each of these having a potential to affect the values and how the values should be interpreted. This not-transferred information (i.e., the semantic context) remains locked up in the sender's software source code and database structure, which captured the original values, if it is captured at all.

In order to provide a sustainable solution for semantic interoperability, the concept of multilevel model-driven software development introduced in the late 20th century by the *open*EHR Foundation [59] has been modernized and improved for the 21st century through the *Multi-Level Healthcare Information Modelling* (MLHIM) project, which produced the MLHIM specifications [60], published under a Creative Commons License.

The advantage of MLHIM over other healthcare IT standards is that the syntax and semantics of a concept are defined such that they can be exchanged between the sender and receiver. This is done by using the ubiquitous eXtensible Markup Language (XML), which has tools for processing on all platforms and programming languages, thus making it the *lingua franca* for information exchange. The simplest concept on how this information exchange can be performed with full semantic interoperability with MLHIM is described in these steps.

A healthcare domain expert (i.e., physician, physical therapist, nurse, cardiologist, etc.) describes a set of phrases that represent a healthcare concept. A knowledge modeler, which may or may not be the same domain expert, frames each phrase in the context of a common Reference Model (for syntactic interoperability) and adds links to controlled vocabularies and/or ontologies in order to express the meaning (semantics) of the phrase. The phrases are combined in a Domain Model that includes additional semantic links and metadata descriptions about the use, misuse and provenance of the model. This Domain Model is then expressed in a computable form as an XML Schema known in MLHIM as a Concept Constraint Definition (CCD)[1]. As a consequence, when data is exchanged between two systems, the data must be valid against the CCD that describes the syntax and semantics for it. This approach provides a data instance (or message) as well as a model to validate it against to prevent lost or incorrect semantics as a result of the data exchange.

Since MLHIM has a common Reference Model, systems can be designed to automatically import and export data instances that conform to CCDs. However, systems that currently exist, not based on MLHIM, may still use MLHIM CCDs to define data extracts for exchange.

A key advantage of the MLHIM approach is that CCDs are reusable but are not defined in a top-down, bureaucratic environment. The reason for this bottom-up, merit-based approach is based on the realization that healthcare is consensus driven at the macro level, as expressed in clinical guidelines. However, at the micro level of everyday practice there are wide variations and very little consensus among domain experts [61].

If the issue of semantic interoperability is addressed with proper rigor, it becomes clear that the only place that complete semantics can be captured is at the point when the data was captured; thus, semantics cannot be faithfully, added later [62]. By using a bottom-up, multi-level approach and linking the data instance (message) back to the defining CCD, both the data and the Domain Model can be shared between systems for full human and computer interpretation.

In the context of XML, each of the phrases that compose a CCD are represented as a *complexType*. In MLHIM, these are called Pluggable complexTypes (PcTs), since they are reusable across many CCDs. The Concept Constraint Definition Generator (CCD-Gen) allows the knowledge modeler to explore examples of PcTs and CCDs on www.ccdgen.com, with several examples of how it is possible to take definitions from other data dictionaries such as the US National Cancer Institute, Common Data Element project and representing them as PcTs. The CCD Library also provides example CCDs, XML data instances as well as an HTML form providing a graphical view into how user interfaces can be built for systems based on MLHIM.

4.1. Questions

1. Define with your own words the multilevel model-driven approach.

[1] A CCD can be validated against the Reference Model using open source and commercial XML tools available on the market. This provides a complete validation chain from instance data to CCD to Reference Model to the W3C XML model.

2. What are the main differences you can identify between the openEHR and the MLHIM approaches to multilevel modeling? If necessary, perform a web search on both specifications' website for additional information.
3. Is it possible to represent any controlled vocabulary concept using the multilevel model-driven approach? Elaborate.

5. Future Work and Perspectives

The future of health informatics depends largely on the overcoming of the currently prevailing paradigms in this social space, and the acceptance of technological innovations that effectively solve the complex problem of semantic interoperability. This will require a cultural change that must necessarily include the adoption of new business models in the medical software industry, the true democratization of political bodies responsible for setting healthcare IT standards, the renewal of the curricula of undergraduate and postgraduate courses in health informatics and the evolution of attitudes towards the acceptance of true and effective technological innovation.

An important aspect in this regard concerns the adequacy of healthcare applications to their everyday users, especially the healthcare providers at the point of care. Conventional electronic records have proved poorly adapted to these users workflow patterns. There is systematic evidence on the very low level of use of such software at this level of attention. This is an important point to address because this is where most of the decision intelligence in healthcare occurs. The community of healthcare application users and independent analysts are currently the voices calling for changes in the academic and industrial establishment of healthcare IT. The most frequent demands in this community concern the development of mobile health applications (mHealth) and the adaptation of EHRs to user interfaces and workflows similar to the social networks.

The technology presented in this Chapter, so far, seems to be the only approach that allows the development of medical applications that combine these two requirements (mHealth and social network user experience) without the creation of a huge and confusing heathcare Big Data silo. Since the infrastructure is already defined by the MLHIM specifications, for the development of mHealth applications based on this technology, it is necessary, at this time, improving the user (knowledge modeler) experience for applications such as CCD-Gen,. This will increase the community of developer of clinical models adapted to the reality of each point of care, but still able to share syntactically coherent and semantically valid data.

Conclusion

The achievement of semantic interoperability is an essential requirement for the cost-effective adoption of information technologies in healthcare. The importance of controlled vocabularies cannot be minimized in the achievement of this goal. However, the previous experiences have shown that the implementation of controlled vocabularies in conventional software is not enough to provide semantic interoperability between healthcare information systems. The wider adoption of multilevel, model-driven software development solutions has the potential to overcome the current challenges in healthcare IT, thus enabling the development of patient-centered, semantically coherent, longitudinal healthcare information ecosystems.

TECHNICAL GLOSSARY

Classification: According to the ISO 17117 Standard, a "terminology which aggregates data at a prescribed level of abstraction for a particular domain".

Clinical Care Classification (CCC): A nursing terminology that identifies the discrete elements of nursing practice, provided by the American Nurses' Association (ANA) since 1990.

College of American Pathologists (CAP): A not-for-profit corporation established in 1946 that certifies pathologists in the United States, being also responsible for the development of the SNOMED Reference Terminology (SNOMED-RT), one of the components of the modern SNOMED-CT.

Controlled Vocabulary: According to the ISO 17117 Standard, a "set of terms intended for clinical use".

Creative Commons License: A public copyright license that enable the free distribution of an otherwise copyrighted work, originally released by Creative Commons, a US non-profit corporation since 2001.

Data Silo: A computerized dataset that cannot share semantically valid data with other applications.

Diastolic Blood Pressure: Pressure exerted by circulating blood upon the walls of blood vessels during the cardiac diastole (relaxation of the cardiac muscle).

Domain Model: The multilevel model-driven technology data models, defined by combination and restrictions of the Reference Model components that are necessary to define a given domain concept.

eXtensible Markup Language (XML): A markup language that defines a set of rules for encoding documents in a format that is both human-readable and machine-readable, defined in the free open XML 1.0 Specification and other related specifications, produced by the World Wide Web Consortium (W3C) since 1998.

Health Level Seven (HL7): HL7 Inc. is a US company that develops and maintains the HL7 specifications, converted into an US American healthcare IT standard with the Health Insurance Portability and Accountability Act (HIPAA) of 1996.

Healthcare Application: Computerized information systems applied to the healthcare domain.

Healthcare Concept: A definable idea pertaining to the healthcare domain.

Healthcare Domain Expert: A healthcare professional with a specialized knowledge on a specific area of healthcare sciences (e.g., cardiology, nursing, general practice)

Healthcare Information Technology (HIT): Application and implementation of Information Technology (IT) to the execution and registration of inputs, processes and outcomes in healthcare.

Healthcare Setting: An institution and its facilities where healthcare is provided (e.g., hospitals, clinics, medical offices).

Healthcare Specifications: Expression usually adopted to refer to healthcare IT specifications, comprises a given set of documentations, software code and related resources that inform the development of healthcare applications.

Healthcare Standard: Expression usually adopted to refer to healthcare IT standards, comprises the subset of healthcare IT specifications and related resources that are developed, adopted or approved by a Standards Development Organization such as the International Standards Organization (ISO).

Healthcare Workflow: Formal and informal definition of work processes in healthcare settings, such as clinical care processes.

International Classification for Nursing Practice (ICNP): A classification of phenomena, actions and outcomes that describes nursing practice, established in 2000 by the International Council of Nurses (ICN).

International Classification of Diseases – Clinical Modification (ICD-CM): A classification for diagnoses and reason for visits used in United States' healthcare settings, based on the WHO's ICD, provided by the Centers for Medicare and Medicaid Services (CMS) and the National Center for Health Statistics (NCHS).

International Health Terminology Standards Development Organisation (IHTSDO): An international not-for-profit organization that owns and administers the rights to SNOMED-CT and related terminology standards.

International Statistical Classification of Diseases and Related Health Problems (ICD): Controlled vocabulary developed and maintained by the World Health Organization (WHO), organizes the human diseases by types (Chapters), with codes associated to each diagnosis.

Knowledge Representation: Expression of concepts from a specific domain (such as healthcare) in a format that can be interpreted by computers or other humans.

Logical Observation Identifiers Names and Codes (LOINC): Terminology developed and maintained by the Regenstrief Institute, mostly composed of terms for laboratory diagnosis.

Metadata: data providing information about one or more aspects of a given data.

Metathesaurus: the UMLS repository of controlled vocabularies

Multi-Level Healthcare Information Modelling (MLHIM): An XML-technology, multilevel model-driven specification, derived and evolved from the openEHR specifications by Tim Cook, an individual entrepreneur and inventor, in association with the Brazilian National Institute of Science and Technology – Medicine Assisted by Scientific Computing (INCT-MACC) since 2009.

Multilevel Model-Driven Development (MMDD): Software development approach composed of a minimum of two levels, the Reference Model, the information infrastructure, and the Domain Model, the definition of constraints to the Reference Model that expresses the data model.

National Health Service: the United Kingdom's publicly funded, national healthcare system, established in 1947.

National Subset: A set of SNOMED-CT terms that is appropriate to a particular national State, including specificities related to language, dialect, healthcare system and context.

Natural Language Processing (NLP): Area of interface between computer science and linguistics that studies and develops way of enabling computers to understand, process and reproduce the human language-based communication.

North American Nursing Diagnosis Association (NANDA): A professional organization of nurses establisehd in 1982 that develops and maintains the NANDA terminology of nursing diagnoses.

Nursing Interventions Classification (NIC): A classification of nursing activities as a part of a nursing care plan, provided by the American Nurses' Association (ANA) since 1990.

Nursing Outcomes Classification (NOC): A classification system which describes patient outcomes sensitive to nursing intervention, provided by the American Nurses' Association (ANA) since 1991.

Omaha System: A healthcare terminology mostly adopted by nursing professionals, consisting of an assessment, intervention an outcomes components originally developed by the Visiting Nurse Association of Omaha since 1973.

Ontology: According to the ISO 17117 Standard, an “organization of concepts for which a rational argument can be made”

openEHR Foundation: A not-for-profit company established by the University College London (UK) and the Ocean Informatics Pty Ltd (Australia) in 1999, responsible for the development and maintenance of the openEHR specifications, the first multilevel model-driven specification released in 2002 (release 0.9).

Patient Care Data Set (PCDS): A terminology to represent clinical data in patient care information systems. Mostly used by nursing professionals, it was originlly developed at the University of Virginia, now being maintained by the Vanderbilt University Medical Center.

Perioperative Nursing Data Set (PNDS): a healthcare terminology specific for the field of perioperative nursing, provided by Association of periOperative Registered Nurses (AORN) since 1993.

Permanent Universal Resource Locater (PURL): A web address that acts as permanent identifiers in the face of a dynamic and changing Web infrastructure.

Post- Coordination: An *a posteriori* combination of SNOMED-CT terms.

Pre-Coordination: An *a priori* composed SNOMED-CT term.

Programming Language: An artificial language designed to communicate instructions to a machine, particularly a computer.

Reference Model: The information infrastructure of multilevel model-driven technologies, in which all the structural components and the semantic expressive framework that are necessary for the persistence of any type of data, are defined.

Regenstrief: The Regenstrief Institute, Inc. is a healthcare informatics research institute established in 1969 in association with the Indiana University, responsible for developing and maintaining the LOINC terminology.

Semantic Context: The meaning (or semantic content) each word (isolated or in combination in sentences) expresses in a possible context of use.

Semantic Interoperability: Ability that computerized information systems (applications) need to have in order to exchange and compute across, semantically valid data.

Semantic Link: a symbol that indicates the connection among semantic nodes with semantic relations.

Semantic Mapping: Transformation of data elements from one namespace into another namespace on the Semantic Web, performed by a semantic mapper.

Semantic Network: A graph that represents semantic relations between concepts.

Software Maintenance: Activities and processes related to the adaptation of a given piece of software to the user's requirements, including updates, versioning, database migration amng others.

Structured Query Language (SQL): A purpose-specific programming language designed for managing data persisted in relational databases.

Systematized Nomenclature of Medicine – Clinical Terms (SNOMED-CT): The most comprehensive healthcare terminology, managed by the IHTSDO and formed in 1999 by the convergence of CAP's SNOMED and the NHS's Clinical Terms

Systolic Blood Pressure: Pressure exerted by circulating blood upon the walls of blood vessels during the cardiac systole (contraction of the cardiac muscle).

Terminology: According to the ISO 17117 Standard, a "set of terms representing a system of concepts within a specified domain".

Unified Medical Language System (UMLS): a set of controlled vocabularies managed by an application suite maintained by the US National Library of Medicine (NLM).

World Health Organization: A specialized agency of the United Nations (UN) established in 1948 that operates in the field of international public health.

REFERENCES

[1] Halamka, J; Overhage, JM; Ricciardi, L; Rishel, W; Shirky, C; Diamond, C. Exchanging health information: local distribution, national coordination. *Health Affairs* 2005 24, 1170-1179.

[2] Ortiz, E; Clancy, CM. Use of information technology to improve the quality of health care in the United States. *Health Services Research* 2003 38, xi–xxii.

[3] Bates, DW; Gawande, AA. Improving safety with information technology. *New England Journal of Medicine* 2003 348, 2526-2534.

[4] Bates, DW; Cohen, M; Leape, LL; Overhage, JM; Shabot, MM; Sheridan, T. Reducing the frequency of errors in medicine using information technology. *Journal of the American Medical Informatics Association* 2001 8, 299-308.

[5] Nash, M; Pestrue, J; Geier, P; Sharp, K; Helder, A; McAlearney, AS. Leveraging information technology to drive improvement in patient satisfaction. *Journal of Healthcare Quality* 2010 32, 30-40.

[6] Bolton, LB; Gassert, CA; Cipriano, PF. Technology solutions can make nursing care safer and more efficient. *Jorunal of Healthcare Information Management* 2008 22, 24-30.

[7] Hillestad, R; Bigelow, J; Bower, A; Girosi, F; Meili, R; Scoville, R; Taylor, R. Can electronic medical record systems transform health care? Potential health benefits, savings, and costs. *Health Affairs* 2005 24, 1103–1117.

[8] Wu, S; Chaudhry, B; Wang, J; Maglione, M; Mojica, W; Roth, E; Morton, SC; Shekelle, PG. Systematic review: impact of health information technology on quality, efficiency, and costs of medical care. *Annals of Internal Medicine* 2006 144, 742-752.

[9] Heeks, R; Mundy, D; Salazar, A. Why health care information systems succeed or fail. Information Systems for Public Sector Management Working Paper Series no. 9

[online]. 1999 [cited 2013 September 24]. Available from: http://unpan1.un.org/intradoc/groups/public/documents /nispacee/unpan015482.pdf.

[10] Freudenheim, M. The ups and downs of Electronic Medical Records. The New York Times. 2012 [cited 2013 October 16]. Available from: http://www.nytimes.com/ 2012/10/09/health/the-ups-and-downs-of-electronic-medical-records-the-digital-doctor.html?pagewanted=all&_r=0.

[11] Schmidt, DC. Model-driven engineering. *IEEE Computing* 2006 39, 25-31.

[12] Martínez-García, M; Hernández-Lemus, E. Health systems as complex systems. *American Journal of Operations Research* 2013 3, 113-126.

[13] de Lusignan, S; Pearce, C; Shaw, NT; Liaw, ST; Michalakidis, G; Vicente, MT; Bainbridge, M; International and European Medical Informatics Association and Federation Primary Care Informatics Working Groups. What are the barriers to conducting international research using routinely collected primary care data? *Studies in Health Technology and Informatics* 2011 165,135-140.

[14] Jha, AK; Desroches, CM; Campbell, EG; Donelan, K; Rao, SR; Ferris, TG; Shields, A; Rosenbaum, S; Blumenthal, D. Use of electronic health records in U.S. hospitals. *New England Journal of Medicine* 2009 360, 1628-1638.

[15] Raths, D. Shifting away from silos. The interoperability challenges that hospitals face pale in comparison to the headaches plaguing state departments. *Healthcare Informatics* 2010 27, 32-33.

[16] Dehaghani, SM; Hajrahimi, N. Which factors affect software projects maintenance cost more? *Acta Informatica Medica* 2013 21, 63-66.

[17] Meinert, DB. Resistance to Electronic Medical Records (EMRs): a barrier to improved quality of care. *Issues in Informing Science and Information Technology* 2005 2, 494-504.

[18] Ash, JS; Bates, DW. Factors and forces affecting EHR System Adoption: report of a 2004 ACMI discussion. *Journal of the American Medical Informatics Association* 2005 12, 8-12.

[19] Kaplan, B; Harris-Salamone, KD. Health IT success and failure: recommendations from literature and an AMIA workshop. *Journal of the American Medical Informatics Association* 2009 16, 291-299.

[20] Ganguly, P; Ray, P; Parameswaran, N. Semantic interoperability in telemedicine through ontology-driven services. *Telemedicine Journal and E-Health* 2005 11, 405-412.

[21] Knaup, P; Bott, O; Kohl, C; Lovis, C; Garde, S. Electronic patient records: moving from islands and bridges towards electronic health records for continuity of care. *Yearbook of Medical Informatics* 2007 16, 34-46.

[22] Ingenerf, J; Reiner, J; Seik, B. Standardized terminological services enabling semantic interoperability between distributed and heterogeneous systems. *International Journal of Medical Informatics* 2001 64, 223-240.

[23] Bodenreider, O. Biomedical ontologies in action: role in knowledge management, data integration and decision support. *Yearbook of Medical Informatics* 2008 17, 67-79.

[24] Kalra, D; Blobel, BG. Semantic interoperability of EHR systems. *Studies in Health Technology and Informatics* 2007 127, 231-245.

[25] Nachimuthu, SK. Vocabulary metadata service for terminology servers to handle variations in design of various biomedical terminologies. *AMIA Annual Symposium Proceedings* 2008, 1062.

[26] Ryan, A. Towards semantic interoperability in healthcare: ontology mapping from SNOMED-CT to HL7 version 3. *Proceedings of the Second Australasian Workshop on Advances in Ontologies* 2006 72, 69-74.

[27] Lewis, GA; Morris, E; Simanta, S; Wrage, L. Why standards are not enough to guarantee end-to-end interoperability. *Seventh International Conference on Composition-Based Software Systems* 2008, 164-173.

[28] Laurenti, R. Analysis of information on health data: 1893-1993, a hundred years of the International Classification of Diseases. *Revista de Saúde Pública* 1991 25, 407-417.

[29] Mezzich, JE; Salloum, IM. Towards innovative international classification and diagnostic systems: ICD-11 and person-centered integrative diagnosis. *Acta Psychiatrica Scandinavica* 2007 116, 1-5.

[30] Rey, G; Aouba, A; Pavillon, G; Hoffman, R; Plug, I; Westerling, R; Jougla, E; Mackenbach, J. Cause-specific mortality time series analysis: a general method to detect and correct for abrupt data production changes. *Population Health Metrics* 2011 9, 52.

[31] World Health Organization. *International statistical classification of diseases and related health problems - 10th revision*. Edition 2010. Geneva: World Health Organization ; 2010.

[32] Surján, G. Questions on validity of International Classification of Diseases-coded diagnoses. *International Journal of Medical Informatics* 1999 54, 77-95.

[33] Chute, CG. Clinical classification and terminology: some history and current observations. *Journal of the American Medical Informatics Association* 2000 7, 298-303.

[34] Rothwell, DJ; Cote, RA; Cordeau, JP; Boisvert, MA. Developing a standard data structure for medical language: the SNOMED proposal. *Proceedings of the Annual Symposium on Computer Application in Medical Care* 2003, 695.

[35] International Health Terminology Standards Development Organisation. *SNOMED CT Starter Guide*. The Hague: IHTSDO; 2014.

[36] Chiang, MF; Hwang, JC; Yu, AC; Casper, DS; Cimino, JJ; Starren, J. Reliability of SNOMED-CT coding by three physicians using two terminology browsers. *AMIA Annual Symposium Proceedings* 2006, 131-135.

[37] Cooke, M; Irby, DM; O'Brien, BC. *Educating physicians: a call for reform of medical school and residency*. San Francisco: Jossey-Bass; 2010.

[38] Demner-Fushman, D; Chapman, WW; McDonald, CJ. What can natural language processing do for clinical decision support? *Journal of Biomedical Informatics* 2009 42, 760-772.

[39] Forrey, AW; McDonald, CJ; DeMoor, G; Huff, SM; Leavelle, D; Leland, D; Fiers, T; Charles, L; Griffin, B; Stalling, F; Tullis, A; Hutchins, K; Baenziger, J. Logical observation identifier names and codes (LOINC) database: a public use set of codes and names for electronic reporting of clinical laboratory test results. *Clinical Chemistry* 1996 42, 81-90.

[40] McDonald, C; Huff, S; Deckard, J; Holck, K; Vreeman, DJ. *Logical Observation Identifiers Names and Codes (LOINC) users' guide*. Indianapolis: Regenstrief Institute; 2013.
[41] Maedche, A; Staab, S. *Ontology learning*. Berlin Heidelberg: Springer; 2004.
[42] Smith, B; Ashburner, M; Rosse, C; Bard, J; Bug, W; Ceusters, W; Goldberg, LJ; Eilbeck, K; Ireland, A; Mungall, CJ; The OBI Consortium; Leontis, N; Rocca-Serra, P; Ruttenberg, A; Sansone, SA; Scheuermann, RH; Shah, N; Whetzel, PL; Lewis, S. The OBO Foundry: coordinated evolution of ontologies to support biomedical data integration. *Nature Biotechnology* 2007 25, 1251-1255.
[43] Noy, NF,; Shah, NH; Whetzel, PL; Dai, B; Dorf, M; Griffith, N; Jonquet, C; Rubin, DL; Storey, MA; Chute, CG; Musen, MA; BioPortal: ontologies and integrated data resources at the click of a mouse. *Nucleic Acids Research* 2009 37, W170-W173.
[44] Coenen, A; Marin, HF; Park, H; Bakken, S. Collaborative efforts for representing nursing concepts in computer-based systems: international perspectives. *Journal of the American Medical Informatics Association* 2001; 8, 202-211.
[45] Park, HA; Cho, I. Education, practice, and research in nursing terminology: gaps, challenges, and opportunities. *Yearbook of Medical Informatics* 2009 19, 103-108.
[46] Bakken, S; McArthur, J. Evidence-based nursing practice: a call to action for nursing informatics. *Journal of the American Medical Informatics Association* 2001; 8, 289-290.
[47] Warren, JJ; Coenen, A. International Classification for Nursing Practice (ICNP): most-frequently asked questions. *Journal of the American Medical Informatics Association* 1998 5, 335-336.
[48] Braga, CG; Cruz, DDALM. The Taxonomy II proposed by the North American Nursing Diagnosis Association (NANDA). *Revista Latino-Americana de Enfermagem* 2003 11, 240-244.
[49] Bowles, KH; Naylor, MD. Nursing intervention classification systems. *Journal of Nursing Scholarship* 1996 28, 303-308.
[50] Johnson, M; Maas, M. The nursing outcomes classification. *Journal of Nursing Care Quality* 1998 12, 9-20.
[51] Moss, J; Damrongsak, M; Gallichio, K. Representing critical care data using the Clinical Care Classification. *AMIA Symposium Proceedings* 2005, 545.
[52] Barrera, C; Machanga, M; Connolly, PM; Yoder, M. Nursing care makes a difference: application of the Omaha System. *Outcomes Management* 2003 7, 181-185.
[53] Lu, D; Street, W; Currim, F; Hylock, R; Delaney, C. A data modeling process for decomposing healthcare patient data sets. *Online Journal of Nursing Informatics* 2009 13, 1-26.
[54] Westendorf JJ. Utilizing the Perioperative Nursing Data Set in a surgical setting. *Plastic Surgical Nursing* 2007 27, 181-184.
[55] McGonigle, D; Mastrian, K. *Nursing informatics and the foundation of knowledge*. Burlington: Jones & Bartlett Publishers; 2011.
[56] Hardiker, NR; Hoy, D; Casey, A. Standards for nursing terminology. *Journal of the American Medical Informatics Association* 2000 7, 523-528.
[57] Blobel, B. *Analysis, design, and implementation of secure and interoperable distributed health information systems*. Amsterdam: IOS Press; 2002.

[58] Elkin, PL; Brown, SH; Carter, J; Bauer, BA; Wahner-Roedler, D; Bergstrom, L; Pittelkow, M; Rosse, C. Guideline and quality indicators for development, purchase and use of controlled health vocabularies. *International Journal of Medical Informatics* 2002 68, 175-186.
[59] Kalra, D; Beale, T; Heard, S. The openEHR foundation. *Studies in Health Technology and Informatics* 2005 115, 153-173.
[60] Cavalini, LT; Cook, TW. Use of XML Schema Definition for the development of semantically interoperable healthcare applications. *Lecture Notes in Computer Science* 2014 8315, 125-145.
[61] Grimshaw, JM; Russell, IT. Effect of clinical guidelines on medical practice: a systematic review of rigorous evaluations. *Lancet* 1993 342, 1317-1322.
[62] Greenes, RA; Peleg, M; Boxwala, A; Tu, S; Patel, V; Shortliffe, EH. Sharable computer-based clinical practice guidelines: rationale, obstacles, approaches, and prospects. *Studies in Health Technology and Informatics* 2001 86: 201-205.

About the Authors

LUCIANA TRICAI CAVALINI, MD, PhD. Physician with PhD in Public Health. Professor at the Department of Health Information Technologies, Medical Sciences College, Rio de Janeiro State University, Brazil. Professor at the Department of Epidemiology and Biostatistics, Community Health Institute, Fluminense Federal University, Brazil. Coordinator of the Technological Development Unit in Multilevel Healthcare Information Modeling. Coordinator of the Emergent Group in Research and Innovation on Healthcare Information Technologies.

JOYCE ROCHA DE MATOS NOGUEIRA, CRN, MSc. Nurse with MSc in Public Health. Project Manager at the Technological Development Unit in Multilevel Healthcare Information Modeling, Rio de Janeiro State University, Brazil.

TIMOTHY WAYNE COOK, MSC. Advanced Electronics Technologist with MSc in Health Informatics. Creator and core developer of the Multilevel Healthcare Information Modeling (MLHIM) specifications. Chief Technological Officer at MedWeb. International Collaborator at the National Institute of Science and Technology – Medicine Assisted by Scientific Computing.

In: Knowledge Engineering
Editor: Alfonso Perez Gama
ISBN: 978-1-63463-909-5

Chapter 3

Cognitive Approach and Its Application to the Modeling of Strategic Management of Enterprises

Robert A. Karayev*

Institute of Control Systems of National Academy of Sciences of Azerbaijan, Azerbaijan

Abstract

The paper discusses the difficulties of choice strategies of enterprises development in modern complicated turbulent environments. Ill-structured (by G. Simon) and the dynamic nature of the problem of choice restricts the opportunities to use traditional widely known DSS-tools (SWOT & PEST, BSC, CCB, SODA, SAM, SAST, SCA, BCG, GE / McKinsey, Shell / DPM, MD ASQ et al.). New prospects for solution of the issue open ideas and methods such as "cognitive modeling" which today is major component of the global trend of world science - "NBIC Convergence". Some progress in terms of development and use of cognitive DSS-tools of strategic management was achieved over the past two decades. However it becomes apparent (and some "bottlenecks" are caused by complex phenomenology of modern management), that it is difficult to formalize. The paper presents the methodology of cognitive modeling and cognitive DSS-tools oriented to deal with? this kind of "bottlenecks". The purpose of the article: a) present the short overview of the main provisions and basic tools of the developed methodology, and b) present the main results obtained in process of development, and testing research prototypes of cognitive models for three companies with different structure and dynamics of their macroeconomic environment.

Keywords: Enterprise strategy, dynamic analysis, cognitive approaches, cognitive models

* e-mail: karayevr@rambler.ru.

1. Introduction

The task of choosing strategies faced by the managers of enterprises in today's turbulent business environment can be fully attributed to the tasks of management of ill-structured problem situations [1], i.e., to problems not amenable to exact formally mathematical analysis.

In recent years as promising support tools for solving this kind of tasks are considered the cognitive models [2, 3, 4, 5, 6, 7, and 8].

The article contains the results of the development and testing of cognitive models to assess strategic perspectives of three concrete enterprises that are significantly different in structure and dynamics of macroeconomic environment and internal microeconomic conditions.

In these projects is not intended to create working models.

Developments worn research character and were performed by three independent groups.

Below are:

(1) A general description of the cognitive modeling of management strategies, reflecting the features of the economic management in an uncertain economic environment;
(2) A conceptual scheme of the task from the standpoint of intelligent "model theory" (knowledge-based) solvers of ill-structured problems;
(3) Brief description of cognitive models of the strategies established as part of the executed projects;
(4) Some of the most important in our view, the results which, although correlated with the features of specific enterprises, may be of interest to developers of strategies for other enterprises.

Conclusions presented in the final part, reflect not only the opinion of model developers, but also the opinion of employees of enterprises.

2. Cognitive Approach

2.1. Common Characteristics

Cognitive approach is a method of studying and managing problem situations basing on formation and study of their cognitive models [2, 5, 7, 9, and 10].

Cognitive model is complex, and includes

1) Cognitive map of a problem situation, reflecting the mental models of experts regarding the structural and functional organization of this situation;
2) Methods of analysis of cognitive map, allowing investigating the structural properties of the problem situation and carrying out model experiments in order to search the optimal (in some sense or other) management strategies for problem situation

Cognitive revolution happened in 1950-1960s. The first cognitive research center was established in Harvard in 1960. This date is indicated as the development of cognitive science, which includes philosophy, cognitive psychology, neurophysiology, anthropology, linguistics and theory of artificial intelligence.

Methodology of cognitive modeling is addressed for analysis and decision-making in complex ill-structured situations. The first applied versions of this methodology were suggested by R. Axelrod [11]. Modern trend of the cognitive approach are well reflected at Proceedings of the International Conferences of ICCM series [12].

A specific feature of the cognitive modeling method differing from traditional methods is the possibility of conducting multi-factor and multi-criteria analysis and management of development of ill-structured situations (combining vitally important stages of divergence, convergence and transformation of project cycle [25]) that is not possible through traditional mathematical and statistical calculus.

2.2. Cognitive Map

Cognitive map is a structure (network) of cause and effect relations between the components of the system under survey and its surrounding environment, reflecting the explicit understanding (mental models) of expert(s) about the structure and functioning of this system [7, 26].

In the context of control problems the ontology of cognitive map are:

1) Basic factors (concepts) characterizing the control object and its environment according to the representation of subject of control.
2) as well as cause and effect relations between basic factors.

Such a factor division lets realize wide range of model experiments, for instance, construction of different alternative strategy versions, to prognoses the utility's behavior (its goal form) for every strategy version, to prognoses the utility's behavior in various dynamics of external environment factors, and etc.

2.3. Methods of Analysis of Cognitive Maps

Methods of analysis of cognitive maps are the sets of methods which allow various kinds of model experiments on cognitive maps, associated with studies and virtual management of problem situation.

Efforts of scientists are currently focused on the development of methods of analysis, that allow:

a) To investigate the most important structural properties of the problem situations (consistency of target factors, priority of control actions, dynamic stability of management strategies, etc.);

b) Predict the development of the problem situation under various management strategies (self-development, controlled development) and under various scenarios of environmental change.

Cognitive modeling is a periodic process and consists of several interrelated stages main of which are: cognitive structuring and development of cognitive map of surveyed situation; structural analysis of cognitive map; scenario based modeling of situation development (self-development and controlled development).

2.4. Stages of Cognitive Modeling

2.4.1. Cognitive Structuring

Stage provides for the definition of the factors that characterize the internal situation at the enterprise and PEST-factors of environment influencing the enterprise development.

The cognitive structuring stage is formed as a cognitive map (CM) describing a set of basic factors of the enterprise and its environment and cause and effect relations between them. Currently common feature for all researches on cognitive modeling is the use of cognitive maps based on the digraph (signed or weighed) [27].

For each factor its value (or tendency of change) characterizing the subject, event or process associated with the given factor is determined. For cause and effect relations, character and strength of interrelation between basic factors is determined. Values of appropriate variable are given on the basis of a linguistic scale, i.e., in words in a native language and each is denoted by a corresponding figure in the interval [0; 1].

Example of a cognitive map of the strategic management of the enterprise is given in [28].

Ibid is given an example of linguistic scale.

In this stage the basis to set the basic factors also are determined: subset of target factors and subset of controlled factors, also, initial values and/or tendencies of change of basic factors. Factors relating to the enterprise or to external environment, which the management of the enterprise may influence on, are selected as controlled factors.

2.4.2. Structural Analysis of Cognitive Map

This analysis is implemented to study structural features of CM which are important from the point of view of management practice. Such features include:

1. Non-conflicting purposes. The main point of the non-conflicting purposes vector is to ensure that desired change of some target factors does not result in undesirable change of others.
2. Non-conflicting purposes and controlled factors. Managing the situation is the change of controlled factors to the extent that would result in desired change of target factors, i.e., in the direction of planned dynamics. In connection with this, effectiveness of influence of controlled factors on targets of the company, and conformity of controlled factors with the targets of the company are surveyed. Acceptable effectiveness of controlled factors is determined by the degree and

character of their influence on the target factors. Conformity of controlled factors with targets vector means that no change of them should cause change in any of the targets in undesired direction.

At present a range of mathematical methods of structural analysis of CM has been developed [10, 27]. However, in practice, structural solutions achieved through these formal and mathematical methods require interpretations in the subject area, which are not always possible.

2.4.3. Scenario Based Modeling of Situation Development

This is conducted for comparative analysis of the trajectories of the situation development in different incoming managing impacts and different scenarios changes of environment.

Modeling may be conducted in a mode of self-development and in a mode of manageable development. In the most studies the dynamics of development is modeled using the apparatus of linear dynamical systems [27].

Self-development implies maintaining existing tendencies of factors and in essence, it is extrapolation of current situation taking into account mutual influences of basic factors.

Managed development of situation implies purpose targeted influence on one or several managed factors. Impulsive change of current value of the factor which is transferred to other factors through the chains of impacts serves as management.

Modern concepts of cognitive approach to the management of enterprise (purposes and crucial definitions, CM structuring principles and adequacy criteria, types of CM and their analysis methods) are described in [2, 6, 10, and 12]. In the framework of these concepts cognitive strategy modeling is strategy modeling based on cognitive maps (CM), which search for optimal (in one sense or another) strategies of enterprise development.

Systemization of CM and their analysis methods are given in [10, 27, 29, 30, and 31].

Systemization of principles and methods of reliability assessment of CM, which allows to block typical errors of explication of expert knowledge and to raise adequacy of CM are given in [32, 33]. Depending on conditions and limitations of strategy development task the appropriate CM types and their analysis methods can be chosen.

3. A Cognitive Methodology for Developing of Enterprise Strategy

3.1. Enterprise Strategy

To the question posed by M. Porter, "What is strategy?" [34], currently, there are many answers. Many different definitions of "enterprise strategy" have been proposed [35 – 45].

Analysis of these definitions shows that in the most general form "enterprise strategy" may be interpreted as follows.

Enterprise strategy is a general plan of action that defines the priorities of strategic objectives, resources and sequence of steps to achieve strategic objectives. The main objective of the strategy is to move the enterprise from its current state to a desired future state [69].

The task of search an optimal strategy in today's turbulent economy is extremely complex. It can be fully attributed to the class of ill-structured problems [1], the solution of which is located outside the traditional theory of strategic management of enterprises. Solution of such problems requires fundamentally new approaches and new support tools. One of the most promising approaches is based on the ideas and methods of the cognitive paradigm.

Among the first attempts to use cognitive technology to solve tasks of strategic management is referred SODA methodology [48]. According to the authors of SODA, the methodology is general and can be used to study complex situations in a variety of problem areas. Unfortunately, the phenomenology of the situation in each of the problem areas wears always specific character and requires the creation of their problem-oriented methodologies.

In developing the problem-oriented methodology of cognitive support in the first place, it is important to establish a conceptual scheme of the task, which defines the statement of the task and task-solving scheme in representations of the cognitive approach.

3.2. Conceptual Scheme of Strategy Development Task

Conceptual scheme of general task of the ill-structured objects management was offered by acad. D. A. Pospelov [48]. Strategy development task is a particular case of general task and in terms of cognitive approach it can be presented as follows:

$$P(G,M):\ S^0 \Rightarrow S^c \big|_{U(P)}$$

where $P(G, M)$ – is full knowledge of task;

G – Cognitive map of the task;

M – Methodology of support, which bases on the modern postulates of strategy Management and includes methods of choice of business-conception of Enterprise (M_b), methods for design of cognitive map (M_d), method for analysis of Cognitive map (M_a);

S^o – the current state of enterprise, installed via cognitive map;

S^c – the goal state of enterprise, installed via cognitive map;

U (P) – Optimal (in one sense or another) strategy that determine strategic steps sequence, leading from S^o to S^c.

Depending on the character of macroeconomic environment (stable/unstable) two task versions are possible: static and dynamical. In static version the search of effective strategy is to choice one strategic step leading from S^o to S^c. In dynamical version the search of effective strategy is to choice of strategic steps sequence leading from S^o to S^c.

This and other methods of analysis are used: “method of searching priority impacts”, “method of scenario-based analysis of the dynamics of the situation”, “method of analysis of dynamic stability of strategy”, and others.

Leading method to search optimal strategies in turbulent environment is the scenario-based method of dynamic analysis of a problem situation. This method allows searching the target situation on the set of alternative strategies for various environments' development scenarios.

The mechanism of scenario-based dynamic analysis was developed by us [49, 50, and 51] and is different from the classical cognitive model of linear dynamical systems [27].

Applied versions of dynamic analysis models, especially dynamic analysis models of enterprise's strategy require the adjustment of the "strategic step" definition. Each of strategic steps is action which changes the situation. The changes on each step can be realized by operators, which are described in the Table 1. Here the list of operators is divided into signed cognitive map (SCM) and weighted cognitive map (WCM).

Table 1. Operators of strategic step

Operators	Types of CM	
	WCM	SCM
1. Change the values of some managed vertices (factors) at a certain time	•	•
2. Add a new vertex (factor) and the new arcs to it and from it at certain time	•	•
3. Change sign of some arc at a certain time	•	•
4. Change weight of some arc at a certain time	•	
5. Add an arc between existing vertices (factors) at a certain time	•	•
6. Add a new contour (which increases or decreases deviation) at a certain time		•

The use of these management operators can construct numerous strategic alternatives, which reflect various scenarios of situation development. As soon as the fixed set of strategic alternatives is determined, you can define the statement of strategy selection task. It may have different formulations and configurations of target form of problem situation. For example,

1) Searching optimal strategy (the shortest, the cheapest, and etc.) which meets normative restrictions in some parameters of utility's internal and external environment;
2) Searching a strategy, which maximizes (minimizes) the values of some tops (for instance, profit of enterprises, market share of enterprises, product quality, pollution of environment, and etc.) in case of restrictions in values of some other tops (for instance, financial resources, time resources, human resources, and etc.);
3) Searching a strategy, which doesn't let every variable of enterprise have excessively large or excessively little value (it is called "dynamically stable" strategies).

Designed mechanism of scenario-based dynamic analysis is based on the

- "general theory of impulse processes" on digraphs (signed and weighted) [27],
- Theoretical model of non-linear (non-monotonic) dynamical systems [52],
- Algorithms of strategic planning of knowledge-based solvers by the "direct wave" and by "reverse wave" [48, 52],
- principles and methods of scenario planning [53, 54, 55, 56, and 57].

The mechanism of this type removes many limitations of theoretical schemes and approximates the management practices to the leading postulates of modern pragmatic management (of the 21st Century):

Postulate 1. The management from the future [58];
Postulate 2. Knowledge-based processing of uncertainty [26, 58, 59, and 60];
Postulate 3. The requisite of variety of control mechanism [61];
Postulate 4. Strategy is general path rather than precise steps [47, 48, and 62].
Postulate 5. Hierarchical modeling (planning) strategies under various PEST-scenarios of development of the environment (pessimistic scenario, inertial, optimistic).

Process of constructing strategy is iterative and ends when reaching a satisfactory result, which is under defined restrictions, managed to achieve target state of a problem situation.

4. Examples of Cognitive Strategy Modeling

The attempts of cognitive modeling which we did make were concerned with the solution of management tasks in three research projects:

Project 1. Strategy perspective assessment of offshore-oil Company, functioning conditions which are characterized with typical current tendencies: downturn of world oil prices, global financial crisis, increase of governmental impact, toughening of ecological standards. The work was implemented together with Petroleum Engineering Department of A&M Texas University (College Station, Texas, USA) in the framework of constructive cooperation agreement.

Project 2. Exposure of crucial competences for strategic development task of telecommunication companies, which deal with development, installation and service of industrial, administrative and medical information systems, iP-and CTi- systems – telephoning for communication statement and corporative clients.

Project 3. Analysis of management efficiency in poultry enterprise of one of the holdings. The task was specified by critical situation, which occurred due to the increase of raw materials and feed prices, decrease of finished product prices, the raise of competitive pressure, the difficulties in obtaining commercial credits, lack of qualification of managerial staff, drop of income share, which is considered for refinancing the enterprises (especially because of corruptibility of controlling units, and etc.).

Now let's learn brief characteristics of developed cognitive models for above mentioned projects. The main characteristics of developed cognitive models are: business-concept of strategy, defined due to the results of strategic diagnosis of enterprises; structure type of cognitive map, which describes the logic of business-concept; methods of design and analysis of cognitive map; the scale of values and pace of change of factors of cognitive map.

Characteristics of cognitive models, which were developed in the mentioned projects, are described in the Table 2.

Table 2. Characteristics of Cognitive Models, developed in Projects 1, 2, 3

Project number	Business-concept	Structural type of cognitive map	Methods of design and analysis of cognitive maps	Scales for estimating the values of factors and its trends
Project No 1	"Resource-oriented" [63]	Weighted digraphs [27]	**Methods of design**: SWOT & PEST-analysis. Determinacy analysis [64]. Implicational repertory grids of the C. Hinkle [65]. Matrix interactions [25]. Methods of experimental psychosemantics and nonmetric multidimensional scaling [66, 67]. **Methods of analysis:** Models of linear dynamics of the F. Roberts [27]. Methods of scenario planning [49, 50, 55].	Bipolar linguistic Five-point rating scale
Project No 2	"School competency" [68]	Matrix Diagrams of American Society for Quality [69]	**Methods of design:** Ishikawa diagrams [70]. VRIO-analysis [71]. Reference model of business-processes of the telecommunication companies eTOM.4.0 (Enhanced Telecom Operations Map), International Telecommunication Union. "The model of IS consumer opinion" (IBM, USA). "Model of resources" (ASQ). **Methods of analysis:** Methods of matrix analysis [72]. Analytic hierarchy model [73].	linguistic Nine-point rating scale
Project No 3	"Migration Strategy" [1]	Weighted digraphs [27]	**Methods of design**: SWOT & PEST-analysis. The strategic map of the Kaplan-Norton [74]. Methods of experimental psychosemantics and nonmetric multidimensional scaling [66, 67]. **Methods of analysis**: Model of scenario-based nonlinear (non-monotonic) dynamics [49, 50, 51].	Bipolar linguistic Five-point rating scale

CONCLUSION

The experiments of cognitive strategy modeling and testing in the above-mentioned projects showed that in practical tasks of economic spheres cognitive modeling faces the same issues which the other intelligent technologies faces. These are "the width of problem definition", robustness when "paradigm shift", necessity of specialist-mediator (knowledge engineer, meta-interpreter - cognitivist), necessity of support tools on the development and maintenance stages, and etc.

In general, the experiments of cognitive modeling and testing showed the following:

1. In case of cognitive modeling of strategies the general principals of design of the cognitive map proposed in [10, 25] requires modification reflecting methodological features and concept determined by theory of strategic planning of enterprises.

2. Cognitive modeling of strategies acquires a practical importance only in the framework of strategy planning methodology which includes phases of macro-economic and marketing analysis [50, 51]. Ignoring these phases reduces cognitive models of strategies into mathematical objects which are far from reality of economic practice.
3. The issue of choice of management scheme of problem solving caused wide discussion. At first, we applied the scheme proposed by specialists of Institute of Management Problems of RAS [10].

But analysis showed that proposed scheme implements algorithm of "situation-decision" type, i.e., implements not strategic, but reactive style of management and can't be used for generation of strategy in unstable environment. For such kind of problems are needed the schemes which implements algorithm of "situation-strategy-decision" type. Consequent researches showed that the issue of development of such scheme type is not trivial and it can be considered as one of directions for further improvement of cognitive approach.

4. Cooperation with employees of the enterprises showed that they didn't have well-defined opinion regarding adequacy and efficiency of cognitive models of strategies. At the same time, 8 out of 11 demonstrated active interest and considered that cognitive modeling is promising and useful technology. Our observations showed that the cognitive modeling is useful support tool, which stimulates cognitive and creative activity of strategy developers in most complicated phase of "strategic thinking" [47, 51, 75], in phase with afferent synthesis of strategy.
5. Set of methods directed to the increase of reliability of cognitive models on the stages of identification, conceptualization and CM-formalization of problematic knowledge [2, 3, 5, 29, 30, and 31], can be extended at the expenses of including popular methods developed for analogous purposes in theory of industrial and architectural projecting [25], in experimental psychology [66, 67], and knowledge engineering [33].
6. In all three projects, we faced with a situation that differs from the usual of theoretical schemes. Mental models of enterprises managers proved to be completely inadequate. It became clear that in the process of constructing cognitive maps of enterprises, leading role should belong to the knowledge engineer (cognitivist) who owns the theoretical foundations of strategic planning and skills of cognitive modeling simultaneously.
7. Experience working in three specific projects has shown that the problems with the choice of strategies here were due to the lack of strategic planning skills and difficulties of mental modeling of multifactor development of events in conditions of turbulent environment. This situation seems to us, is typical for most small and medium-sized enterprises. In this context, urgency of creation of cognitive support tools is no doubted. However, the effectiveness of these tools is still a big question. In each specific case serious work is needed to achieve sufficient adequacy of cognitive models, and character of this work is far from the populist estimates published in numerous recent works.

TECHNICAL GLOSSARY ON KE

Problem is defined as a situation in which there are two states: one is called the existing condition, and the other, the desired state. Spacing between current and desired states forms what is called the problem situation.

Ill-structured problem is a problem in which the composition of elements and relationships between elements is known only partially and have mixed (quantitative & qualitative) character.

Resolution of these problems is most critical for our today's world and is the most important area for the apps abilities of managers, supervisors and specialists on management. The concept "ill-structured problem" was introduced by G. Simon (1973).

Cognitive approach, actively developed in the modern theory of management, is a method of studying and managing ill-structured problem situations basing on formation and study of their cognitive models. Cognitive models allows us to overcome the "curse of uncertainty" by using cognitive abilities (perception, representation, cognition, understanding, explanation) of management subject. Today, application areas of the cognitive approach are: sociology, political science, biology, ecology, industry, business, education, healthcare, military conflicts, emergencies, government, etc.

Cognitive approach to solving complex, ill-structured problems, historically owes its name to the notion of "cognitive map", which originally appeared in psychology and was subsequently transferred to the sociology and political science, and another "new" science.

Cognitive model includes:

1) cognitive map of a problem situation, reflecting the mental models of experts regarding the structural and functional organization of this situation;

2) methods of analysis of cognitive map, allowing to investigate the structural properties of the problem situation and to carry out model experiments in order to search the optimal (in some sense or other) management strategies for the problem situation.

Cognitive map is a structure (network) of cause and effect relations between the basic factors (concepts) of the problem situation reflecting the cognitive representations (mental models) of expert(s) about the structural and functional organization of problem situation.

In the context of problem management, the ontologies of cognitive map are:

1) basic factors characterizing the management object and its environment according to the representation of the management subject,

2) as well as cause and effect relations between basic factors.

Technically, classical cognitive maps are directed graphs with signed arches. In formal notation, a cognitive map M is a triple, $M = (C, E, S)$, where C is a set of nodes, or factors, E is a set of signed arches, and S is a tool that reflects the nature of the causal relations between factors (signed, weighted, temporal, functional, logical).

Basic factors. Conceptually, the basic factors are the factors that (1) define and limit the observed phenomena and processes of the problem situation, and (2) interpret the subject of management as essential key parameters, signs, of these phenomena and processes. Various publications also use the terms "concept", "parameter" or "variable". Factor (from lat. *factor* - acting, producing) cause a driving force of some process, phenomenon, defining its character or its separate properties. In the context of enterprise management task, basic factors are the set of the essential key factors of the managed problem situation, including a subset of the target factors of enterprise, subset (managed and unmanaged) of internal factors of the enterprise, and subset of the enterprise environmental factors.

Methods of analysis of cognitive maps are the sets of methods which allow various kinds of model experiments on cognitive maps, associated with studies and virtual management of the problem situation.

Efforts of scientists are currently focused on the development of methods of analysis, that allow:

a) to investigate the most important structural properties of the problem situations (consistency of target factors, priority of management actions, dynamic stability of management strategies, etc.);

b) predict the development of the problem situation under various management strategies (self-development, managed development) and under various scenarios of environmental change.

Cognitive modeling is a series of model experiments on cognitive maps carried out in order to study the problem situation and the choice of optimal strategy to translate the situation from its current state to a desired state. Specific of cognitive modeling is that the formal mathematical methods of analysis are applied to models that describe the subjective vision of the situation. However, the orientation on the tradition of the standard approach to the methods of processing of human knowledge often leads to the fact that in a number of works, declared dependence on man has little effect on the content, methods and results of research, or almost no effect on them. This is evident, for example, when compared with other "non-cognitive" expert methods and techniques to support decision making. Actually human, cognitive component of the "cognitive" modeling in this case is outside of the scientific knowledge and arguments considered by the "common sense" outside the norms of control over their validity. Extreme position here is to treat cognitive methods just as a kind of mathematical modeling methods.

Hierarchical planning. Planning for problem solving in which at first it's searched the approximate plan (strategic plan), by which it's searched the fundamental answer of reachability goals. Then this plan is gradually refined (tactical plan), taking into account the specific characteristics of the current situation and the state of the planning system.

DSS-tools (SWOT & PEST analysis, **BSC** - Balanced Score Card, CCB - Change Control Board, **SODA** - Strategic Options Development and Analysis, SAM - Software Asset Management, SAST - Strategic Analysis in Science and Technology, SCA tools, BCG matrix, GE/McKinsey model, Shell/DPM model, Matrix Diagram of American Society for Quality, etc.)

(*All these acronyms are opened on the Internet*)

NBIC. In 2006, the U.S. National Science Foundation, under whose auspices carried the lion's share of research in America, released a report that predicts the development of science in the next 50 years. Report was named **"NBIC –convergence"** (http://www.nbic.info/): (N – nanotechnologies, B – biotechnologies, I – Information Technologies, C – cognitive technologies). The report defined main trends in the world science coming decades.

Information technology revolution began in the 60s of the twentieth century, the rapid progress of biotechnology turned in 90s, nanotechnology – at the beginning of the XXI century. Now beginning to develop rapidly cognitive technologies, including technology and cognitive control of complex objects of various natures (industry, business, banking, education, medicine, biological resources, defense industry, regions, military and political conflicts, emergencies, crises in economy, etc.).

Today's complicated management objects are characterized by four major features: multifactor, highly dynamic, limited information and statistical resources, and most importantly, high role of mental (cognitive) opportunities (capacity) of control subjects.

In this context, the thesis becomes relevant that the 21st century can be called the century of “high hume”, as opposed to the 20th century – century “high-tech”.

SODA (Strategic Options Development and Analysis) is one of a number of approaches developed in the UK Operational Research (OR) community over the past 30 years to assist strategic decision-making.

1. Eden C (1989). Using Cognitive Mapping for Strategic Options Development and Analysis. In: Rosenhead J (ed). *Rational Analysis for a Problematic World.* Wiley: Chichester

2. Eden C and Ackermann F (2001). SODA – The Principles. In: Rosenhead J and Mingers J (eds). *Rational Analysis for a Problematic World Revisited 2001.* Wiley: Chichester

3. Rosenhead J and Mingers J (eds) (2001). Rational Analysis for a Problematic World Revisited. Wiley: Chichester

References

[1] Simon, H. (1973.) The Structure of Ill-structured Problems. *Artificial Intelligence, volume 4,* pp. 181-202.

[2] Eden, C. (1988). Cognitive Mapping: a Review. *Eur. Journ. Oper. Res, volume 5. number 3,* pp. 1-13.

[3] Eden, C. (1992). On the Nature of Cognitive Maps. *Journ. of Management Studies, volume 29 number 3*, pp. 261-265.

[4] Westcombe, M., Pidd, M., Mackenzie, A., Warren, I., & Sommerville, S. (2002). Problem Solving Dialogue: Cognitive Mapping and IBIS. Working paper MS01/02. Management School, Lancaster University, UK. http://www.comp.lancs.ac.uk/computing/research/cseg/projects/wisdom/ (accessed 25.07.2014).

[5] Huff, A. S. (1990). *Mapping strategic thought.* Chichester: Wiley.

[6] Schellinck, J., & Webster, R. (2013). Cognitive models: Understanding their critical role as explanatory and predictive hypothesis generators in cognition research. Proc. of the IEEE Intern. Conf. on Cognitive Modeling (ICCM-2013).

[7] Russell, R.D. (1999). Developing a process model of entrepreneurial systems: a cognitive mapping approach. *Entrepreneurship Theory and Practice, volume 23 number.3*, pp. 65-85.

[8] Hodqkinson, G. (2001). Cognitive process in strategic management: Some emerging trends and future directions. *Handbook of industrial, work&organizational psychology* (pp. 416-441). London: SAGE Publication 2.

[9] Eden, C. (1989). Using Cognitive Mapping for Strategic Options Development and Analysis. In: Rosenhead J. (Ed.), *Rational Analysis for a Problematic World* (pp. 127-141). Chichester: Wiley.

[10] Proc. of the Intern. Conf. "Cognitive Analysis and Management of Development of Situations" (2007). CASC'2007. M.: Institute of Control Problems of RAS. http://window.edu.ru/resource/144/51144 (accessed 25.07.2014).
[11] Axelrod, R. (1976). The Structure of Decision. In R. Axelrod (Ed.), *Cognitive Maps of Political Elites* (pp. 405-427). Princeton: University Press.
[12] IEEE Proc. of the Intern. Conf. on Cognitive Modeling (ICCM) series:
[13] ICCM 2013: Ottawa, Canada (proceedings)
[14] ICCM 2012: Berlin, Germany (proceedings)
[15] ICCM 2010: Philadelphia, USA (proceedings)
[16] ICCM 2009: Manchester, UK (proceedings)
[17] ICCM 2007: Ann Arbor, USA (proceedings)
[18] ICCM 2006: Trieste, Italy (proceedings)
[19] ICCM 2004: Pittsburgh, USA (proceedings)
[20] ICCM 2003: Bamberg, Germany (proceedings)
[21] ICCM 2001: Fairfax, USA (proceedings)
[22] ICCM 2000: Groningen, Netherlands (proceedings)
[23] ECCM 1998: Nottingham, UK (proceedings)
[24] EuroCog 1996: Berlin, Germany (proceedings).
[25] Jones, J. (1982). *Design Methods*. New York, Toronto, Chichester: John Wiley&Sons.
[26] Swan, J. (1995). Exploring knowledge and cognitions in decisions about technological innovation: mapping managerial cognitions. *Human Relations, volume 48 number 11*, pp. 1241-1270.
[27] Roberts, F. (2011). *Discreet mathematical models with application to social, biological and ecological issues*. New Jersey: Prentice-Hall, Inc.
[28] Karayev, R.A. (2014). Cognitive approach to the analysis and choice of innovation strategies of the enterprises. Journal of Investment and Management, volume 3 number 1, pp.1-6.
[29] Westcombe, M. (2002). Problem structuring: the process of SODA modelling. Proc. of the ACM Hypertext Conference: Workshop on Facilitating Hypertext-Augmented Collaborative Modeling. University of Maryland, MD, USA.
[30] Decision Explorer TM User's Guide, Version 3. (1997). Glasgow: Banxia Software Limited.
[31] Decision Explorer™ Reference Manual, Version 3.1. (2000). Glasgow: Banxia Software Limited.
[32] Dorner, D. (1996). *The Logic of Failure: Recognizing and Avoiding Error in Complex Situations*. Basic Books Publ.
[33] Waterman, D. (1986). *Guide to Expert Systems*. Addison-Wesley Publ.Co., Inc.
[34] Porter, M. (1996). "What is Strategy?". Harvard Business Review, volume 7 number 3, *pp. 42-57.*
[35] *Nickols, By Ed. (2012). Strategy definitions and meaning. References on strategy. http://www.nickols.us/strategy_definition.htm* (accessed 25.07.2014)
[36] Strategy (1967). B. H. Liddell Hart. Basic Books.
[37] Strategic Planning (1979). George Steiner. Free Press.
[38] The Rise and Fall of Strategic Planning (1994). Henry Mintzberg. Basic Books.
[39] The Concept of Corporate Strategy, 2nd Edition (1980). Kenneth Andrews. Dow-Jones Irwin.

[40] Competitive Strategy (1986). Michael Porter. Harvard Business School Press.
[41] Top Management Strategy (1980). Benjamin Tregoe and John Zimmerman. Simon and Schuster.
[42] Strategy: Pure and Simple (1993). Michel Robert. McGraw-Hill.
[43] The Discipline of Market Leaders (1994). Michael Treacy and Fred Wiersema. Addison-Wesley.
[44] "Customer Intimacy and Other Value Disciplines" (Jan-Feb 1993). Michael Treacy and Fred Wiersema. Harvard Business Review.
[45] "The Span of Control" (May-June 1956). Lionel Urwick. Harvard Business Review.
[46] Mintzberg, H. (1994). *The Rise and Fall of Strategic Planning*. N. Y.: Free Press.
[47] Pospelov, D.A. (1986). *Situational Management: Theory and Practice*. Moscow: Nauka (in Russian)
[48] Karayev, R.A., Ismaylov, S. F., & Sadhikova, N.Y. (2003). Models of scenario analysis. *Trans. of the Nat. Acad. of Sci. of Azerbaijan. Series of phys.-math. and techn. sciences, volume XXIII number 3*, pp. 33-36 (in Russian).
[49] Karayev, R.A. et al. (2004). Forming of corporate enterprise policies by means of fuzzy cognitive maps. *Trans. of the Nat. Acad. of Sci. of Azerbaijan. Series of phys.-math. and techn. sciences, volume XXIII number 2*, pp. 37-54 (in Russian). http://www.science.az/cyber/pdf/2004-2-24.pdf (accessed 25.01.2014).
[50] Karayev, R. A., Safarli, I. I., Abdurahimov, T. F., & Naghiyev, M. A. (2010). Cognitive analysis and company's innovative project management. *Informative-management systems, volume 4 number 47*, pp. 37-43 (in Russian).
[51] Osipov, G.S. (1998). Dynamics in knowledge-based systems. *Trans. of the Russian Academy of Sciences. Theory and system of management, number 5*, pp. 24-28 (in Russian).
[52] Balston, B., & Wilson, I. (2006). *The Scenario Planning Handbook: Development strategies in uncertain times*. Harlow: Pearson.
[53] Lindgren, M. & Bandhold, H. (2009). *Scenario planning. The Link Between Future and Strategy*. N. Y.: Palgrave MacMillan.
[54] Nickols, F., & Ledgerwood, R. (2005). The Goals Grid. A New Tool for Strategic Planning http://www.nickols.us/strategic_planning_tool.pdf (accessed 25.07.2014).
[55] Ogilvy, J.A. (2002). *Creating Better Futures: Scenario Planning as a Tool for a Better Tomorrow*. Oxford University Press.
[56] Michel, G. (2001). *Creating Futures: Scenario Planning as a Strategic Management Tool*. N.Y.: Economics.
[57] Ansoff, I. (1965). *Corporate Strategy: An Analytical Approach to Business Policy for Growth and Explanation*. N. Y.: McGraw Hill.
[58] Grant, R. (1996). Toward a knowledge-based theory of the firm. *Strategic Management Journal, number 17* (*Winter special issue*), pp. 109-122.
[59] OECD Science, Technology and Industry Scoreboard 2011: Innovation and Growth in Knowledge. http://www.oecd.org/sti/oecdsciencetechnologyandindustryscoreboard2011innovationandgrowthinknowledgeeconomies.htm (accessed 25.07.2014).
[60] Holsapple, C., & Whinston, A. (1996). *Decision Support Systems: A Knowledge-based Approach*. Minneapolis: West Publishing Co.
[61] Ashby, W. (1956). *An Introduction to Cybernetics*. London: Chapman and Hall.

[62] Makridakis, S. (1990). *Forecasting, planning, and strategy for the 21st century*. N. Y.: Free Press.
[63] Grant, R.M. (1991). The resource-based theory of competitive advantage: implications for strategy formulation. *California management review, volume 33 number 3*, pp. 114-135.
[64] Chesnokov, V.C. (1987). *Determinacy Analysis*. Moscow: Nauka (in Russian).
[65] Fransella, F., & Bannister, D. (1977). *A manual for repertory grid technique*. London: Academic Press.
[66] Borg, I., & Groenen, P. (2005). *Modern Multidimensional Scaling: theory and applications* (2nd Ed.). New York: Springer-Verlag.
[67] *Nonmetric Multidimensional Scaling Programs:* by Mark Steyvers. *http://www.granular.com/MDS/* (accessed 25.07.2014)
[68] Prahalad, C. K., & Hamel, G. (1990). The core competence of the corporation. *Harvard business review*, May-June, pp.79-91.
[69] Abbasov, A.M., Karayev, R. A., & Safarli, I.I. (2006). Method identification of key management competencies telecommunications companies. *Trans. of the Nat. Acad. of Sci. of Azerbaijan. Series of phys.-math. and techn. sciences, volume XXIII number 3*, pp. 15-20 (in Russian).
[70] Statistic methods of quality improvement. (1990). In Hitosi Kume (Ed.) (translation from Japanese). Moscow: Nauka (in Russian).
[71] Barney, J. (1997). Looking inside for competitive advantage. In A. Campbell, K. Luchs (Ed.), *Core competency-based strategy* (pp. 13-29). London: Intern. Thomson Business Press.
[72] Markus, M., & Mink, H. (1972). *The review under the theory of matrixes and matrix inequalities*. M.: Nauka (in Russian).
[73] Saaty, T. L. (1980). *The analytic hierarchy process: Planning, priority setting, resource allocation*. N.Y.: McGraw-Hill.
[74] Kaplan, R. S. & Norton, D. P. (1996). *The Balanced Scorecard: Translating Strategy into Action*. Harvard Business School Press.
[75] Marakas, G. (1999). *Decision Support Systems in the twenty-first century*. New Jersey: Prentice-Hall, Inc.

About the Author

ROBERT A. KARAYEV (born on 1939)Dr., Professor, head of the Laboratory of the Institute of Cybernetics of the National Academy of Sciences, Azerbaijan, Az1141. Baku, 9, B. Vahabzade str. e-mail: karayevr@rambler.ru.

Research interests: knowledge-based technologies, cognitive technologies, applied systems analysis.

Application Areas:

1. Ecological problems of the Caspian Sea (Environmental Impact Assessment, EIA in a transboundary context, strategies recovery stocks of sturgeon of the Caspian Sea, etc.) 2. Expert systems

industrial purpose. 3. Cognitive analysis innovation strategies of the small and medium-sized enterprises.

4. Cognitive analysis strategies of regional ICT-management and SME (Sollow's Paradox solution).

Developments. Membership of international organizations:

1. In 1990 I received a grant of the State Committee on Science and Technology of the USSR and the Scientific Council AS USSR on the Complex Problem "Artificial Intelligence" for create a "Tool complex for the development and maintenance of intelligent CAD" (Competition project No 720).
2. In the area of intelligent technologies I work since 1985. In 1986-1989 my team was developed first in the former USSR commercial expert system ESM-1800 (analogue of the expert system XCO-R1 (McDermot team from Carnegie Mellon University and DEC Co.)). The system is implemented in the Scientific and Production Association ELECTRONMASH (Kiev), as well as in a number of scientific& research institutes and design organizations of the former Soviet Union.
3. The works in the area of cognitive technologies are conducted by us since 2001. In 2003, the project "Fuzzy cognitive maps for the generation and analysis of managerial decisions" was awarded a Diploma of Russian Academy of Sciences and Grant of the International Scientific Foundation on Economic Researches acad. N.P. Fedorenko (Project No 2003-41).
4. Scientific supervisor of the Research Project "Development of scientific bases on Environmental Impact Assessment (EIA) in the Caspian Sea region (at the modern stage)". Institute of Cybernetics. Baku. 2013.
5. In the period of 2005-2007 I was a member of World Conservation Union/Species Survival Commission/Sturgeon Specialist Group.
6. Currently I am also a professor of International Ecoenergy Academy.
7. Publications - more than 190 work in the areas of applied ecology, knowledge-based and cognitive technologies.

In: Knowledge Engineering
Editor: Alfonso Perez Gama

ISBN: 978-1-63463-909-5

Chapter 4

IN PURSUIT OF HIGH QUALITY ACCREDITATION IN HIGHER EDUCATION

Alfonso Pérez Gama[*]
Fundación de Educación Superior Bogota, Colombia

ABSTRACT

We face the process of High Quality Accreditation in two ways: one, involving a large amount of information (big data), including issues as: self-assessment, high quality, statistics, indicators, surveys, and field-work (process engineering), during several periods of time. The other one, related to the information contained about High Quality: which involves the development of an intelligent architecture based on both knowledge and models for competitiveness. The engine for this architecture is integrated by mathematical and computational models for dynamic and structural analysis of academic governability. It especially considers the processes of High Quality Accreditation (HQA), which demands great effort with the participation of numerous people and faculty members, and compliance with government regulations.

The architecture makes the walkthrough, top down and bottom up, easy: from macro to micro level of data (and vice versa), covering all processes of the university in order to verify full compliance with accreditation rules, policy and quality assurance of the entire academic program. These architectures allow us to follow up the progressive enhancement in search of the academic excellence.

Keywords: High quality architecture, intelligent architecture, self-assessment, higher education, accreditations of high quality, governability, competitiveness, productivity

[*] Corresponding author: www.usanjose.edu.co.

1. INTRODUCTION

The pathway to high quality is paved with significant achievements and overcoming of great obstacles. The macroscopic information is presented in Sections 3 and 4. The main informational components integrate the architecture as follows:

- The related business enterprise model whose functions are peculiar to it, and are related to the functions, which are typical of the university mission.
- The related to the management component as support.
- The ICT architecture.
- The SIFES (MIS, Management Information Systems, for Higher Education in FESSANJOSE)
- The documentation repository.
- Infrastructure.
- The quality and self-assessment.

Understanding the self-assessment, as a process or management tool through which the FESSANJOSE, with a critical review and reflection, made into its university formation system, considering its relationship to the external sector. To achieve the education (through the use of propaedeutic cycles) of a Professional Technical, Technology, and Professional University Education, for building new horizons in quality of life, welfare and equity, and social and economic development, the full compliance with the accreditation regulations, policy and quality assurance of the programs we are offering is required. Accreditation is a part of quality assurance certifying the result of a quality assessment or evaluation.

The institutional self-assessment model proposed by the CNA (National Accreditation Council of Colombia), which has four major components (factors, characteristics, variables and indicators), in turn, raises definitions such as:

- The factors are groupings that affect quality;
- The variables are attributes of the characteristics;
- The empirical referents indicators are variables; the features are the central component of the model, they are the evidence of the quality of an institution or program.

The features are general and specific predicates, something that exists; is an institution, a process, a program, or a service.

In Sections 5, 6 and 7 we present our mature intelligent enterprise architecture – model driven, with 360° vision, accompanied by an executive survey on structural aspects, functional and non-functional of the FESSANJOSE, on the road to High Quality (HQ). We retrieved the best practices for HQA that we have designed and implemented for the purpose mentioned before. Also we have developed intelligent architecture based on knowledge and models for the competitiveness, productivity and high quality supported in our experiences, which are discussed; the architecture engine is formed by mathematical and computational models for dynamic and structural analysis of academic governance. Computational and mathematical models are hypotheses about reality and allow us to analyze the complex world in a more structured and coherent way. These architectures allow us to follow up the progressive enhancement in search of academic excellence.

2. HIGHER EDUCATION CRISIS

The complexity of the problems of Higher Education (HE), have been focused on the poor levels of quality, competitiveness and productivity, with a high incidence of accelerating propensity to dropout, attrition of quality and elevated costs in the education sector in Colombia.

2.1. Challenges of HE

Colombia has also suffered a digital divide (delay) and social (poverty), internal struggles that have bled this country in the last 60 years. One of the challenges is to achieve peace and harmony to promote social development and technical progress. Sustainable economic development and economic growth with quality of life: these challenges are great in terms of competitiveness.

In recent publications such as the World Economic Forum[1] (WEF), Colombia is ranked 92 among 138 at science and math, so, how can we compete in these times of globalization?

The Organization for Economic Cooperation and Development (OECD), and the World Bank (WB), have both warned that students have graduated college in Colombia with serious deficiencies in Mathematics, Physics and Literacy. In order to improve the quality of HE in this country, both these institutions just put the Government of Colombia through an extensive study. They made 63 recommendations to the sector, including the creation of a grade 12° for ME (media education).

In the Program for International Student Assessment (PISA), among 44 participating countries, Colombia was in the last position, after a test of ability to solve problems of the XXI century, on 85,000 15-year-old students, 9,000 of them Colombians. The proof of the PISA was basically an optional test of creative problem solving, in which the Latin American countries were not in good standing with other regions of the world such as Asia, for example.

A recent study, which was conducted by MEN-COMPARTIR FOUNDATION[2], focuses on Teaching as a guarantor of the Constitutional Right to Education. It has generated many expectations on specific support, but there are many questions: Are we going to continue educating using methods and tools of the nineteenth and twentieth century? Obviously we believe that education is the key to face backwardness and poverty. How to do we take advantage of this moment? The study focuses on the Colombian teachers and proposes the improvement of teachers to raise the quality of education. This study proposes important incentives for educators including the sponsorship of major studies.

---

[1] http://www3.weforum.org/docs/WEF_GlobalCompetitivenessReport.

[2] Fundación Compartir. *Following The Teaching Excellence: Improving the quality of education for all Colombians* (Spanish) www.fundacioncompartir.org.

2.2. Competitiveness

It is a lifelong process. Colombia is stuck in the rear positions worldwide (67th), according to the world ranking of WEF Progress; it has been disappointing since the National Competitiveness Agenda paradoxically has created modern institutions (one public and other private) with a multitude of isolated and unrelated policies, with little enforcement capacity and little private participation in the design of policy. For this social Sector of Education, it is a very serious problem: it is an issue of great prevalence aggravated by low investment in STI (Science, Technology and Investigation), the issue of competitiveness and productivity of public education is virtually unknown although it has been claimed as a substantial element of quality and is insufficient. The local Observatory for STI[3] mentions that the rate of the GNP (gross national product) related to Science and Technology inversion is 0.17%, which is 20-30 times less than the leader countries. The latter reveals a fragility in the STI sector in Colombia.

The government proclaims high educational coverage but the problem is poor education quality, which severely distorts the educational service and the labor market especially in Technical and Technological Education.

3. Enterprise Information Architecture for HQ

3.1. Information Architecture Justification

Educational Architecture is a statement towards determination to develop a system incorporating high quality and competitiveness, and opening the channel of communications between those involved. It facilitates planning, management and execution for the strategic development of the University. It can also be seen as the expression of persistent characteristics and principles that support the higher education system to guide acceptable permanent changes.

It enables verification and comparison of whether the implementation of the academic and administrative system is in accordance with the architectural description. Many innovations have been the result of our careful study and insight at the architectural level.

Generally the university enterprise architecture is composed of Strategies, Academic and Organizational Processes, Human and Technology resources, Intellectual Processes, infrastructure and other architectures. It enables coherence and consistency among architectures.

3.2. Information Architecture Description

1. The architecture includes a business enterprise model, which relates to the functional items that are typical of a university mission.

---

[3] www.ocyt.org.co/

2. This component allows us to have access to Institutional and Strategic Plans for each Academic Program, and Intellectual Assets as Production: Papers, Books, Software SIFES, etc.
3. Includes items related to the management component as support to the internal and mission process.
4. The ICT architecture: PLANESTIC, The PROGRAM VIRTUAL Self-Assessment
5. The MIS (SIFES[4]): functionalities, their MODULES and Documentation; The architecture for early warning; FESSJ-ADVERTOR and LINK ME-HE; Knowledge mobility with other institutions in Colombia[5];
6. The quality and self-assessment architectures, which are discussed later.
7. The documentation repository Center. Government and Internal Regulations, Master documentation of entire academic programs, etc.
8. Infrastructure: Computer Technology, Facilities, Buildings and Labs.

4. Institutional Self-Assessment

4.1. Regulations

Gross guidelines have been given by the CNA of the Colombian MEN. It should be noted that they are in full compliance with the accreditation policy and quality assurance programs we run, emanating from Law 30, Law 1188 of 2008, and Decree 3462, among others, including the Guidelines for the Accreditation of Undergraduate Programs, January 2013, and the resolution of Initial Conditions: 002 Agreement in April 2013 from the MEN.

4.2. Description of the Architecture of Self-Assessment

The institutional self-Assessment model proposed by the CNA has four major components:

- Factors (between 8 and 10), which are groupings that affect quality:
  1. Mission, Institutional and Program Project;
  2. Students;
  3. Teachers;
  4. Academic Process;
  5. National and International Visibility;
  6. Research;
  7. Institutional Welfare;
  8. Organization Management;
  9. Impact of Graduates in the Environment;
  10. Physical and Financial Resources.

[4] FESSANJOSE MIS for HE (Spanish).

[5] Universidad Tecnologica del Choco, Agreement 0071 2013; Joint to INFOTEP and Comfenalco Cartagena, are being benefited over 30,000 students in all different headquarters.

- The features (40 to 42) are measurable properties, which are the features model component by way of expression of the quality of an institution or a program. These are general and specific predicates, a component, of whether an institution is an academic or organizational process or a service. For example in the Student factor, features are: 1. Mechanisms of Selection and Admission; 2. Admitted Students and Institutional Capacity; 3. Participation in Integral Formation; 4. Student and Academic Regulations.
- The aspects (181-243) are relative values associated to empirical variables. For item 1, mentioned above, the aspects to investigate are: 24 Special requirements for admission to programs that merit it; 25 Admission Policies and exceptional mechanisms that are made public; 26 Profiles of mechanisms supported by exception; 27 Systems and evaluation mechanisms and processes of admission and preselecting, including the implementation of the results of this Assessment; 28 Admitted to each admission process of the last four cohorts, by application of general rules or by applying exception mechanisms.
- The quantification mechanism is through online surveys to all involved (students, administrators, teachers) oriented interviews, data analysis, and information systems of the University or the Government.

In this information enterprise architecture, we developed a Scalogram Multivariate Matrix with fuzzy values for self-Assessment (degree of completeness): The size of the Self-Assessment matrix for one year is 230 rows (aspects) by 45 columns (academic and administrative process). We evolved the matrix from a qualitative model from another with metrics. We applied the same methodology of the architecture of curriculum coherence. The self-assessment can be quantified by the well-known process of Artificial Intelligence (AI) known as defuzzification that we have used on many occasions. In the future we may extend inter-temporal analysis.

4.3. Objectives of Self-Assessment

- Set to Imperative: the quality
- Generating continuous improvement processes
- Creating open thinking of changes: the Society´s own knowledge
- Projecting new and improved academic and administrative processes
- Assessing and maintaining the quality of customer service (students, teachers, parents) internal and external
- The continuous improvement of developing plans with national and international visibility
- Unifying the processes and procedures effectively and efficiently with productivity.
- Determining the Self as the organizational process (academic and administrative) to integrate within the Matrix Process optimization purposes using our knowledge architecture.
- The architectural approach allows us to analyze and evaluate information in a well-structured way with Vision 360°.

- It also allows us to browse the entire administrative and academic information of the University (walking-through: from top down to bottom up)
- Greatly, the applied method facilitates the strategic alignment of the different units to the final strategy: High Quality.
- The congregation of information reduces the complexity of the analysis and design of coherent institutional improvement plans.
- Self-Assessment itself, managed as an organizational process, facilitates organizational metrics with a linear programming model and Leontief input-output, which extends its value.
- With self-assessment as a process variable, i. e. allowing to quantify the incidence of Self-Assessment in terms of quality, academic sustainability, student dropout, and many others.

5. High Quality in Tertiary Education

5.1. Quality Architecture

Quality has its ethos in an HEI. The accreditation of HQ is the verification of the completeness of the whole institutional quality, which has many different sides, and is a complex problem to determine. It is a system whose components are integrated flexibly towards educational excellence. To self-diagnose the current state allows us to determine the distance to our perfection limit. The HQ of the HE is necessary but not sufficient to achieve sector competitiveness.

These innovative developments have been the result of long submittance processes to the education authorities, of all our programs including: 3 educational levels (Professional Technician, Technologist, and University Professional); and several areas: Engineering, Business Administration, Design and Arts, and also Sports. In total, more than 30 programs in the last 6 years, with accountability to education authorities and with rigorous academic peers, to meet quality standards for obtaining the Qualified Registry, as required in the rules of the MEN in Colombia. Also, there is our outcome of huge experiential learning as an Academic Pair with the National Intersectional Commission for Quality Assurance in Higher Education (CONACES), and CNA [15].

The QA (See Figure 1) has four main components, in our way of looking:

- Educational Plans which define the Mission and Vision horizons, the use of university autonomy accompanied by self-assessment, the governability (Figure 5) that focuses on the feasibility of making necessary decisions and also continuous improvement (See section B, below).
- The global curriculum typical of the knowledge society and educational openings with modern educative processes, which are focused on personal autonomy of student learning and competence-based integral education. One of its components is the Internationalization In House. We started this process several years ago in FESSANJOSE. Nowadays we have the support and accompaniment of the MEN, with the most important universities like La Salle and Rosario. Also recently we have

gained mentoring by representatives of University of Yale and Kentucky State University inside the program of International Mentoring, provided by the MEN. Accreditation could be an important tool to enhance and improve cross-border education. The term Accreditation describes the process of certification and the results of it as mentioned before.

- Research and Innovation to develop the capacity to produce knowledge and innovation capacity. The knowledge architecture is discussed in Section C (below), which allows us to quantify knowledge production and also the accumulation of Intellectual Knowledge[6].
- The infrastructure refers to the required intellectual capital and knowledge assets, the financial resources including technological ones and total quality: from the beginning to the end in the pursuit of excellence.

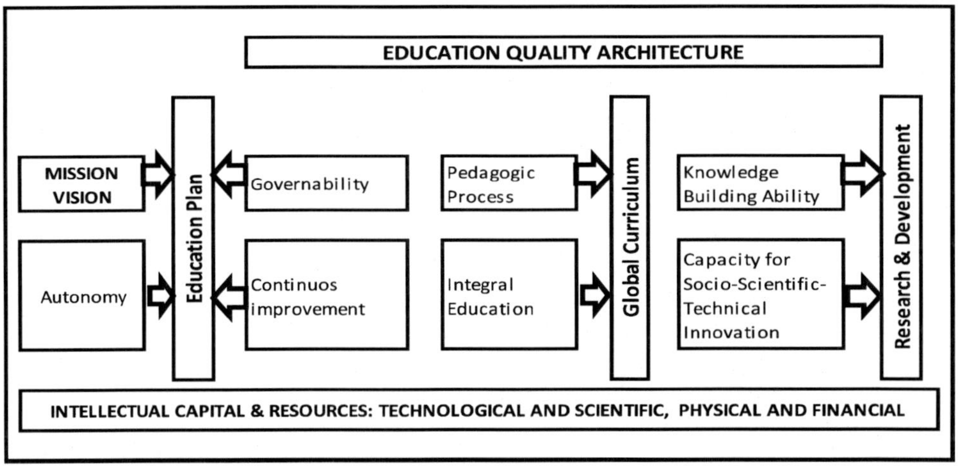

Figure 1. High Quality Architecture.

The governability architecture, in Figure 5, is discussed in Section 5.

5.2. Governability: Knowledge for All

The integrated architectures and models for the knowledge society promise to be a tool for analyzing and quantifying the Competitiveness of Higher Education in this country, with our best potential for high quality accreditation by the HEI. The methodological framework for learning and development prototypes, which we developed at FESSANJOSE, is displayed below.

[6] Our knowledge production can be seen in www.Colciencias.gov.co San Jose International Research Group –Cod 0084828 - We were recognized in 2010, classified and categorized in 2014, by COLCIENCIAS: Colombia National Institution of STI.

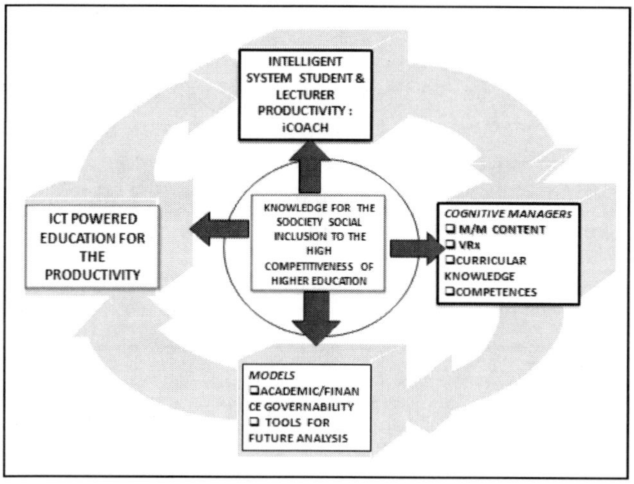

Figure 2. Knowledge for all.

Figure 2 above highlights the methodological framework for learning and development of prototypes, which allowed us to identify problems and provide answers with the same engineering rigor. It summarizes our research efforts, which proposes solutions that combine intelligent virtual environments both as a computational and mathematical model for the purpose of providing systematic answers to the problem of dropouts and repetition in Higher Education.

5.2.1. Governability

It is a concept that goes beyond what an administration is and it is associated with conditions of institutional capacity to deliver educational goods and services, the ease of decision-making, the management of new intellectual capital and related items to meet the needs of government, business and society in general.

It is affected by the overload of demands and social requirements and also by factors such as trust, participation and consensus building. University Governance and Financial Sustainability are closely associated. They are not a matter exclusively of educators. Sustainability is not a purely financial issue, but finance is a strategic component of the strength of educational institutions.

A model of corporate governance is the composition: consistent, coherent, concerted, committed, and participatory; it is assumed by the set of systems and actors, about ways of thinking, decision making, acting and learning, that shows an Institution in the different dimensions of its strategy.

Also the governability problem is related to the mobility of students between the cycles of formation and the levels of the productive sector as well the establishment of an education TP (Technician Professional) –T (Technologist) with international competitiveness and quality.

5.3. Continuous Improvement

This architecture is not a simple conceptual and methodological improvement, but an innovation in the comprehensive and coherent treatment of the concurrent problem of Desertion-Permanence-Repetition-Quality, in two-ways: in the use of creativity in the analysis of problems and the use of creativity in the solution of problems. One consequence is the possibility of dynamic analysis, as illustrated in Figure 3.

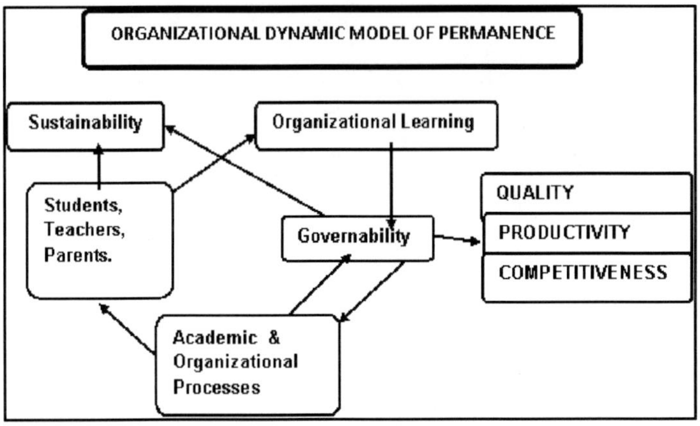

Figure 3. Permanence Dynamic Analysis.

$Y = f(X)$

ϵ: Competence Areas

$X =$
- X_1= Multiple Paradigms: social interactionism, constructivism, discovery learning Bruner, Ausubel Meaningful Learning.....
- X_2= dimensions: biological, cognitive, affective, praxeological
- X_3= ICT

Y:
- **Y_1= Pedagogical strategies set**
- **Y_2= Pedagogic process strategies**

Figure 4. Pedagogic computational Model.

The model focuses on organizational governability with its impact on financial sustainability, generation of knowledge and institutional learning (starting from Young Seed Research Groups) to QUALITY, PRODUCTIVITY AND COMPETITIVENESS. The core mission focuses on student productivity (supported by an intelligent system), teacher productivity (supported by an intelligent handler of competencies and an intelligent courses-contents generation, and also the system for coherence and curriculum optimization[7].

5.4. Pedagogic Model and Integral Education

5.4.1. Pedagogic Model Description

In strategic alignment with the IEP (Institutional Educational Project), the pedagogical model promotes the development of multiple intelligences to develop during the preparatory stage of cycles as an axiological aspect of the subject in his/her LIFE PROJECT.

It encompasses the strategy and pedagogical decisions rules, which are an important component of the institutional navigation chart, the IEP, and more specifically, the aims and objectives for strategic processes and action plans, focusing on skills training for evaluation and permanent control. A pedagogical model is part of the corporate strategy, drawn on pedagogical mediation of ICT and the support of the new theories of learning in virtual environments known as computational mathematics (from Greek manthenein μανθάνειν: to learn). The Consolidated Pedagogical Model promotes strategies that are required for the design and implementation of the whole pedagogical process inside the HEI.

The pedagogical model of the FESSANJOSE is configured from its constituent principles, which correspond to the following, regarding the conception of the subject (person) and training:

- It is framed within the lineaments of Colombian Education Law
- It is established by the conceptions of the person, from the perspective of integral education.
- Under the vision of the documents, the four pillars, and the seven lessons for the future education, of Delors and Morin [18], the ones we provide in relation to the conception of education.
- About the conceptions for the project life skills, profession, education and communication. From the perspective of social inclusion, human development and welfare.
- In connection to educational and pedagogical concepts: The developing skills to generate meta compressions and understandings from the reflections.
- From the question of education strategy.
- Through the significance of meaningful learning experience.
- Through interaction in teaching
- From the perspective of the intelligence of the persons looking for multiple intelligences.
- Through understanding the pedagogical models.
- Located epistemologically, from practice and practice in the constructivist model.
- Through strategies and active classroom participants.
- From problem solving.

[7] 1-2014-677 07/01/2014: USANJOSE-CURR-COHE, System to Analyze, Optimize the Curriculum Coherence of the Propaedeutic Cycles in Higher Education. SOFTWARE REGISTRATION Book 13-Volume 41-Part 205.DNDA, Colombia National Directorate of Copyrights.

- From generation projects that facilitate learning through the acquisition of knowledge and problem-solving situations. Through the interactions of subjects (teachers and students) and the relationships established and the recognition achieved.

5.5. Knowledge Architecture

5.5.1. Conceptualizing

The Knowledge architecture can be defined as the set of strategic design decisions that affect the structure, intelligent behavior or functionality of the system as a whole. The HEIs are the natural space where the ethos of knowledge can be developed and the Intellectual Capital (IK) can be accumulated. The inadequacy of the MIS to incorporate knowledge is no secret. In fact it is shared by many authors that well over half the market value is explained by the IK in companies of the Third Millennium. Traditional systems do not account for the IK and only estimate the book values vs. market values when selling is focused on negotiation processes. On the other hand, there are already quite a few financial models of the knowledge economy that consider the IK. For the universities it is a critical issue for the competitiveness of HE.

5.5.2. Knowledge Process

A process is defined as an activity that takes place in ongoing stages to produce a result or a specific group of them coherently. It is a set of activities that transforms inputs into a product or a service with customer value.

A knowledge process is a sequence of iterative activities characterized by having measurable inputs/outputs and value added activities, including organization, staff, equipment, procedures and materials required to produce a result: knowledge, intellectual assets and intelligent performances.

5.6. Metrics for Knowledge Production and Innovation

5.6.1. Educational Innovation or Innovation ICT?

It is a unanimous consideration that there has been practically no technical or scientific change that did not impact pedagogy. The education sector has been profiled in two ways, sometimes contradictory: a changing and modifying way, since the education sector has to educate future generations with scientific, social and technological changes, and the other, the conservative way, given that it must preserve social and cultural structures, which it favors.

But it is also noted that behind it are the benefits of such changes. These days of rapid obsolescence is when the education sector will require more innovation, and is when to take advantage of developments in other sectors, enabling the transformation of practices of appropriation of knowledge from different components of science and cultures.

The question remains whether innovative activity in computer science education should be the set of social research, i.e., the progress of scientific basis, or else its origin as in the progress of the computer, according to the possibilities of profit to be contemplated.

5.6.2. Mathematical Knowledge Architecture

The Mathematical Knowledge Architecture is presented in Table 1, which comprises the matrix of Leontief Input-Output (innovated to the knowledge Society) in a system either at the micro level (i.e., a program of study) or a higher-level institution or a country. This architecture has 3 components:

- The inter-sector industry subset, including the Knowledge Sector
- The restriction and threshold values: real world facts.
- Various objective functions.

The model was integrated with linear programming to analyze together the services of Education in the Tertiary Sector of the economy (trade and services), with the primary sector and the manufacturing sector.

The optimization criteria are shown schematically in Figure 5, which shows the levels of students in HE related to students permanence/ desertion(dropout).

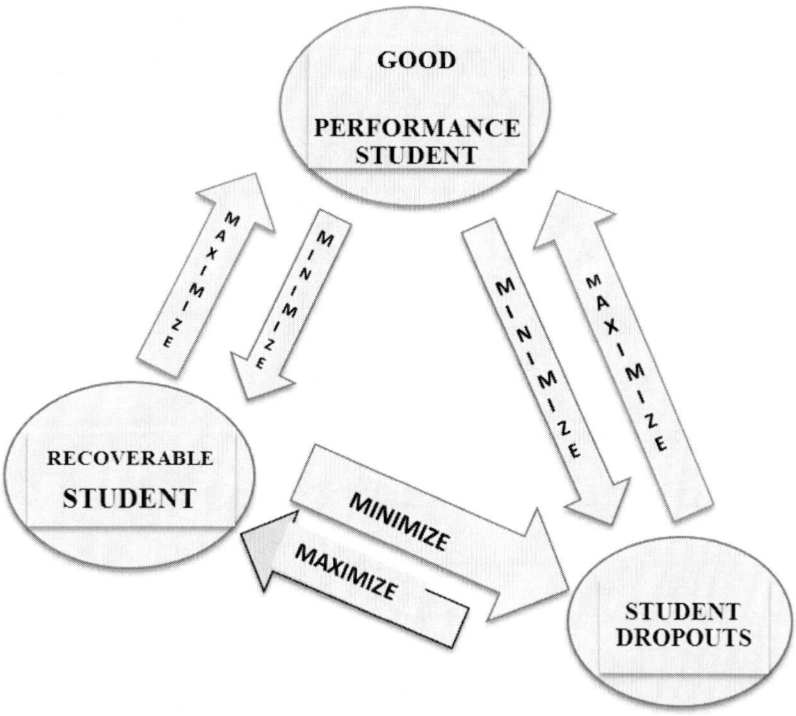

Figure 5. Academic Governability.

The governability deals with control of the flows within these levels of students, outlined and quantified in the multiple objective functions. It seeks to maximize the number of students performing well, given the facts of the world of HEI (restrictions, limits), which is one of the indicators of quality, pre excellence. The academic governance also implies the control flows that are contrary to policy optimization. The model also generates information on the costs of flows of students.

Table 1. Knowledge Architecture

Leontief Multisectorial Linear Programmming		Primary	Manufacture Industry	Higher Education						Rest of Commerce & Services y Crecimineto	Households	Government	Exports	Imports	Rest of Final Demand				RHS
				Basic Sciences	Professional Basics	Socio-Humanistic Sciences	Communications	Found. Scientific Technical	Social Projectn & Research						Physical Capital	Intelectual Capital	Others		
Industry & Knowledge ECONOMY	Primary Sector																	=	0
	Manufacture Industry																	=	0
Higher Education	Basic Sciences															k1		=	0
	Professional Basics															k2		=	0
	Socio-Humanistic						(I - A)				-H	-G	-1X	-1M	-df1	k3		=	0
	Communications															k4		=	0
	Found. Scientific Technical															k5		=	0
	Social Projection & Research															k6		=	0
	Rest of Commerce, Services & TICs															k7		=	0
	Remunerations	f1	f2	f3	f4	f5	f6	f7	f8	f9	-1							=	0
	Government	t1	t2	t3	t4	t5	t6	t7	t8	t9		-1						=	0
	Exports	ex1	ex2	ex3	ex4	ex5	ex6	ex7	ex8	ex9			-1					=	0
	Imports	m1	m2	m3	m4	m5	m6	m7	m8	m9				-1				=	0
	Rest Added Value	r1	r2	r3	r4	r5	r6	r7	r8	r8	-1							=	0
	Restrictions and Thresholds																		
FIT	Seats			q1	q2	q3	q4	q5	q6									≤	b1
	Human Resource			l1	l2	l3	l4	l5	l6									≤	b2
	Capacity			v1	v2	v3	v4	v5	v6									≤	b3
	Minimun Coverage			j1	j2	j3	j4	j5	j6									≥	b4
	Multiple Objective Functions																		Z
CRITERIA	STUDENT LEVEL			q1	q2	q3	q4	q5	q6									=	Opt
	Repetition Avoided			l1	l2	l3	l4	l5	l6									=	Max
	Desertion Avoided			v1	v2	v3	v4	v5	v6									=	Max
	Gross benefits			j1	j2	j3	j4	j5	j6									=	Max

$$f(X, D_f) = 0 \quad (1)$$

D_f Is the final demand: Households, Inversion, Government, Δ Inventories including Intellectual Capital, Rest of the world…

Political function issues:

$$\text{Max } Z = f(\Delta Students\ Level) \quad (2)$$

$$(I - A)X - D_f = 0 \quad (3)$$

$$\text{F (resources)} \leq b_i \text{ availability} \quad (4)$$

5.7. Strategies Analysis

Among the questions that can be analyzed and quantified running the knowledge architecture would be:

What would be the cost of changing a student from one level to another?
What would be the opportunity cost of losing a student from a higher to a lower level?
What type of management strategies: economic, academic or pedagogic, respond better in order to maximize the number of students who graduate school?
Which strategy is more responsive to the maximization of repetition avoided?
How an institution responds to the demands faced in improving the quality of curricular and economic competitiveness?
How much does it cost for an institution to improve its quality and competitiveness?
What is the cost of the Internationalization process?
How much does it cost for an institution to improve global competitiveness?
What additional financial and technological resources does an institution need to maintain good government?
What is the value of intellectual capital accumulated in a university?

6. Intelligent Educational Architecture

Architecting implies the organization of subsystems or components to obtain new or better functionalities. If such component is knowledge based, we obtain intelligent behavior.

6.1. Space

We developed our architecture of maturity regarding the HE problem space we used, as displayed in Figure 4. The categorization of agents of this model includes family parents, students, teachers who are the kernel, the universities, the professional unions, the industry and the Government. Students and Teachers are individually represented. This architecture has allowed the knowledge mobility of several universities in Colombia [13].

6.2. The Computational Model of Architecture

Computational representation is required for obvious reasons but we need to recognize the impossibility of mathematical expression as a determined and closed expression. The variables involved are objects, arrays (in terms of function coverage by level and area), vector (technological level), fuzzy variables (e.g., performance management) and scalar. Their inputs and outputs give data flows simply, to express different forms usually unstructured e.g., a problem to solve or a plan of action to follow:

The architecture scheme could also be represented by a set of simultaneous equations given multiple inter and intra relations of the system as MIS inter-temporal analysis. However the scheme described above indicates in itself, a much richer and fertile performance to meet the demands of the corporate governability system, and is intended to suit individual conditions of an executive–user. The computer left its position as a simple data repository and calculator, to become an expert assistant, playing a much more important role.

Y = f {problems, needs, performance, technological level, management level}

The results of the architecture (i.e. outputs)

$$Y: \begin{bmatrix} \text{Governability} \\ \text{Plan-Roadmap} \\ \text{High Quality} \end{bmatrix}$$

Governability: [(Teachers, Students, Resources, Continuous Improvement)]

Road Map: [(Strategic Orientation, Mission, Vision, Action Plan, Prospective Articulation)]

High Quality: [(Self-Assessment, Competence Educational Model, Pedagogical Consolidated Model, Accumulation of Intellectual Capital and Assets Innovation)].

Figure 1. Architecture Computational Model.

6.3. Models for Intervention

The intelligent architecture, knowledge based, has allowed us to define several intervention models for student remediation of several kinds: academy, psychology, economy and related. The Intervention Model implies:

- Protocol for raising awareness: Family Parents workshops for adapting to university life, funding for HE, sexuality, etc.
- Academic difficulties protocol: study skills and time management; test and sensitization to teachers and students about learning and cognitive styles; academic monitoring.
- Protocol for the prevention of depression: Test of the Beck inventory; ID on symptoms of depression for parents and students.
- Reinforcement design workshops on basic communication and Mathematics skills to be applied to freshman students who use to perform the induction process in the first half academic period.
- Design workshops for generating skills for analysis and understanding of text, and also Basic Math
- Integral plan: training mentoring.

Our architectures [10] were included in Colombia's Successful Experiences in Desertion.

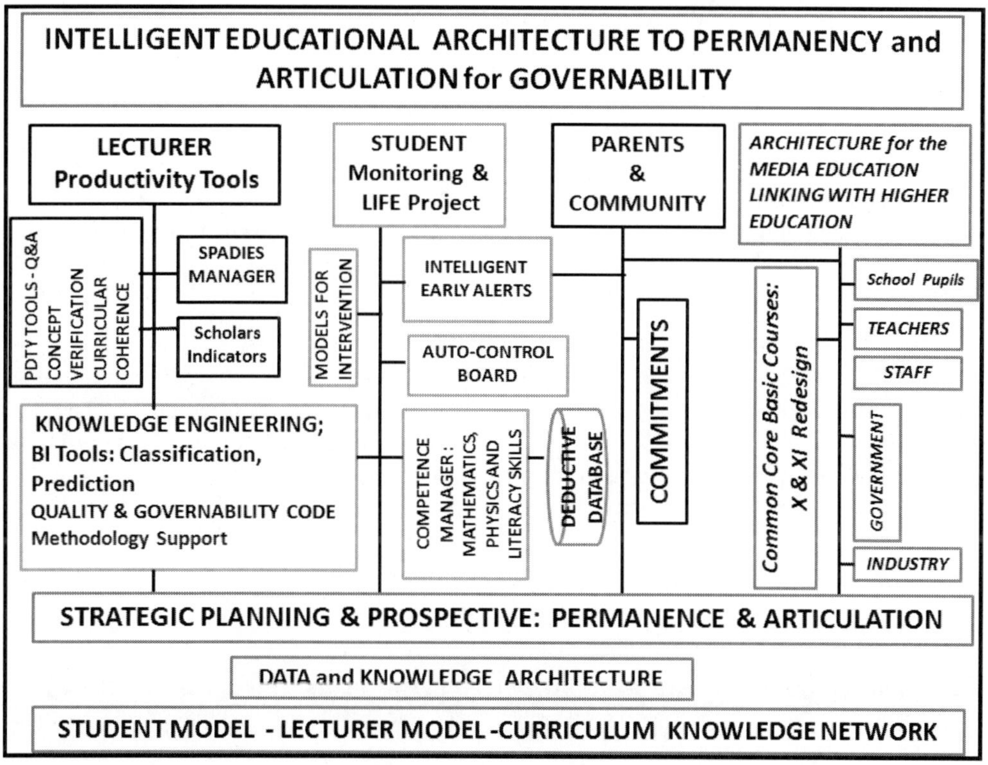

Figure 2. Intelligent Educational Architecture.

6.4. Lecturers and Teachers

The widespread use of different architectures as discussed in this paper provided a space to analyze and find optimal and feasible solutions, given the high complexity of the educational sector.

The teacher side includes authoring tools for content generation, and verification of concepts and knowledge.

6.5. Student: Early Alerts

Early alerts software[11] for each student, approached from different fields, starting from the risk characterization of SPADIES[12] (System for Dropout Prevention in Higher Education in Colombia, developed by MEN) and thus, detailed tracking of students who are at high risk.

There is another area of focus for alerts regarding attendance for teachers and students with a daily log of this assistance, which is carried out electronically giving us an indication of both students who have stopped attending for a certain time, and teachers on the rate of absence that may promote a decline in academic quality. Another item has to do with the student´s academic performance and payment methods, to make an accompaniment for these issues.

The Model monitors students by dependencies with protocols and determines routines, with online guides to improve Math & Reading and Writing skills, including support and protocols for the use and monitoring, ICT-based.

6.6. Student: Self- Control Board

Student Self-control board: is a student-centered tool, used to monitor his/her own progress and individual information, competencies, academic and administrative information.

6.7. Student-Teacher: Knowledge Engineering Tools

Business Intelligence (BI) tools are required for mining and knowledge discovery for classification and prediction in terms of risk and desertion (dropout). It has been an important data analysis tool used to improve the models for intervention.

6.8. Competence Manager: iCOACH

The design and implementation of iCOACH, a knowledge-based intelligence tool, is a high computing instrument used to follow each student in the first academic term of the

[11] 1-2014-647 on 07/01/2014: USANJOSE ADVERTOR-HE- SOFTWARE RECORD; REGISTERED: Book 13 - Volume 41, Part 203; DNDA, Colombia National Directorate of Copyrights.

[12] http://spadies.mineducacion.gov.co/spadies/

engineering faculty at the FESSANJOSE, specifically in the areas of Math, Physics and Reading-Writing Skills. The software architecture has 3 main parts: Edumatic builder (a productivity tool for the Teacher and competence manager), the Student Model, and the third one is the knowledge base for concept verification. Several previous works have preceded this project, so our methodology and related items are very experienced. A prototype was built [12] to demonstrate the iCOACH validity and applicability and was also used as an instrument of academic productivity for competence management.

6.9. Linking ME HE

There are various kinds of Articulation between processes, cycles and levels of education, and of these, with Industry, Government and Society. The most serious problem is the articulation of ME with HE.

Also there are other complications: joining educational coverage with the same quality of education; the articulation between the propaedeutic cycles uniting the various integrative skills.

Similarly, we could try other extensions to articulate quality educational excellence; to articulate the dimensions of the productivity, quality and competitiveness of the education sector (which requires relevant education), to reach an ongoing process as a mediation to articulate the Information Society to the building of the Knowledge Society, where leading countries are engaged.

It has been a constant and ongoing activity to improve student skills in math, physics, and reading and writing, which allowed high school attendees to enter HE and shows success in curricular flexibility and a substantial improvement in the State tests. This component allows students in high school institutions to have an articulation agreement with the University, to access the 3rd level once the student has completed his/her ME.

6.10. Strategic Planning

The STRATEGIC PLAN articulated with the Prospective, allows definition of the roadmap to align human, physical and technological efforts toward HE Competitiveness, comprising: SWOT matrix, Critical Success Factors, Strategic Orientation, Strategic Map, Prospective and Scenarios Desertion, and ME-HE Addressing Articulation.

A major product is a Handbook of Quality and Governance in Student Drop and Permanence, including the definition of institutional policies [5].

7. Discussion

7.1. About Our Developed Architectures

- The architectural methodology illustrates how a complex system can be developed and articulated in order to show the governance and relations to actors, major subsystems, and software to obtain new, important and better functionalities. This architecture conforms a big system as a whole, organized and complex.

- The architectural approach allowed us to analyze and evaluate a large volume of academic and administrative information, in a well-structured way, with a 360° view. It also allowed us to view the entire administrative and academic information of the University (walking-through: from top down to bottom up)
- Overall, the applied method facilitated the strategic alignment of the different units to the final strategy: High Quality. It also provided the synchronization of the academic and administrative process, establishing common referents to the whole community.
- The congregation of information at different levels of aggregations reduced the complexity of the analysis and design. It even facilitated institutional improvement plans coherently.
- Self-assessment itself, managed as an organizational process, facilitated with organizational metrics, the linear programming model and the Leontief input-output, extended its value for optimization purposes.
- Another important contribution is the model of Self-Assessment for HE, according to the CNA, for which we use some tools for BIG Data management and visualization, through a multivariate fuzzy matrix–dashboard with an Architectural Vision, 360°.
- With self-assessment as a process variable, i.e., it allowed quantifying self-Assessment in terms of quality, academic sustainability, student desertion (dropout) and other information, thanks to the knowledge architecture.
- Finally we consider that the information enterprise architecture is the Institutional memory.

7.2. Synthesis: Outcomes of the Architecture

As shown before, in Figure 7, we summarize the following outcomes:

- The accreditation of High quality is the verification of the completeness of the whole Institutional Quality towards excellence: Our architecture helps us visualize, diagnose and quantify our approach to academic excellence.
- These experiences have been cataloged by the MEN as successful and allowed us the mobility of knowledge we are implementing in several universities in Colombia [13]
- Regarding methods of HE, which are changing rapidly, we are facing new challenges both at institutional and at individual levels. Due to the increase in national and international competition, institutions are struggling to offer attractive academic programs with HQ Accreditation for learners by employing modern ICT based e-learning.
- These architectures allow us to follow up the progressive enhancement in search of academic excellence.

7.3. Conclusion and Future Work

Knowledge is one of the most important expressions of human intelligence, in order to:

- Confront problems and determine to solve them
- Address the complexities of human beings, society and the world
- Cope with shortages of food and resources that we were given, as limited.
- In short, knowledge appears in the Third Millennium as a cognitive tool for large applications and uses in the Knowledge Society.
- We have presented dual architecture models for handling HQ in HE: One is related to the large knowledge, data and information. The other is to verify the completeness of the requirements for accreditation purposes by National and International Agencies. Both of these are combined in one tool.
- Perhaps the most important innovation regarding the inter-industrial Leontief model is including the knowledge sector.
- Production can be quantified in both knowledge and intellectual assets, in addition to its accumulation.
- These experiences have been cataloged by the MEN as successful and allowed us the mobility of knowledge. We are implementing them in several universities in Colombia [13].
- The Quality Architecture has been framed as a systemic one, to respond to the main problem of HE. The Accreditation process is a byproduct of this endeavor.

We try to address the complex problem of Educational Quality, including

- The joint HE - ME due to poor preparation of young people who will enter the HE in Colombia.
- The different actors in the process: teachers, students, parents, government, industry and others.
- We use complex tools, as befits the nature of the problem, such as ICT, Artificial and Computational Intelligence, Knowledge Engineering, and different kinds of architectures: Data, Information, ICT and Intelligent knowledge-based Software Engineering from many others.
- New constructs are conceptualized as Educational Intelligence as a set of analogous to BI (Business Intelligence) but with its own specific constructs.

7.4. Future Work Purposes

They are related to enrich intelligent architecture with Machine Learning constructs.

We will improve the methodological and software experiences and developments to achieve a professional version to offer it to the academic community, local and international. We are addressing this professional development of our tools, presented in this Chapter, to give it broader social use, which can be adapted to the specific needs of each HEI. To this end we are seeking international resources to support our innovation and research initiatives.

Given that the complexity of knowledge is caused by the dynamic nature of enterprise systems of the III Millennium, and especially by how HEI in general evolves, this brings challenges to the achievement of semantic inter-operability and the maintenance of managerial information & knowledge systems. Therefore the urgent adoption of vocabularies has been required, primarily terminologies and ontologies for KE (knowledge engineering) and KM (knowledge management). It is a way to standardize HEI knowledge representation models, as the knowledge has its ethos inside the University. In this book we included a technical glossary related to KE and KM in each Chapter.

8. Acknowledgment

Special thanks to Dr. Jorge Enrique Franco Gallego of the National Ministry of Education. Our gratitude to FESSANJOSE, to Lecturers and Officers, especially to the SAN JOSE EIDOS International & Research Team, including Guillermo Hoyos, Claudia Caro, Martha Rozo, Carlos F. Pareja, Mandina Quizza, Hugo Medina, Olga Forero, Byron Perez Gutierrez, Dr. Marco Eric Perez-Hernández and especially to Dr. Giovanni Rozo Pardo, to all of them, our debt of thanks.

9. References

[1] *American International Journal of Contemporary Research*, Vol. 3, No. 4, April 2013 Application of Quality Assurance & Accreditation in the Institutes of Higher Education in the Arab World (Descriptive & Analytical Survey), Dr. Mohammed Ahmed Mohammed Hamdatu et. al. College of Science & Humanities Shaqra University - KSA.

[2] "Handbook on Enterprise Architecture". Springer; 1 edition (November 5, 2003). (International Handbooks on Information Systems). 7- ISBN-10, 3540003436. ISBN-13: 978-3540003434.

[3] Tertiary Education in Colombia; Reviews of National Policies for Education: Tertiary Education In Colombia - OECD AND IBRD/THE WORLD BANK 2012

[4] Perez Gama Alfonso, Andrey Alvarez Gaitán, Marco Antonio Pérez Compendium of Quality and Government, Student Desertion and Permanence –(Spanish); Fundación de Educación Superior San Jose BOGOTA Febrero 2013; ISBN: 978-958-46-1442-1.

[5] Perez Gama Alfonso, Analytical Models for Tertiary Education by Propaedeutic Cycles Applying Knowledge Engineering and Knowledge Management; BOOK Title: "New Research on Knowledge Management Models and Methods"; Published BY INTECH - OPEN ACCESS PUBLISHER, ISBN 979-953-307-226-4.

[6] Perez, Gama Alfonso; Guillermo, Hoyos Gómez; Byron, Alfonso Perez Gutiérrez. Knowledge for the Society: Social Inclusion to the Superior Education High Competitiveness: A Knowledge-Based Governability Model for the Higher Education in Colombia by Propaedeutic Cycles;. IEEE EDUCON 2011 Annual AMMAN JORDAN. ISBN: 978-1-61284-641-5

[7] Perez, Gama Alfonso; Andrey, Ali Alvarez Gaitán. Intellectual Assets and Knowledge Method: A Contribution; Book Chapter published by Springer Heidelberg, London, BOOK Title: Advances in Intelligent Systems 172 ISSN 2194-5357; Eds Lorna UDEN et al.

[8] Modelo Analítico-Inteligente de los Ciclos Propedéuticos; Incluido en el BANCO DE EXPERIENCIAS SIGNIFICATIVAS EN EDUCACION SUPERIOR; Ministerio de Educación Superior, Bogotá 2010. http://www.colombiaaprende.edu.co/

[9] FODESEP National Meeting of Success Cases on Desertion for Higher Education-Bogota September 2013 Prevention and Remediation of Desertion System Towards the Academic Improvement: An Approach Bio-Psycho-Socio-Techno-Scientific to address Desertion and Permanence in Higher Education. September 2013; (Spanish) Ministry of National Education- Bogotá

[10] FESSANJOSE is part of Internationalization Accompaniment Project awarded by the Ministry of National Education supported by the YALE UNIVERSITY and KENTUCKY STATE UNIVERSITY.

FESSANJOSE under the "National Agreement to Reduce Student Attrition in Higher Education", which was signed on November 22, 2010, executed the 755 Agreement with the MEN, which aimed at strengthening policies, strategies and actions of the anti-dropout program that promotes our institution in favor of the desertion of young people enrolled and in accordance with the social project that promotes access to Higher Education. (Spanish)

[11] MEN Convocation 2013: NATIONAL AGREEMENT TO REDUCE STUDENT DROP OUT. Projects directed to transfer strategies that promote the permanence and graduation in higher education. (Spanish)

[12] Perez Gama Alfonso: Education Software Architecture: Facing Student Desertion in Colombia Higher Education with an Intelligent Knowledge Based Coaching System: et al.; IEEE ANDESCON 2010 Bogotá Colombia. ISBN 978-1-4244-7172-0.

[13] Bahamon Lozano Jose Hernando: La Gestion estratégica en el contexto de la Universidades Colombianas. Factores que inciden en su incorporación, aplicación efectiva e institucionalización, PhD Thesis U de Sevilla, España; Marzo 2013

[14] Consejo Nacional de Acreditación -CNA- (enero de 2013). Lineamientos para la acreditación de programas de pregrado. Obtenido de CNA.gov.co: http://www.cna.gov.co/

[15] María José Lemaitre editor; et al. Educación Superior en Iberoamérica Informe 2012 universia CINDA - Aseguramiento de la calidad en Iberoamérica. ISBN 978 956 7106-60-8

[16] Villanueva Ernesto Fernando: Alcances y Perspectivas de los Sistemas de Aseguramiento de la Calidad Educativa En América Latina; La Educación –Revista Digital, OEA Enero 2019; n 142

[17] Morin, Edgar: Seven complex lessons in education for the future. UNESCO, Paris.

10. Technical Glossary on KE

ARCHITECTURE: Architecting implies the organization of subsystems or components to obtain better and/or new functionalities. If any component is knowledge-based we obtain an intelligent behavior. The Architecture-multilayer approach is itself a system of systems (SoS) that ensures compliance with government policies, rules and standards in a highly complex social institution with intellectual assets and knowledge processes, which are usual to a university.

ARTIFICIAL INTELLIGENCE: It is the systematization and processing of knowledge; increases the efficiency of a system; it is the added value for e-commerce to the organization. Enables the company to stand and survive successfully and be competitive. It refers to doing more with less: the challenge of today. It is the field of computer science, which is related to symbolic reasoning, problem solving and computational systematization of human intelligence. It provides automatic systems for learning and for making autonomous decisions, such as robotics.

COMPUTATIONAL INTELLIGENCE: According to the IEEE this branch was removed from computer science and is a higher stage of artificial intelligence. It focuses on bio-inspired, swarm intelligence, cellular automata, and neural networks, among other systems. It is mainly based on computational logic systems, software, abstract patterns, and soft-computing.

FUZZY LOGIC: Form of reasoning also called inexact reasoning, which can be used with uncertain or partial information. Feature of human thought when the limits of a set or system are not well defined or delimited. It also relates to linguistic contexts.

ICT: The convergence of information technologies, the cognimatics, computing and telecommunications (particularly the Internet and computer networks) with its technological base, information or "content" that is acquired, stored, handled, transported and is transmitted through them. The technological basis includes hardware and software components and also nanotechnology, microelectronics technology, computing, and telecommunications.

ICT ARCHITECTURE: Intensive use of ICT deepens the integration and re-composition of processes within and between organizations that are part of the architecture involved. The systems that enables the operation of processes, side by side with skilled human capital, must be dynamically re-architecturalized (i.e., reconfigurable). This reconfiguration capability can be developed with the evolution of integration and application technologies, particularly via the WEB and the composition of modern software techniques.

INFORMATION ARCHITECTURE: Is the engineering, art and science of categorization, structure, organization, taxonomizing and classifying data and information to help users locate and manage that information and also to support the use and capabilities of search. By balancing the characteristics and requirements of users, content and perspective i.e., Questions Top down, & Bottom up Answers.

INTELLECTUAL ASSETS: In modern business it is an intangible asset represented by information, software, and expertise that give the organization an important value. As an example we have the know-how, licenses, patents, copyrights ©, etc. Also associated with INTELLECTUAL CAPITAL is a set of Intellectual Assets of a company. It refers especially to those represented by knowledge, management skills and competencies of various kinds, resident in the human resources of an organization or frozen in software.

KNOWLEDGE: It refers to instructions, procedures, rules and content to address complexity and troubleshooting. It is required for business survival. Refers to How to do a task? Which is correct? The harmonic blend of information and experience, i.e., the combined theory with practice makes true knowledge. The knowledge representation is a surrogate for human reasoning.

KNOWLEDGE BASE: A related set of facts, observations, tasks and procedures description, and statement coded patterns, assumptions and knowledge representation rules, which enable the intelligent agent or expert system to autonomously make decisions and solve problems effectively and support them with explanations and analytical justification based on the stored material.

KNOWLEDGE ENGINEERING: Branch of engineering that deals with the organization, representation, use and application of knowledge to design, build and deploy intelligent agents and Expert Systems. The KE is considered the top step of systems engineering.

KNOWLEDGE REPRESENTATION: Is the process of structuring knowledge for problem solving. It also refers to the methods used to encode, store and retrieve knowledge in a KB (knowledge base). It is a substitute for the human reasoning process.

MODEL: Abstract representation, structured, simplified schematic of reality, as a hypothesis. It encompasses the functionalities of the systems, for analysis and dynamics.

SOFTWARE ARCHITECTURE: The IEEE Software Architecture standard (1471-2000) states that "The Software Architecture is the fundamental organization of a system formed by their components, the relations among them and the context in which they will be established, and besides the principles that orient their design and evolution". The Software Architecture deals with the design and the software structures, and their establishment at high level. It is the result of integrating a certain number of components of adequate form, in order to obtain better and new functionalities as well as non-functional requirements, such as the quality, the reliability, the usability, the scalability, the portability, the availability, the systems interfaces, etc.

11. QUESTIONS

1. What are the purposes and objectives being sought for quality architecture?
2. Design quality architecture in your institution. Identify which components to integrate and define the results to be obtained from that architecture.
3. Establish architecture differences between data, information and knowledge.
4. Review the functions of a data steward in a modern organization. What could be the functions of a Knowledge steward?
5. Identify intellectual assets in your organization. What metrics would you suggest to quantify that IA?
6. The traditional MIS are evolving toward MIKS (Management Information and Knowledge Systems). What managerial innovations bring advantages to modern organizations?

About the Author

ALFONSO PEREZ GAMA
japerezg@ieee.org

Master of Science Computer Science (Artificial Intelligence) UNIVERSITY OF ESSEX, United Kingdom (British Council Honor Scholarship – James Rooke); Magister on Systems Engineering at the UNIVERSIDAD NACIONAL DE COLOMBIA Bogota; Graduate Economy Program, PEG UNIVERSIDAD DE LOS ANDES, Bogota; Electronics Engineer, UNIVERSIDAD DISTRITAL FRANCISCO JOSE DE CALDAS Bogota.

IEEE Institute of Electrical and Electronics Engineers: Life Senior Member; Former Colombia Computer Society Chapter Chair, Education Society Colombia Chapter Chair,

Member of:

The New York Academy of Sciences, NYAS

The International Association of Software Architects, IASA

The International Input Output Association, IIOA

The; International Council on Systems Engineering, INCOSE

The Colombia Systems Engineering Association, ACIS

UNIVERSIDAD NACIONAL DE COLOMBIA: Tenure Professor and University Master Fellow (Retired). Director of EIDOS Research Project sponsored by COLCIENCIAS and CYTED-D;

Universidad DISTRITAL: Tenure Professor Graduate Programs in Engineering

Currently FUNDACION DE EDUCACION SUPERIOR SAN JOSE, Science & Technology Advisor; Director of the International Research Team SAN JOSE EIDOS; Current Research: ANALYTICAL and COMPUTATIONAL INTELLIGENT MODELS FOR THE PROPAEDUTIC CYCLES of the SUPERIOR EDUCATION IN COLOMBIA, Sponsored by COLCIENCIAS, the Ministry of National Education, FODESEP and the EU (European Union).

This work was selected as a Colombia Successful Case and included in the National Bank of Significant Experiences in Superior Education July 2010- by the Ministry of National Education- Also a Case of Successful Best Practices in Higher Education: Student Permanence and Desertion 2011-2012: This project was sponsored by the Ministry of National Education (Contract 755 2011), Bogota Colombia.

1990- Now: National and International Academic Pair: Ministry of Colombia National Education and IEEE

HONORS and Awards:

JAMES ROOKE Honor Scholarship granted by British Council. 1986-1988.

IEEE Colombia Section: 2012 Roberto Valenzuela IEEE Life and Achievement;

City University Francisco Jose de Caldas IEEE Student Branch 50 Years with Professional Excellence Recognition;

IEEE Distinction: Colombia LMG Chair as one of the 10 Top OUTSTANDING AFFINITY

GROUP 2009, 2010, 2011, 2012 and 2013;
IEEE Education Society Awards 2013: DISTINGUISHED CHAPTER LEADERSHIP AWARD.

San Jose Higher Education Foundation AWARD TO THE SCIENTIFIC MERIT, 2013.
Many papers published (close to 300) include several books and several book translations to Spanish for McGraw Hill.

In: Knowledge Engineering
Editor: Alfonso Perez Gama
ISBN: 978-1-63463-909-5

Chapter 5

OBTAINING ROUTE MAP FOR HIGHER EDUCATION, STUDENT PERMANENCE WITH INTELLIGENT TOOLS

Alfonso Pérez Gama*[*], *Luis Giovanni Rozo Pardo*[†],
***Martha Isabel Rozo Arteaga*[‡],**
***Claudia Lucía Caro Gómez*[§]**
***and Guillermo Hoyos Gómez*[#]**
Fundación de Educación Superior San José, Colombia[‖]

ABSTRACT

Nowadays, there is a growing interest in providing computer based facilities for improving the educational methodologies. Knowledge engineering and Artificial and Computational intelligence have emerged as the most promising technologies to develop systems for improving the students and teachers' productivity, learning and assessment processes as well as enhancing the student-teacher interaction. We refer to educational systems that allow intelligent technologies to be adopted by faculty members. Other areas to mention are Agent-based educational environments, Educational robotic systems, Intelligent Evaluation of learning systems, Cognitive engineering tools for learning, Applications in real environments, intelligent training and coaching systems, Knowledge-based communities, Management and curriculum support systems, and Neural-Computational models applied to education.

In the previous Chapter 4, we presented a High Quality Accreditation architecture tool in connection with the complexity of the problems of Higher Education (HE), focused on the poor levels of quality, competitiveness and productivity, with a high incidence in the accelerating propensity to student dropout, attrition of quality, and the elevated costs in the education sector in Colombia.

[*] japerezg@ieee.org.
[†] lgrozop@unal.edu.co.
[‡] bienestar@fessanjose.edu.co.
[§] claudiacarogomez@hotmail.com.
[#] rectoria@fessanjose.edu.co.
[‖] www.usanjose.edu.co.

In this Chapter we introduce some tools developed and other complementary developments that have been implemented for several Higher Education Institutions (HEI) in pursuing the student permanence Rout Map, especially tools for strategic planning coordinated with prospective, as well as a system for establishing curricular coherence with the competences and optimization of a study plan; these tools were built with end user computing.

Keywords: High quality architecture, route map, self-assessment, higher education, strategic planning, prospective, scenarios, curricular coherence, student model of intervention, student self-control

1. Introduction

Having established our framework and the functionality of the architecture in Chapter 4, we have decided to present separately some of the methodological tools and developed constructs supported by the SAN JOSÉ FOUNDATION OF HIGHER EDUCATION (FESSANJOSE) and the National Ministry of Education (MEN), for their implementation in several HEI through institutional agreements and written contracts already completed.[13] We propose that the international community be aware of these developments and especially that they can make their own implementations.

In this chapter we integrate the architectures as the next figure points out:

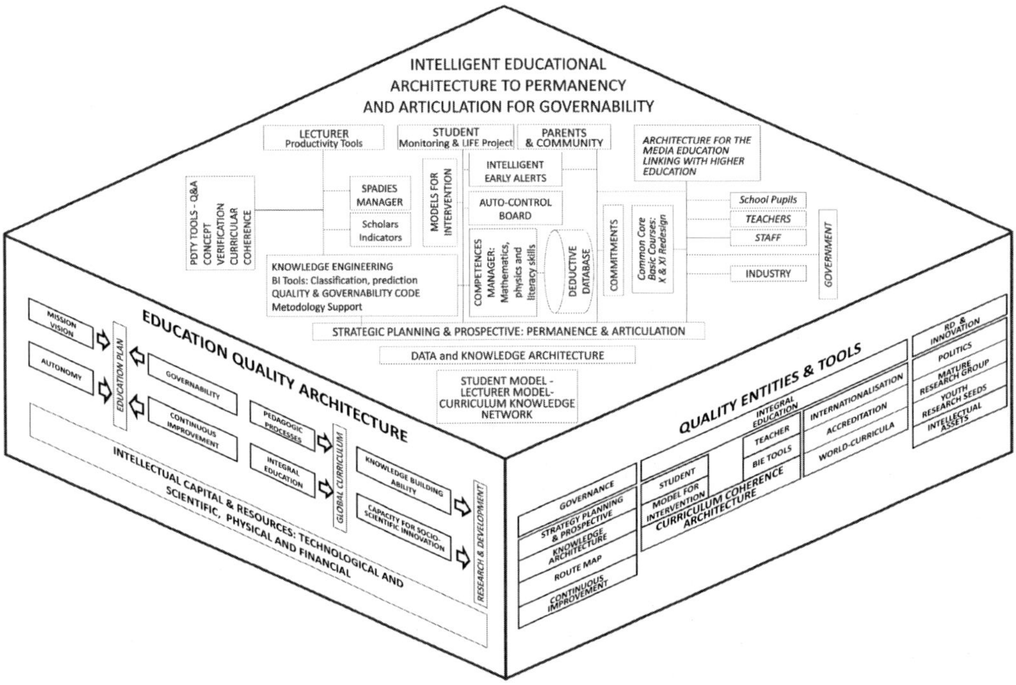

Figure 1. Tridimensional Architecture of High Quality for Higher Education.

[13] Primarily with the Technological University of Chocó and COMFENALCO University Foundation of Technology in Cartagena, both in Colombia.

This three-dimensional view reflects the integration of the quality architecture, the main intelligent architecture and the space of constructs, to be presented in this chapter. Among the tools developed, we highlight those related to strategic planning and curriculum coherence system.

2. High Quality Entities in Education

2.1. High Quality

It provides the synchronization of academic and administrative processes, establishing common referents to the whole community. It is the compliance of the whole Institutional Quality towards the EXCELLENCE. The architectures help us visualize, diagnose and quantify, as we are approaching from now to the academic excellence.

The dimension of high quality in terms of Means – Ends including tools, is displayed in next Figure 2.

Quality Architecture represented as a scheme could also be represented by a set of simultaneous equations given multiple inter and intra relations of the system as Management Information Systems (MIS) inter-temporal analysis. However the scheme described in Chapter 4 indicates in itself, a much more rich and fertile performance to meet the demands of the corporate governability system, and is tending to suit individual conditions of an executive–user. Then the computer left its condition of a simple data repository and calculator to become an expert assistant, playing a much more important role.

The main architecture is displayed in Section 5.6.2 of the Chapter 4. Computationally the expression for the functionalities is showed as follows:

$\mathbf{Y} = f$ {problems, needs, performance, technological level, management level}

$\mathbf{Y}$ is the output vector, which represents the outcome of the Architecture (i.e., output-functionalities): Governance, Plan-Road Map and High Quality.

The entities of the high quality in Education are visualized in the Figure 2.

2.2. Governance

Related to public life and economic and social progress (including education), it is a broader idea than government. It is associated with the conditions of the institutional capacity to deliver the educational goods and services in special the related to Welfare Model of Intervention, the ease for decision making, the management of the new intellectual capital and related, to meet the needs of government, business and society in general.

Tools Developed: Knowledge Architecture. (See Chapter 4, Section 5.5).

2.3. Model for Intervention

2.3.1. Student Intervention Model Discussion

Early alerts software[14] for each student, approached from different fields starting from the risk characterization of SPADIES[15] (System for Dropout Prevention in Higher Education in Colombia, developed by MEN) and thus, provides detailed tracking of students who are at high risk.

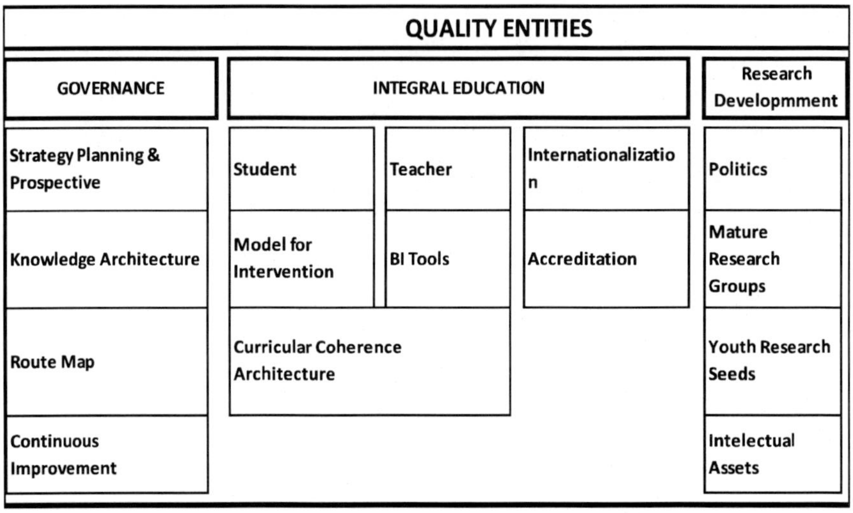

Figure 2. Quality Entities & Tools.

There is another area of focus for alerts regarding the attendance of teachers and students with a daily log of their classes assistance, which is carried out electronically, giving us an indication of both students who have stopped attending for a certain time, and teachers on the rate of absence that may promote a decline in academic quality. Other item has to do with student's academic performance and payment methods, to make an accompaniment in these respects.

The Model monitors students by dependencies with protocols and determines routes (MODEL FOR INTERVENTION), with online guides to improve Math and Reading & Writing skills, including ICT-based support and protocols for the use and monitoring.

The Welfare Department has been leading the process for several years. It seeks to identify the most influential risk factors in student attrition, generating strategies defined in our model of intervention from the three major guiding of what should be the Institutional Wellbeing:

- the integral education,
- the quality of life, and
- the building of academic community, enabling to provide early prevention from Student Desertion alerts.

[14] 1-2014-647 on 07/01/2014: USANJOSE ADVERTOR-HE-SOFTWARE RECORD; REGISTERED: Book 13 - Volume 41, Part 203; DNDA, Colombia National Directorate of Copyrights.

[15] http://spadies.mineducacion.gov.co/spadies/

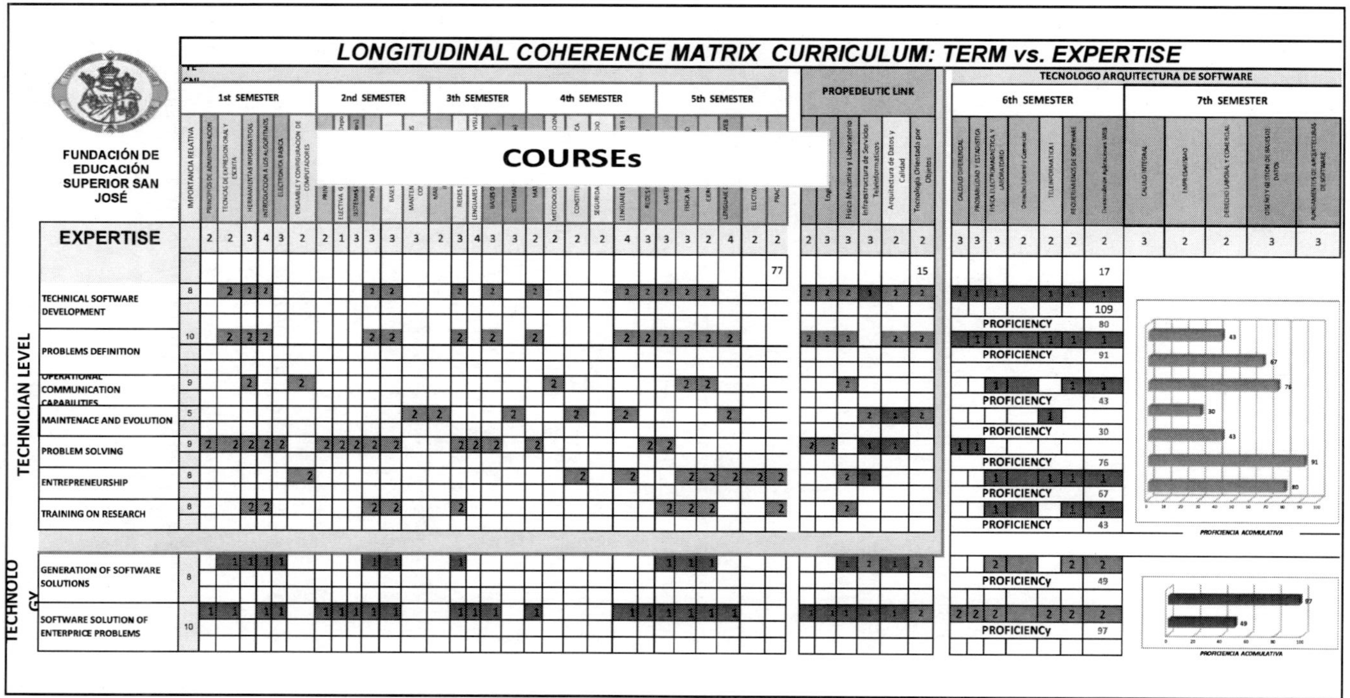

Figure 3. Student Self Control based on the Curricular Coherence Matrix.

The Institutional Welfare Department was established as a body to support the academy, formed by a group of professionals committed to the generation of process improvement, supported by research. Guidance counselors allowed to carry out preventive actions related to dropout, focusing its efforts on the aforementioned identification of early warnings such as persistent absences, poor academic performance and techno-bio-psycho-social problems. It's directed and supported by national and institutional policies in HE.

As part of early dropout prevention three tests are applied to the admission of students which is guided by the following mission-critical activities:

(A) The first project is the Vocational and Professional Guidance through the test of Vocational Orientation. This test the students' expectations about the career to which are presented along with their academic interests and career curriculum aims.

(B) Furthermore, as part of the techno-bio-psycho-social intervention, it counts on the Beck inventory [1], which enables us to inquire about symptoms of moderate to severe depression in first semester students, since symptoms of depression may come to disrupt the academic process resulting in absences from school or academic loss and thereby favoring desertion.

(C) Finally it is counted the Learning Styles tests for which the it is applied the Felder and Soloman [3], based on Felder and Silverman model [2].

The results of these tests are socialized to students and teachers in order to provide new strategies emerging towards the cognitive development of students.

From identification of each specific case, the lines of referral for the Permanency Program arise, which are organized according to the need and/or specific difficulty of students to gain the support and strengthen student retention.

In addition to the preventive activities, a teacher Permanency COORDINATOR is responsible for managing the internal process focused on identifying problems to generate early warnings (individualized and automated). We proceed to personally attend to the student.

All of this has required the cooperation of all sectors that constitute our entire academic community (teachers, parents, students and administrators), without whom we could not perform this process that permeates the academic environment, relationships between all levels, and integral formation, which smoothes the way to the High Quality of the HEI.

2.3.2. Student Intelligent Early Alerts

This software construct has been developed regarding the Intervention Model and also transferred to several Universities in Colombia supported by the *Convocation: National Agreement to Reduce Student Desertion* (2012), Bogotá, National Education Ministry - Projects directed to transfer strategies that promote the permanence and graduation in higher education (Spanish).

2.3.3. Student Self-control

Student Self-control Board: is a student centered tool, to monitor his/her progress and individual information, competencies, academic and administrative information.

2.4. Student-Teacher: Knowledge Engineering (KE) Tools

Business Intelligence in Education (BIE) refers to a great variety of tools that are required for mining and knowledge discovery for classification and prediction in terms of academic risks and desertion probabilities. This has been an important data analysis in order to improve the models for intervention.

We need to detect what is happening with students, who are going to desert?
We need to understand it. Why does it happen?
Could we predict, what would happen with education quality?
How to decide which path to follow (i. e. the route map)?

Business intelligence (BI) is the COLLECTION of architectures, software, techniques, methodologies and tools for the transformation of raw data into significant and useful information and knowledge. The goal of BI is to allow for the easy interpretation of these large volumes of data, identifying new opportunities and implementing an effective strategy based on perception. BI can be used to support a wide variety of business decisions ranging from operational decisions to strategic business decisions including priorities, goals and Route Map directions at the higher level. BIE serves as a strategic factor for a University, generating a potential competitive improvement, which is simply aimed to provide insight information to address academic and managerial problems, e.g.: offering a new program, promotions of fees, provide intellectual assets products, elimination of isolated information sectors, costs optimization, and deserters-students profiling. The goals of a BI exercise include: (1) understanding of a firm's internal and external strengths and weaknesses, (2) understanding of the relationship between different data for better decision making, (3) detection of opportunities for innovation, and (4) cost reduction and optimal deployment of resources.

In the Chapter 4 before, with our Knowledge Architecture we illustrated an example for student model flows and the politics for minimize STUDENT DESERTION AND MAXIMIZE STUDENT PERMANENCE (which are dual problems). The involving variables are non-negatives ones.

Data visualization is seen as a modern equivalent of visual communication. It is not owned by any one field, but rather finds interpretation across many (e.g., it is viewed as a modern branch of descriptive statistics). It involves the creation and study of the visual representation of data. As an illustration we use a dashboard matrix showing fuzzy values between knowledge (study plan) and competences (See section 6). In Self-assessment we use a scale-gram to express the large quantity of descriptive data, most of them in fuzzy values.

Process Discovery is one of the three main types of Process Mining. The other two types of process mining are conformance checking and model extension/enhancement. All of these techniques aim at extracting process related knowledge from event logs. In the case of process discovery, there is no prior process model; the model is discovered based on event logs.

2.5. Road Map

Is related to the action plan: to align human, physical and technological efforts toward HE Competitiveness, comprising: SWOT matrix (Strengths, Weakness, Opportunities and Threats), Critical Success Factors (CSF), Strategic Orientation, Strategic Map, Prospective and Desertion Scenarios, and ME-HE Addressing Articulation.

Tool Developed Strategic Planning and Prospective. (See appendix 12.1).

2.6. Intelligent Competences Coaching, iCOACH

About the design and implementation of iCOACH, it is a knowledge based intelligent tool instrument of high computing to follow up each student in the academic first terms of the Engineering Faculty at the FESSANJOSE, specifically in the areas of Math, Physics and Reading-Writing Skills. The software architecture has 3 main parts: (1) Edumatic builder (as productivity tool for the Teacher and competence manager), (2) the Student Model obviously, and (3) the knowledge base for concept verification. Several previous works have preceded this project mentioned in Chapter 4, so our methodology and related are very experienced. A prototype was built to demonstrate the iCOACH validity and applicability, and also as an instrument of academic productivity for competence managing.

3. Linking ME HE

The articulation is the joint between two rigid systems that enables mobility between the different components that are fragmented. The rigidity was the result of having three educational levels disintegrated and monolithic: there was no concept of SYSTEM. The mobility of knowledge and transit of students is not easily possible, given the severe cohesion and integration of each component that isolates the dam and definitely do not allow communication and governance skills. There are various kinds of articulation between processes, cycles and levels of education, and of these, with Industry, Government and Society. The most serious problem is the articulation of Media Education (ME) with HE.

Also there are other complications: how is the joint of the educational coverage with the quality of education itself; and the articulation between the propaedeutic cycles in the union of integrative skills are promoted, from the basic to the discipline.

Similarly, we could try other extensions as: to articulate quality educational excellence, and articulate the dimensions of the productivity, quality and competitiveness of the education sector (which requires relevant education), to reach an ongoing process as a mediation to articulate the Information Society to the building of the Knowledge Society, in which leading countries are engaged. It has been a constant and ongoing activity to improve student's skills in math, physics, and reading and writing, which allowed high school attendees to enter HE and show success in curricular flexibility and a substantial improvement in the State tests. This component allow students in high school institutions to have articulation agreement with the University to access 3rd. semester once the student has completed his/her ME.

ARTICULATION ME-HE LIFE CYCLE	
PLANNING, ANALYSIS AND REQUIREMENTS	To characterize and recognize directly the socio-cultural and economic context of different educational communities. To identify expectations, interests and motivations ie students from Grade 8th and 9th. To establish real needs of its population. -To Determine the local impact chord relevant programs.
SYSTEM DESIGN BEING TO ARTICULATE	A joint Vacancies shall be generated based on the educational qualification effort between the University and the school is developed, determining strategies, purposes and actions to develop academic-own in the sub-steps of administrative. Curriculum for academic credit and restructuring expertise. PEI adjustments according to the needs of educational settings are made. Vacancies shall be generated based on the educational qualification.
IMPLEMENTING	The startup of the program.
ASSESSMENT	Recognize the perception of students, teachers and Parents regarding the Articulation Program from the Academics, the Institutional Identity, the Vocational Guidance and Professional, the work of the IES and its Impact on student Life Project.
CONTROL AND MONITORING	Early and timely detection of failures, opportunities, changes and new realities

Figure 4. Life cycle of the Articulation between ME-HE.

ARTICULATION ME - HE ARCHITECTURE					
STUDENT	TEACHER	FAMILY PARENT	SECONDARY INSTITUTION	GOVERNMENT	GLOBALIZATION
Data Bio	Salary and category level	Statement of reasons	Past experiences	Laws and Regulations	International Curriculum
Continued Yes/No	Reassessment	Student Life Project	School level	Policies and guidelines	Mobility of students, teachers and programs
Career to study	Working Area	Commitment	Rank	Decision variables Coverage Goal	Bilingual
Productivity	Productivity		Classification and Category		Recognition
Student Life-Project			Internal Policies		
Bilingual			Competitiveness		

Figure 5. System of linking ME-HE.

3.1. Privileges

(1) From simplistic and homogeneous to greater opportunities in education knowledge areas, which ME generates in further strengthening. (2) From the abstract and passive learning to the experiential learning: greater opportunities for experimentation, implementation and practical work. (3) From a simplistic model of education to a market organization of supply and demand for skills with greater access to the HE for further strengthening of the Professional Technician and the Technologist: highest identity, especially in those programs redefined through the use of propaedeutic cycles.

Go towards a better diversification of State Exams, according to new proposals of extensibilities in Secondary Education, with the greatest potential for students: better performance on them.

The architecture of the joint ME HE indicates that the components are integrated to generate the functionality of this Consultancy. It involves modeling Teachers and Students.

4. Knowledge Building Ability

It's about taking ideas through processing; these ideas precede the imagination, which is the ability to place it in mind as creative processes of defining and solving problems; innovation here in a way no one has done before arises. The increased innovation leads to discovering new knowledge whose ETHOS is at the university and is not exclusive to large institutions of Higher Education.

4.1. Research Groups: The International Research Group san Jose eidos[1]

After 7 years of hard effort our team has been appointed as mature research group:

1- Our work has been developed with high academic rigor, disciplined and permanent: its documentation is part of the methodology we use to formalize our ideas and enriching research and innovation by submitting to international contrasting world class events and obviously, systematizing the feedback from international pairs of very high scientific level. We have presented to several convocations of Colciencias[2] since 2008.

2- Three multidimensional worlds constitute the scene of our work: ABSTRACT (mathematical modeling), VIRTUAL (artificial/computational intelligence) and REAL (Problems of Higher Education in COLOMBIA).

3- We focus on intelligent research tools for productivity and competitiveness, mainly for 3 actors: the student, the teacher and the HEI.

4- We address several issues facing the HE: Desertion, Permanence and Repetition, Curriculum Management Skills, Management Skills, Intellectual Capital and National and International Accreditation (i.e., optimization of a Curriculum in the plane Knowledge-Expertise), among others.

5- The purpose is the HE Quality, Productivity and the Student and Teaching Competitiveness in pursuit of the EXCELLENCE.

6- The purpose is to make the work available, including these constructs, to ALL ACADEMIC COMMUNITY for analysis and troubleshooting for the high competitiveness of the education sector.

[1] (Colciencias Code 0084828). Recognized and Classified in C Category at CONVOCATIONS 542 (Aug. 2011) and 640 (Nov. 2014). PROJECTS: FESSJ-PROP, i-COACH, KNOWLEDGE FOR ALL, FODESEP I and II, MEN 2011 Convention 755 with Technological University of Choco, and Convention 0011-2013, 2014, with CARTAGENA COMFENALCO University Foundation of Technology (finished).

[2] National Administrative Department of Science, Technology and Innovation, http://www.colciencias.gov.co/

4.2. Advances

1- Significant achievements in PROBLEM DEFINING, conceptualization and determination of functional/non-functional requirements (analysis).

2- Design of institutional architectures, information, data and software architectures together, with mathematical models: curriculum coherence matrices, Mathematical Programming and Input/Output. It includes the methodological design and implementation of field work in process engineering, cost and intellectual capital.

3- Large variety of prototypes, contributions and national and international publications. The FODESEP economic support and the MEN Assistance in analyzing issues of Attrition-retention. High performance Virtual Education (MEN) was achieved.

4- SUCCESS CASE: “ANALYTICAL MODEL OF INTELLIGENT-propaedeutic cycles”, included in the BANK OF HIGHER EDUCATION IN SIGNIFICANT EXPERIENCES[3]

5- The group is an Accompaniment Project in the Internationalization granted by MEN to FESSANJOSE supported by the Kentucky State University, and the Yale University, and locally accompanied by universities Javeriana, ROSARIO and LA SALLE.

6- MEN Conventions: 755 (2011/2012) Agreement with Technological University of Choco; and 0071 Agreement (2013) with COMFENALCO University Foundation of Technology, Cartagena (completed in 2014).

4.3. Youth Seedlings Research and Innovation

4.3.1. Insertion of Investigative Culture at the FESSANJOSE

The Research Department of San José Foundation for Higher Education since 2008 has implemented a strategy for the promotion and development of research culture in the organization. To fulfill this purpose:

1- Concerning research: an organizational structure built based on knowledge management processes and framed in building an organizational entity: Referrer for each of the academic departments. He/She are teachers who have been consolidating investigative successful teaching practices in the classroom, and have gradually been transformed them into institutional development of skills in research managers, not only students, but also teaching teams of academic programs. Its functions have been aimed at identifying and developing opportunities, potentiating of research projects, from teaching and academic performance of students. The role of the leaders of research has been as facilitators, from a methodological point of view, and managing the relationship with the various networks of academic and research support, locally, nationally and internationally.

Outcome: The Referrer has allowed students and teachers develop skills and competencies for self, towards the promotion of autonomous learning from a constructivist perspective in the context of social interactions that arise between the subjects participating in

[3] “Learning with the Bicentennial”, Bogotá: MEN, Jul. 2010, Alfonso Pérez Gama, Guillermo Hoyos Gómez, Alexis Mena Mena, Leyini Espitia Parra, Miguel R. Ortegón G., Roowan A. Hernández, Ps. Giovanni Rozo Pardo, and Byron Alfonso Pérez Gutiérrez. http://www.colombiaaprende.edu.co/

the processes of seed, showing significant contributions to Integral Human Development and Life Project.

2- Promotion of Investigative Culture: These processes have generated a motivational exercise for developing the research culture, fostering research settings, where students and teachers raise questions about the research, build and develop projects. In short they are spaces to highlight and recognize people, motivating the community to participate in the research process.

4.3.2. Seedlings Awards

Name of Seedlings (SPANISH)	NATIONAL AWARDS	INTERNATIONAL AWARDS	GLOBAL AWARDS
Mariposas de otras tierras	X	X	
Ciclo-montañismo	X	X	
Articular	X	X	x
Una Opción Vital	X	X	
Con-Ciencia	X		
Ecoproyecto de Moda	X	X	
ECOIMPAC	X		
ECODI	X		
Radio y Noticias	x		
Ingenios	x	x	

Figure 6. Achieved awards by the Research Seedlings of FESSANJOSE.

3- Project Seedlings Young Researchers, launched in 2008 for the positioning of the research culture has generated cognitive development of students in subject areas of knowledge, and framed in academic programs at present, so much so that it has generated processes of social appropriation of knowledge and innovation, evident in the participation indicators locally, nationally and internationally.

The Research Seedling ARTICULAR has won several local, national and global awards, as follows:

Year	AMOUNT OF AWARDS
2010	6 Local - 2 national
2011	5 local – 2 national
2012	5 local – 2 national – 2 Global
2013	4 local – 2 national – 1 Global
2014	5 local – 3 national – 2 Global

Figure 7. Table of Awards.

5. STRATEGIC PLANNING

The STRATEGIC PLAN articulated with the Prospective, allows to define the roadmap to align human, physical and technological efforts toward HE Competitiveness, comprising:

SWOT matrix, CSF, Strategic Orientation, Strategic Map, Prospective and Scenarios, Desertion and ME-HE Addressing Articulation.

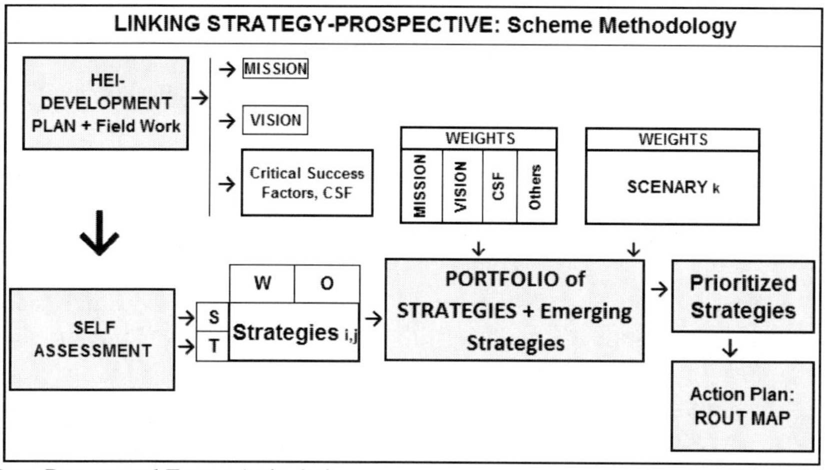

Figure 8. Past, Present and Future Articulation.

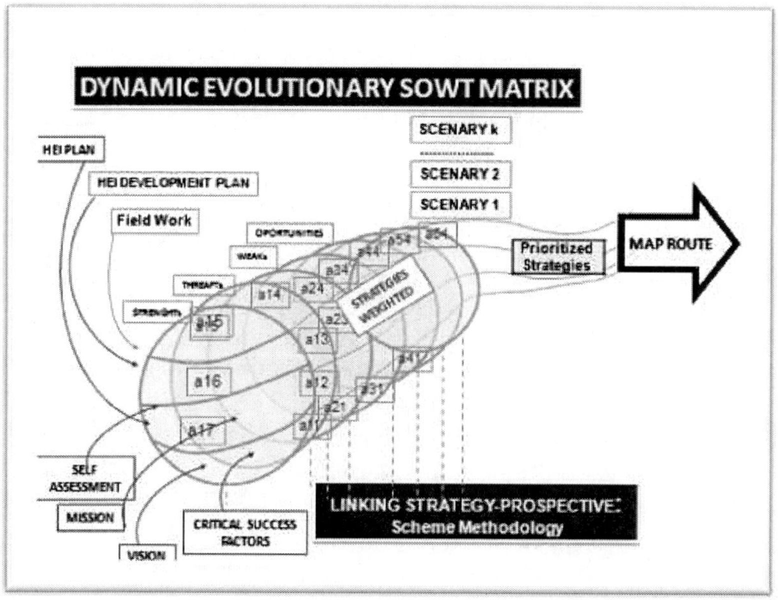

Figure 9. Synthesis for obtaining the Road Map.

A major product is a Handbook of Quality and Governance in Student Drop and Permanence [10], including the definition of institutional policies.

In this way, the system can hold for users the decision process involved, starting from the auto evaluation/determination of the institution's strengths, weaknesses, opportunities and threats, passing by the combination of them pursuing the best strategies that can respond accordingly, and by two quantitative selection process of the proposed strategies based on analyzing different relevant aspects, to finally show conveniently the results in SWOT

Matrices, permitting the explanations of the involved decisions and the selected strategies, and give continuity to the tasks of the Route Map – Mission – Vision of the methodology.

Dynamics evolutionary SOWT matrix is related to the multistep weighting process in order to select strategies primarily. From the above, it is a second filtering process from the point of view of the prospective, where the selected strategies are prioritized, taking into account two or more future scenarios of the institution, with the ultimate goal: to BUILD FUTURE.

5.1. Scenarios for Futures Analysis

They are set descriptions of a system of both its structure and its operation, performance and future situation. Includes event trajectory for moving from an original system ***So*** to the future situation ***Sk***. Both systems must demonstrate systemic coherence. It also refers to the identification of feasible future with the understanding of the series of causalities for each future, identified in such a way that it enables the development of options for dealing with uncertainty.

The Scenarios are an educational tool for organizational learning to create platforms for discussion and analysis of alternative strategies and action plans, improving the thinking of executives and decision makers, to infer requirements and needs in advance, before falling victim of the future, to understand the chain of causality for each future identified, and to develop options for dealing with uncertainty.

5.1.1. Scenarios Objectives

Are the goal definitions of what would be achieved over the state of the world involved, quantified targets or not.

5.1.2. Scenario Building

Build scenarios is the "method of designing, selecting and evaluating situations or options on a system", "writing a detailed image or figure composed of scenes that have a reality about a plan for understanding and analysis" [14]. It is an important path for future building. These scenarios can be ranked by their likelihood, and maximum or minimum, referenced, trend, and policy, among others:

Regulatory Scenario: It Is the most likely scenario of occurrence.

Maximum Scenario: It is the best max-max optimistic scenario.

Minimum Scenario: It is the pessimistic scenario of min-min with undesirable consequences.

5.2. Tool Description

See Appendix in Section 12.1.

6. Intelligent Curricular Coherence Architecture and Competences

6.1. Linear Model of Curriculum Coherence

It refers the logical-cognitive relationships among the architecture parts of an educational system. It is as much an analysis instrument as a linear mathematical structure that communicates (all communication action is a pedagogical one), enabling the justification of a study plan and giving it as an organized and complex totality interlinking the interior and external coherency and consistency.

Among the OBJECTIVES are:

- To manage knowledge enabling a morphologic analysis to a study plan on higher education.
- To eliminate inconsistencies and make viable the curriculum optimization of the PEI.
- To improve the prospective scope of the PEI.
- To quantify the production of the universities in the development of knowledge in students (competence culture) by propaedeutic cycles to redesign the expertise areas in each cycle as well as the know-how.
- To give priority to and classify the competence areas.
- To contribute to develop a curriculum without errors and ambiguities.
- To construct the input/out matrix or as a foundation of the optimization and structural analyses.

Among the objectives and scopes of the curriculum coherence linear model is:

- Non-complex comprehension of the methodology strategy by propaedeutic cycles.
- Optimization of university resources.
- The curricular coherence model is expressed as a matrix which is as much an instrument analysis as a lineal mathematical structure, enabling the justification of a study plan, which gives a sense as an organized and complex totality.

The curriculum coherence is the strategic alignment between a study plan with its objectives, justification, given the purpose and view, duly articulated with the PEI, The *external coherence* refers to the alignment of the educational style of FESSANJOSEJ to the professional profiles and intellectual capital which demand the industry, the government, science, and technology in a global society. The model based on educational processes according to the curriculum study plan, where an assignment (including classes, workshops, tutorials, laboratories etc.) is associated to an expertise unit. The matrix method is of morphological type to obtain a system contradictions free without the unwanted entropy. The coherence also implies harmony, and articulation between teaching and apprenticeship, alignment, and synchronization.

The system diagram of the matrix model is expressed as follows: rows representing expertise of each level against columns in which the corresponding curricula subjects is arranged (See the Matrix below).

The Coherence additionally implies:

- Characteristic: Holistic and integral view i.e., the entire complexity of the curricular system transcends knowledge in all its conceptual administrative, methodological, educational, normative dimensions.
- Academy management is coherent with the PEI when the difference between the achieved in face to the wanted is null, curricular coherence.
- The PEI is the expression of the proper philosophical comprehension of the educational task and it acts as definition of identity, exercising the university autonomy, recognized by the Constitution and Law.

6.2. Matrix Description

Several types of matrices were developed;

Firstly regarding columns: the longitudinal one in time of the study plan (academic semesters); secondly the cross one grouped by curriculum subjects according to their applicability; additionally each cell of each matrix can be expressed as fuzzy values. The groups are: (1) Basic Fundamentals, (2) Scientific and technical fundamentals, (3) Professional Basic, (4) socio-humanistic and business, (5) Professional components, (6) Experimentation Scientific/Technical and (7) Advanced Topics, and thirdly regarding the structure: the input/output for optimization and structural analysis purposes.

The matrix presented below is formed by 4 blocks:

- Technical Labor degree designed for students from basic education (9th grade Secondary School)
- Professional Technical for students from high school (11th grade)
- Technology and
- Professional

6.3. Basic Matrix

In general this matrix A is of MXN for knowledge management, where:

M rows represent the levels of the competence expertise of the curricular organization.

N columns represent the *assignment* subjects (knowledge offering) as functional and unitary areas educational processes involving classes, workshops, tutorials, laboratories ,etc of knowledge of the plan.

Each coefficient (cell), is of the binary type, e.g., can be **ai,j = { 0, 3}**

It is 1, if exists direct implication between the expertise area and each assignment of the cycle study plan. It is 0 otherwise: values fuzzy dashboard in the basic matrix.

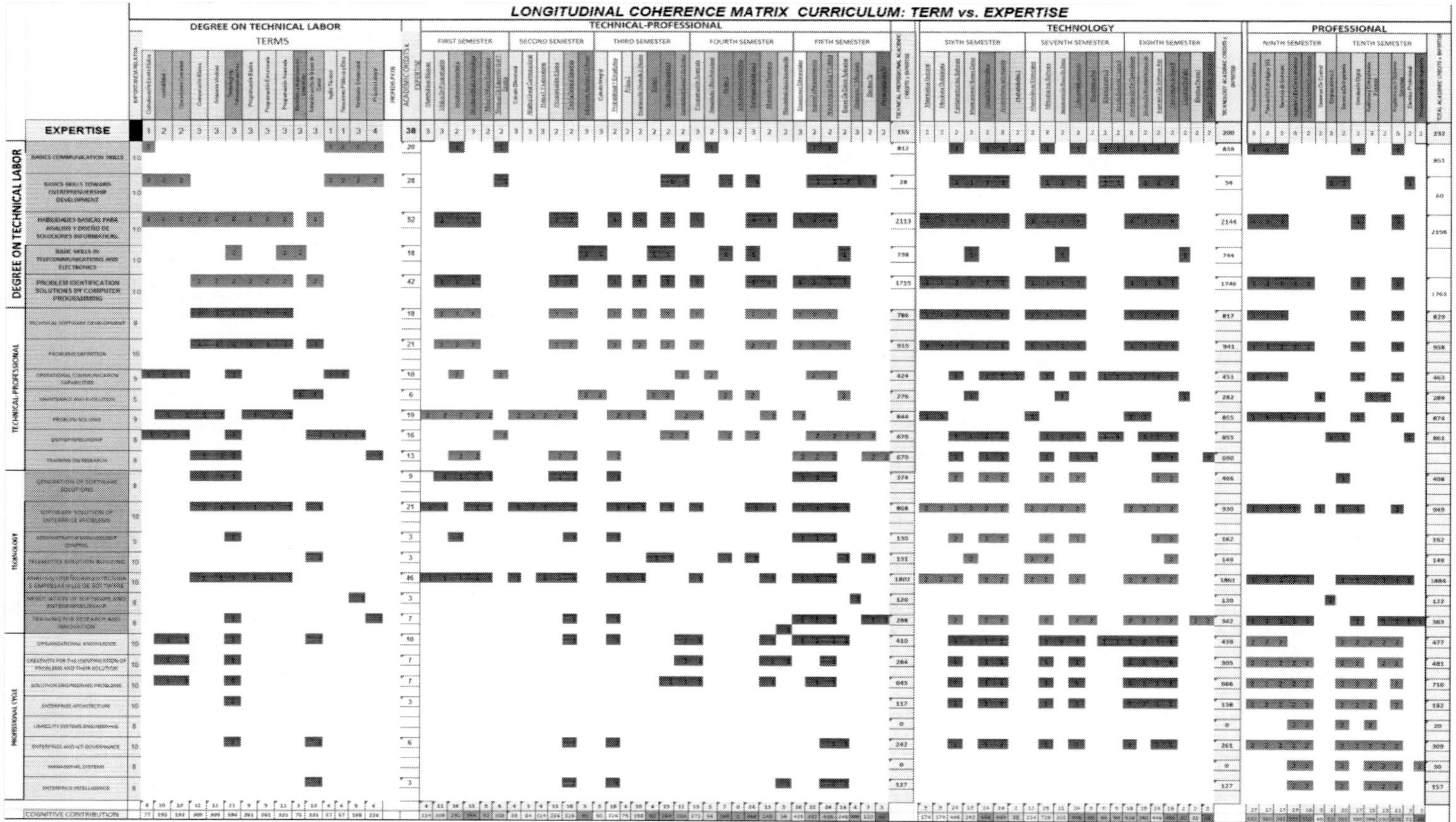

Figure 10. Curriculum Coherence Matrix.

6.3. Basic Matrix

In general this matrix A is of MXN for knowledge management, where:

M rows represent the levels of the competence expertise of the curricular organization.

N columns represent the *assignment* subjects (knowledge offering) as functional and unitary areas educational processes involving classes, workshops, tutorials, laboratories ,etc of knowledge of the plan.

Each coefficient (cell), is of the binary type, e.g., can be **ai,j = { 0, 3}**

It is 1, if exists direct implication between the expertise area and each assignment of the cycle study plan. It is 0 otherwise: values fuzzy dashboard in the basic matrix.

6.4. Fuzzy Matrix

On the other hand, each coefficient (cell) representing the cohesion and coherence of each assignment with the competence, can have other qualitative values / fuzzy logics, i.e.:

A i,j = (null, middle, high) represented by colors in the matrix: [blank, red, blue].

This type of Matrix can be of two classes: the longitudinal in time (i.e., by academic semesters of the study plan and the transversal knowledge, where the curriculum knowledge of the subject is grouped as mentioned above. Below is presented a longitudinal matrix with fuzzy values just specified earlier.

6.5. Curricular Quantification from the Matrix: Cognitive Contribution

From the matrix:

$$\sum_i a_{i,j} n_j = d_j \quad \text{Cognitive Contribution of the } j \text{ Subject}$$

6.6. Other Metrics Obtained from the Matrix: Production

Where **n**j: is the corresponding subject credits **dj** is the cognitive contribution of the j[a] subject for each propedaeutic cycle (columns)

$$\sum_j a_{i,j} n_j = b_i \quad \text{Cultivated Expertise: production } i$$

bi: is the i[a] production expressed as cultivated expertise for each competence unit (rows). For each cycle see below the corresponding values obtained. The degree on Technical Labor on Systems of our Secondary School[1]

[1] Instituto Triangulo – Bogota Colombia.

The expertise demands the specific competence determination or high performance in a domain in each cycle. As an example see Figure 11.

	EXPERTISE	
TECHNOLOGY	GENERATION OF SOFTWARE SOLUTIONS	52
	SOFTWARE SOLUTION OF ENTERPRICE PROBLEMS	123
	ADMINISTRATIVE MANAGEMENT CONTROL	45
	TELEMATICS SOLUTION BUILDING	32
	ANALISIS/DISEÑO/ARQUITECTURAS EMPRESARIALES DE SOFTWARE	109
	NEGOTIATION OF SOFTWARE AND ENTERPRENEURSHIP	5
	TRAINING FOR RESEARCH AND INNOVATION	86

Figure 11. Example of output of Competence in the Professional level of Propaedeutic Cycles.

The expertise approach implyes the competences development as a dynamic continuum and is associated to formation processes during long life of an individual and also are affected by technological changes and social practices. In the knowledge society the competences structure is variable and also intectually more demanded. Shows a measure of how well the different subjects of the Study Plan within a propaedeutic cycle work together to provide a specific expertise of functionality of the competence system displayed above in the transversal curricular coherence matrix.

6.7. Student Productivity

Dropout university rates at national level are critic by its cultural, economic, familiar, and institutional implications. Several Higher Education Institutions have carried out studies, some of them by the Office of Higher Education, evidencing a prevalent and regular problem. For the first time, the design and construction of a tool iCOACH is presented. This one is based in knowledge and is powered by technology on artificial and computational intelligence apart from knowledge engineering as instruments of high information to record each student and assignment of the first semester. The architecture of the system involves three components: an edumatic constructor of tests and exams (professor's tool), a subsystem based on the student's modeling, and in another administration and security modeling. Several developments have preceded this project, which makes of the framework along with its methodology very reliable; on the other hand, it is intended to work according to international standards in order to obtain a good quality of the implemented produced to construct a system for checking the students concept the project was performed within Edumatic, and the synergy Architecture and Software Engineering to set up the planning, the analysis, and the determination of the educational requirements to specify the design of an intelligent and systematic edumatic system with student's cognitive assessment for virtual modality.

6.8. Components

The curricular coherence matrix Several presentation matrices mentioned above were identified and grouped. Each of them is composed of several sub matrices and vectors among which highlights the coherence and technical coefficient sub matrices, for each propaedeutic cycle, the feedback sub-matrix corresponding to the objective cycle which allows quantifying the knowledge articulation of the current cycle of further cycles to strengthen the implicit competences. The feedforward sub-matrix allows quantifying the articulation of the current cycle processes and its feedback to the formation of the superior cycle competences. Within the vectors are those of production or cultivated competence vectors for each cycle and the cognitive vectors, among others. The solution is complemented with a system architecture framework to display the complete outlook of the curricular information or visor 360° of the academic logic, whose complexity deserves to be approached with accuracy methods and techniques.

6.9. Conclusion Remarks on Curriculum Coherence

- The Coherence Architecture is a kind of macroscopic of great quantity of curriculum information and competences, allowing the corresponding knowledge management.
- This initiative sets up a way toward the architectural of information of HEI on account of Colombia Education Law 1188 which is explicit about the curriculum complexity.
- The model seeks to be an institutional learning instrument in the community and handles knowledge, thereby from these experiences is expected that IES go beyond of the simple management of the ICTs.
- It is seen that is entirely feasible an ethos for research and knowledge in the technical and technology institutions. Likewise it is also seen that this policy based on propaedeutic cycles far from being an utopia really enables the democratic way to knowledge as proclaimed in the world summits on information society: Geneva and Tunisia
- The construction of visor 360° not only as analytic instrument but also as support to architectural documentation for High Quality described in Chapter 4th, a long with the model generates great expectation as credit of high quality in Higher Education with the prototype iCOACH, which has been performed. It evident one more time the flexibility of its professional implementation for the national academic community.

7. Synthesis: Outcomes

The chart (Figure 1) summarizes the architectures proposed and developed in Chapters 4 and 5. The cube points the integration of Architecture Quality (top) which is specified in the intelligent architecture displayed in the front view; on the other hand, in side view are the tools built-level of constructs as the deployed conceptual methodologies widely used in various universities.

The model for student involvement has matured and implemented at several universities as mentioned. Involving Parents has empowered the LIFE PROJECT of students, given their commitment to jointly accompany the student.

The university academic climate visualized better in the student permanence, is witnessing the prelude to the HIGH QUALITY, to the extent of have attrition control, student retention, and generating better academic and financial sustainability, except other contingent factors beyond control of our University. This is the way of the Public Policies that are being led by the MEN in Colombia, with various Implementing Strategies to address the attrition of students of higher education, improve and increase the education quality.

This implementation of projects are aimed at the optimization of the capacity of these institutions to design, implement and evaluate strategies for permanence of students' knowledge, *pari passu*, improving the quality and competitiveness.

The MEN understands and promotes that, and it means there are technologies, knowledge and experiences which are transferable to HEI that have needs for process development, resources and strategies, to address the dropout improving the academic and financial sustainability and also the expectations and efforts of the parents. The reality is that social applications are very rare in the world.

Our work has attempted to fill a gap and to be a response in which we have worked with scientific rigor and discipline. As mentioned, our tools are being implemented in several HEI in this country, have proven to be useful for understanding the reality of higher education and the transformation itself of the sector, that facilitate the entry into a knowledge economy.

Thus the mathematical and computational tools make it easy, in a way more than proportionately, the decision making and the definition of policies, building future centered scenarios, both in the evolution of ICT and from science itself.

The dramatic developments of technology intelligence, give meaning to urgent answers needed by society to address crucial problems of higher education such as the High Quality, Student Dropout and Permanence. We have shown that the methodological and instrumental developments are critical success factors in these tasks we are undertaken.

8. Acknowledgment

Our Special thanks to Dr. Jorge Enrique Franco Gallego, of the National Ministry of Education of Colombia. Our gratefulness to FESSANJOSE Lecturers and Officers, especially to the SAN JOSE EIDOS International Research Team, including Francisco Pareja and Carlos Pareja, Alexis Mena, Andrey Alvarez, Mandina Quizza, Hugo Medina, Olga Forero, Marcela Guerrero, Andrés Zea, Gustavo Gil, Prof. Byron Pérez Gutiérrez and Dr. Marco Eric

Pérez Hernández. Our gratitude with Ms. July Andrea Espinosa Sanchez, Karol Martinez and Lucy Marisol Renteria of U. Choco, Ivan Caranton, and Sergio Montoya of U. Comfenalco

9. REFERENCES

[1] Beck, A.T.(1967). *"Depression: Clinical, experimental, and theoretical aspect".* Nueva York: Harper & Row.

[2] Felder, R. M. and Silverman, L. (1988). "*Learning and Teaching Styles in Engineering Education".* Revista Engre Education..

[3] Felder, R.M. & Soloman, B.A. (1991). "*Index of Learning Styles".* http://www.engr.ncsu.edu/learningstyles/ilsweb.html

[4] FESSANJOSE. *"National Agreement to Reduce Student Attrition in Higher Education"*, MEN 755, November 22, 2010, Aimed at strengthening policies, strategies and actions of the anti-dropout program that promotes our institution in favor of the desertion of young people enrolled and in accordance with the social project that promotes access to Higher Education. (Spanish).

[5] FODESEP *"Prevention and Remediation of Desertion System Towards the Academic Improvement: An Approach Bio-Psycho-Socio-Techno-Scientific to address Desertion and Permanence in Higher Education*". *"National Meeting of Success Cases on Desertion for Higher Education".* Bogotá: National Ministry of Education, September 2013 (Spanish).

[6] OECD AND IBRD/THE WORLD BANK (2012). *"Tertiary Education in Colombia; Reviews of National Policies for Education"*: Tertiary Education in Colombia.

[7] Perez Gama, Alfonso. "*Analytical Models for Tertiary Education by Propaedeutic Cycles Applying Knowledge Engineering and Knowledge Management*" In: "New Research on Knowledge Management Models and Methods"; INTECH - OPEN ACCESS PUBLISHER. ISBN 979-953-307-226-4.

[8] Pérez Gama, Alfonso. *"ARCHITECTURE OF DATA, INFORMATION, KNOWLEDGE, ICT AND MANAGEMENT INFORMATION SYSTEMS"* CourseWare Spanish ; Universidad Distrital Francisco José de Caldas – I Edición 2009; FESSANJOSE y ACCIO Asociación Colombiana de Informática, 2009. Libro Electrónico ISBN 978-958-44-5164-7 – Bogotá.

[9] Pérez Gama, Alfonso. *"STRATEGIC PLANNING OF INFORMATION SYSTEMS AND KNOWLEDGE, CONTINUITY, ARCHITECTURE AND GOVERNANCE"* – Courseware (Spanish); Universidad Distrital Francisco José de Caldas – I Edición 1999; XII Edición ACCIO Asociación Colombiana de Informática, 2008. Libro Electrónico – Bogotá, ISBN 978-958-44-1922-4.

[10] Perez Gama, Alfonso, Álvarez Gaitán, Andrey and Marco Antonio Pérez. *"Compendium of Quality and Government, Student Desertion and Permanence"* (Spanish). Bogotá: Fundación de Educación Superior San José, Feb., 2013; ISBN: 978-958-46-1442-1.

[11] Pérez Gama, Alfonso and Álvarez Gaitán, Andrey Alí . *"Intellectual Assets and Knowledge Method: A Contribution".* In: UDEN, Lorna et al (Eds.) Advances in Intelligent Systems, 172. ISSN 2194-5357. London: Springer Heidelberg..

[12] Pérez Gama, Alfonso and Rozo Pardo, Giovanni (Eds.) *"Knowledge Society and Knowledge Industry" Is there a Knowledge Society for the Third World?* –Bogotá: COGNISOCIEDAD 2006. ISBN 958-33-9559-5.

[13] Pérez Gama, Alfonso, Hoyos Gómez, Guillermo and Pérez Gutiérrez, Byron Alfonso. *"Knowledge for the Society: Social Inclusion to the Superior Education High Competitiveness: A Knowledge-Based Governability Model for the Higher Education in Colombia by Propaedeutic Cycles"*. IEEE EDUCON 2011, Annual AMMAN JORDAN. ISBN: 978-1-61284-641-5.

[14] RIVERA PORTO, Eduardo. "Método de Escenarios para la Toma de Decisiones". Alfaomega, 1998.

[15] Rockhart, John f. and Flannery Lauren S., *"The Management of End User Computing"*, in Communication of the ACM, 26 (Oct., 1983), 776-784.

[16] *Tecno-Dialecto Especializado de Cognimática, Planeación Estratégica y Auditoría de Sistemas* – ACCIO Bogotá. Mayo 2007. ISBN 978-958-44-2172-2

10. Technical Glossary on KE

10.1. Articulation

Refers to the linking of 2 or more components, jointing separable parts of a system. In ME-HE refers to create a competences space to establish a continuum. In the same sense, Propaedeutic Articulation refers to the jointing two propaedeutic levels, e.g., Professional Technician with Technology.

10.2. Business Intelligence in Education, BIE

It is the collection of architectures, software, techniques, methodologies and tools for the transformation of raw data into significant and useful information and knowledge. The goal of BI is to allow for the easy interpretation of these large volumes of data, identifying new opportunities and implementing an effective strategy based on perception. BI can be used to support a wide variety of business decisions ranging from operational decisions to strategic business decisions including priorities, goals and Route Map directions at the higher level. It serves as a strategic factor for a University, generating a potential competitive improvement, which is simply aimed to provide insight information to address academic and managerial problems, e.g., offering new program, promotions of fees, provide intellectual assets products, eliminate isolated sectors of information, cost optimization, or deserters student profiling.

10.3. Cognitive Style

Subjective and individual processes through which the subject organizes data and information and is changed during decision making. It also refers to how students perceive the world in their learning process and how they organize and process information and knowledge. It is analogous to cognitive development.

10.4. Critical Success Factors, CSF

These are variables that can influence management decisions which can significantly impact the overall competitive position of firms in an industry, and need to be identified and recognized to support or threaten the achievement of the mission goals of the company and even its existence. These factors should be monitored to ensure the successful implementation of the strategic program. They are also used to guide and motivate key employees to act in ways that make an optimal contribution to the strategy.

10.5. Curricular Coherence

A structural system to determine and analyze the cohesion and coherence of the propaedeutic cycles between competences and the curriculum knowledge. This construct enables curricular knowledge management inside the higher education. Several types of matrices can be developed. Firstly, regarding columns: the longitudinal one (time, semesters); secondly, the cross one, grouped by curriculum subjects (additionally, each cell can be expressed by fuzzy values); thirdly, regarding the structure (the input/output for optimization purposes).

10.6. Emergent Strategy

It refers to strategies that form an unintended pattern that was not initially anticipated or intended in the initial building of the SWOT Matrix. A strategy is considered "emergent" when it rises from the collection of past patterns of behavioural consistencies despite of the lack of intentionality.

10.7. End-User Computing

It refers to computational methods targeted at end users who are not able to create their own software but use tools such as Microsoft Excel.

10.8. Higher Education, HE

Or tertiary education, is the post-secondary education, a non-compulsory final stage of formal education with learning that occurs after secondary education. It is provided by universities, academies, colleges, seminaries, and institutes of technology.

10.9. Media Education, ME

Is the intermediary education level; it normally takes place in secondary schools, after primary education, and may be followed by higher education.

10.10. Multivariate Scale-Gram

Is related to a dashboard matrix used in Multivariate Statistics, which is a form on all sides of the simultaneous observation in Self-assessment and analysis with many variables.

10.11. Mission

Is the definition of objectives and targets, having the organization functions that are proper and are distinguishing it from others in its operations, product differentiation, market and human potential, that makes it possible to achieve its products. Describes the concept of enterprise, its nature, its rationale, and who serves the principles and values upon which the organization wants to work. Define the *what*, or the *raison d'être*, of the company. The mission should be broad enough to include not only what the company is doing now, but it should also include what can reasonably be expected to do in the future. To define the mission requires management to identify the scope of the products and services carefully.

10.12. Process Mining

Is related to techniques that allow for extracting information from event logs, e. g., the transaction logs of a university resource planning system, and can be used to discover models, describing academic/administrative processes, organizations, and products. Process mining is the missing link between model-based process analysis (as the Knowledge architecture) and data-oriented analysis techniques. Using software, its course provides data science knowledge that can be applied directly to analyze and improve processes in a variety of domains.

10.13. Prospective

The prospective is defined as the reflection before executing an action plan in order to anticipate the future. Prospective strategy as proposed is to anticipate future events to meet emerging situations and to develop strategies to define requirements: collect fingerprints from the future to bridge the gap between today and the future. These markers or signs are translated into information requirements of the system TODAY. Their main instruments are the scenarios.

10.14. Self-Assessment

The gross guidelines have been given by the CNA (National Accreditation Commission) of the Colombian MEN. It should be noted full compliance with the accreditation policy and quality assurance of postsecondary academic programs, in a continuing way. It refers to the management: through which managers at all levels evaluate the effectiveness of their educational performance in all areas of responsibility, and determine what improvements are required.

10.15. Strategy

A set of actions chosen to bring about a desired future, such as achievement of a goal or solution to a problem. The term is derived from the Greek word (στρατηγική) for generalship or leading an army. It means action, decision making and resource allocation. It is the pattern, set of decision rules or plan that integrates the main goals and policies of an organization, and establishes a coherent sequence of actions to perform. Strategy as a value component of the strategic planning process, is essential to explain past actions or trends and behaviors or future plans. When questions of strategic nature (i. e., competition, markets, customers, technological change, IT industry, etc.) are raised, it is possible to obtain multiple responses. For the company it is critical the process of strategy formation, i. e., culture throughout the organization.

10.16. Strategic Orientation

Refers to the strategic direction as a course of action or Route Map that leads to the accomplishment of the goals of an organization's strategy

10.17. Strategic Planning

Strategic planning is a tool most preferred by managers in the knowledge society; it is important to order changes; should reach all areas of the business that are involved with the growth of it. It is the window to the future and is the process by which individuals within the organization collect, process and analyze the internal and external information concerning to understand and evaluate the present situation of the organization and its level of competitiveness, to anticipate and make decisions about the direction the company should take to face *the tomorrow* in the process of building the future.

10.18. Vision

Determines how one wants to see the organization in the future and the arena, as wants to see how the competition see it. It is given by the managers and leaders of the organization, must be known by all and give the frame to where they would lead the company. Vision gives the direction of the organization, is the one that links the present with the future of the company. Provides a guide to strategy formulation, and becomes reality through projects and goals that are measurable by management indices or models.

11. QUESTIONS

1. An assumption is that high quality is in direct proportion with the institutional capacity to generate knowledge and innovation: How can BE SHOWN ABOVE, at a university, what is already accredited AS A HIGH QUALITY?

2. Intellectual capital can be measured directly with its own knowledge engineering metrics. Also as the opportunity cost of not having them: Identify 3 intellectual assets of your organization and calculate the opportunity cost of not having them.

3. Experience and good practices of companies that use strategic planning are an indicator of copmany ability for Technology Management. Often they can turn a weakness into a strength in the dynamics of Management. Identify an institution where this opportunity has been given. What steps should been taken in this regard?

4. What is a STRATEGY and what is not? Identify three examples.

5. Prospective is customary as a good practice to design three scenarios. Explain why the normative scenario or better odds of being realized tends to bias the building of the future? Explain

6. From the point of view of computing any number of scenarios could be processed. But the practice has indicated that very low probability events tend to be left out of the roadmap, as happened with the Twin Towers (USA, 911). Identify at least 2 events whose probability of occurrence is very low and what consequences would bypass this analysis.

7. There is a belief that the science of data can lead companies to articulate faster than others to the knowledge society. What competitive advantage is offered to your organization's ability to generate KNOWLEDGE AND INNOVATION?

8. CCIR matrix allows you to manage target the competencies and knowledge of curriculum. This practice will allow you to design more appropriate scenarios in future construction?

9. Build a CCIR Matrix in which micro-skills are included for each subject of the curriculum and see how you can synchronize and strategically align with the target the competencies to the extent that a student progresses in their learning semester to semester.

12. APPENDIX: TOOLS DESCRIPTION

12.1. "Strategic Planning and Prospective Architecture for Determination of Student Permanence RoadMap"

This spreadsheet book tool, firstly illustrates graphically the methodology "Prospective-Strategy Articulation System", in the sheet "1-Artic-Prospective" where also is shown the

"Educational Software Intelligent Architecture for Permanence and Articulation". Then the methodology process can be followed assisted by the System through the 12 sheets:

(1) "SWOT": to write up to 15 of each Strengths (S), Weaknesses (W), Opportunities (O) and Threats (T) that apply by self-evaluation in the institution.

Help	FUNDACIÓN DE EDUCACIÓN SUPERIOR SAN JOSÉ, FESSANJOSE		"No hay buena previsión sino solamente buenas preguntas sobre los medios para alcanzar los horizontes deseados". Simón Nora y Alain Minc. "Planning means no blind execution", Agile Manifesto.	
PROSPECTIVE 2014-2016				
SWOT MATRIX			PERMANENCE & DROPOUT	
	INTERNAL ENVIRONMENT		EXTERNAL ENVIRONMENT	
i	S STRENGTHS	W WEAKNESSES	O OPPORTUNITIES	T THREATS
1	S1 Online programs	W1 Deficiencies in politics of student permanence	O1 Acknowledgement by OEI and MEN/MINTIC Ministries	T1 Local HEI/ICTs competitors (like SENA)
2	S2 Success in ICTs for presencial programs	W2 Lack of an international certification	O2 Great demand for articulation with higher education at the Regional level	T2 Moderate technology obsolescence
3	S3	W3	O3	T3

Figure 12. Building SWOT Matrix.

(2) "SO": to generate the strategies related to the Strengths and the Opportunities (SO). The system shows all of these at the left for the user to consult and determine combinations <S's:O's> (up to 10) in the columns under "COMBINATION", by selecting them from drop-down lists in the cells; the combinations appear in the columns "STRENGTHS" and "OPPORTUNITIES" at right; then, to write for each combination an appropriate strategy that most respond to, at right in the column "STRATEGY". There are two buttons at the upper left corner to localize the window-section for each of the two tasks. Mainly the aim is to maximize the Strengths, profiting maximally from the Opportunities.

(3) "ST": to generate the strategies related to the Strengths and the Threats (ST). The user tasks are similar than for SO, but determining combinations <S's:T's>, to write strategies that most respond to them. Here mainly the aim is to maximize the internal Strengths, mitigating the external Threats.

(4) "WO": to generate the strategies related to the Weaknesses and the Opportunities (WO). Equaly the user determines here combinations <W's:O's> and writing strategies that most respond to them with the aim to obtain maximum profit from the external Opportunities, minimizing the internal Weaknesses.

(5) "WT": to generate strategies related to the Weaknesses and the Threats (WT). The user tasks are similar but determining combinations <W's:T's> and writing strategies that most respond accordingly mainly with the aim to minimize the Weaknesses, mitigating the Threats.

(6) In "Strategy": to review all the strategies just proposed in the previous steps.

(7) In "Transition": to carry a process to select the best strategies, in a first filter. The users are between one and three evaluators. All the strategies are presented in the column "STRATEGIES", grouped by SO, ST, WO and WT. For each strategy there are 5 fileds by evaluator: MISSION, VISION, CSF, PERMANENCE and other, where to write a integer value from 1 to 5 about the aspect. The system calculates the average taking into account whether the aspect has been graded or not. The results are coded by color and the strategies with 4.00 or more pass the filter, are shown at right in the column "SELECTED STRATEGIES", and are reflected in the next levels of the methodology. Here in an upper-

rigth table, the user can edit the ranges of the six color-grades, and the minimum value for approbation. By administrative or development tasks, the aspects can be edited, and other one can be added.

(8) “SWOT-Trans” is to review the state of the SWOT Matrix with the already passed strategies. This matrix is structured as follows:

(9) “2-Prospection-SWOT2014”: to develop the second process of strategies filtering. All the strategies are shown but only the previously filtered are available for a new evaluation. The users have two tasks:

(A) Write a brief explanation of the selected strategies in the column Involved Decisions;

(B) In a group of three evaluators grade between 1 to 5 the already filtered strategies, considering 5 different objectives in each of the following scenarios: MAXIMUM, NORMATIVE and MINIMUM. The system provides the averages in the next columns with a similar color code than in “Transition”, and permits the pass of the strategies with 4:00 or more, which will appear in the column at right, and at the next steps in the methodology.

(10) In “SWOT-Final”: review the definitive SWOT Matrix of the selected strategies.

(11) In “StrategiesMatrix-Def” carefully and clearly explains the selected strategies. All the subsequent process in the methodology, the Route Map – Mission – Vision with which the book is continued.strategies are shown colored according with the selection process; only the finally approved have a text box for the user to write the explanation.

(12) “3-RoadMap2014” shows the diagram of the subsequent process in the methodology, the Route Map – Mission – Vision with which the book is continued.

12.2. “Intelligent Architecture of Curricular Knowledge and Competencies”

Is composed by 11 spreadsheets book tool, the core supported by LONGITUDINAL and EVALUATORS for consulting and editing respectively, the “Longitudinal matrix of curricular coherence: semesters Vs. Expertise”. Besides, the competences and courses sheets supply data and show it to users; and there are two summary sheets.

In terms of the user, the interface has sections for consulting, enter or editing, and administrating. There are three user roles: (1) student, (2) institution-basic, and (3) institution-administrator. The core functionality is available to all, but the student can’t edit the matrix and the institution-basic can’t edit the student model. The institution-administrator can edit academic program, competencies, curses and some parameters.

About the core functionality, the matrix in the rows has the competencies grouped by 4 propaedeutic cycles of a certain study program curriculum; in the supplied example, the cycles are: labor-technician (TL), professional-technician (PL), technologist (T), and professional (P). Each competence has a relative importance quantity assigned. From a template, books can be generated for different academic programs and for personal use of students.

In its columns, the matrix has the courses of the program with their respective number of academic credits, academic group of pertinence, and are also ordered by the propaedeutic cycles and semester.

So, the aim of the matrix is to relate these quantitatively: all competencies (row) and all courses (column), in a certain degree: incidence; the incidence in the LONGITUDINAL sheet

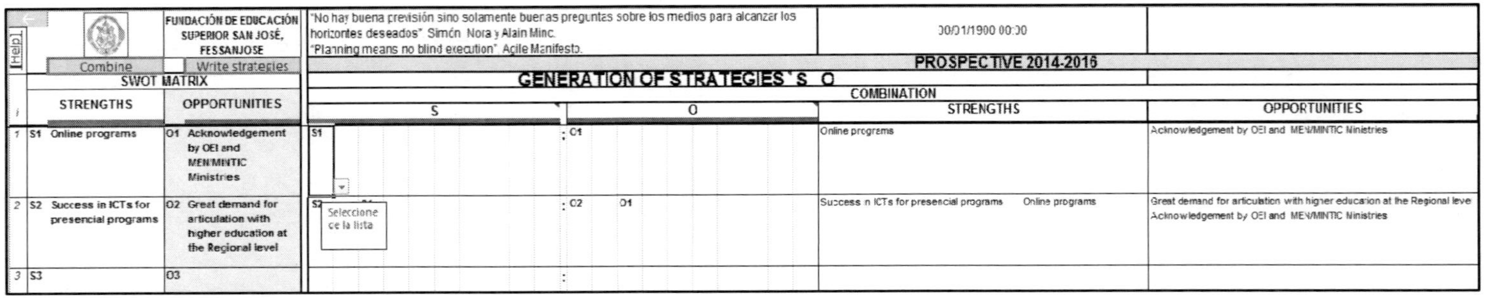

Figure 13. Generating gross strategies.

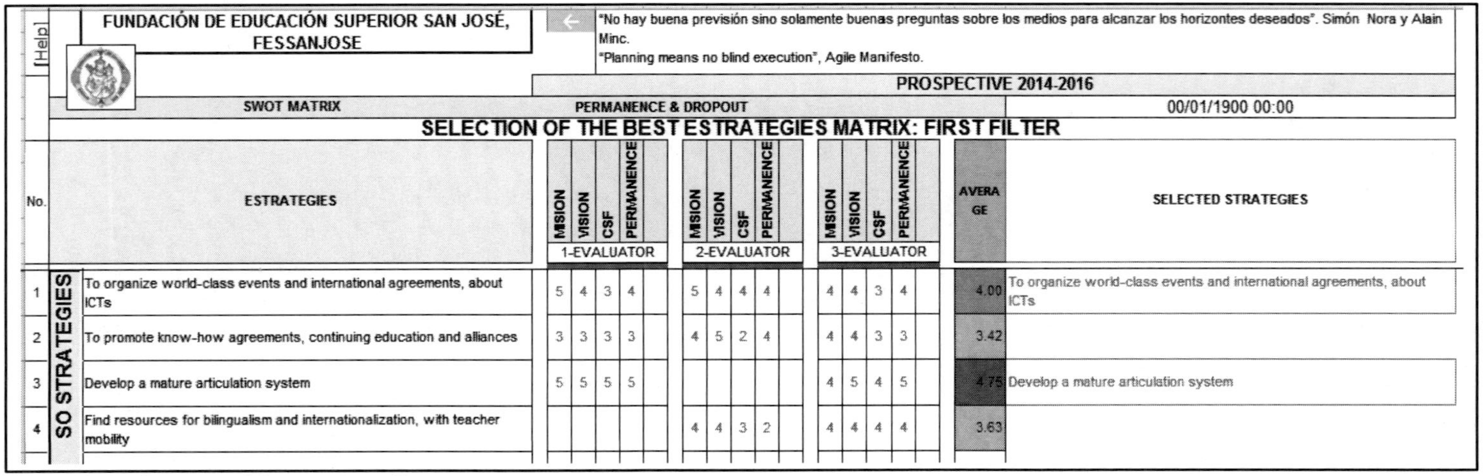

Figure 14. Assignment of fuzzy values: first stage.

		Internal Environment	
		Strengths, S	**Weaknesses, W**
External Environment	**Opportunities, O**	SO Strategies	WO Strategies
	Threats, T	SA Strategies	WA Strategies

Figure 15. SWOT Matrix scheme.

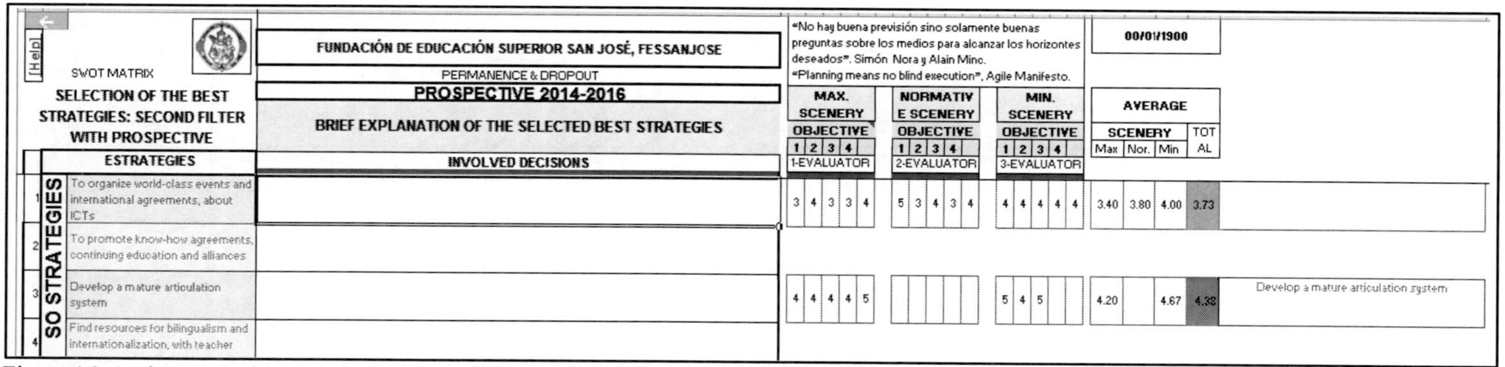

Figure 16. Assignment of fuzzy values: prospective second stage.

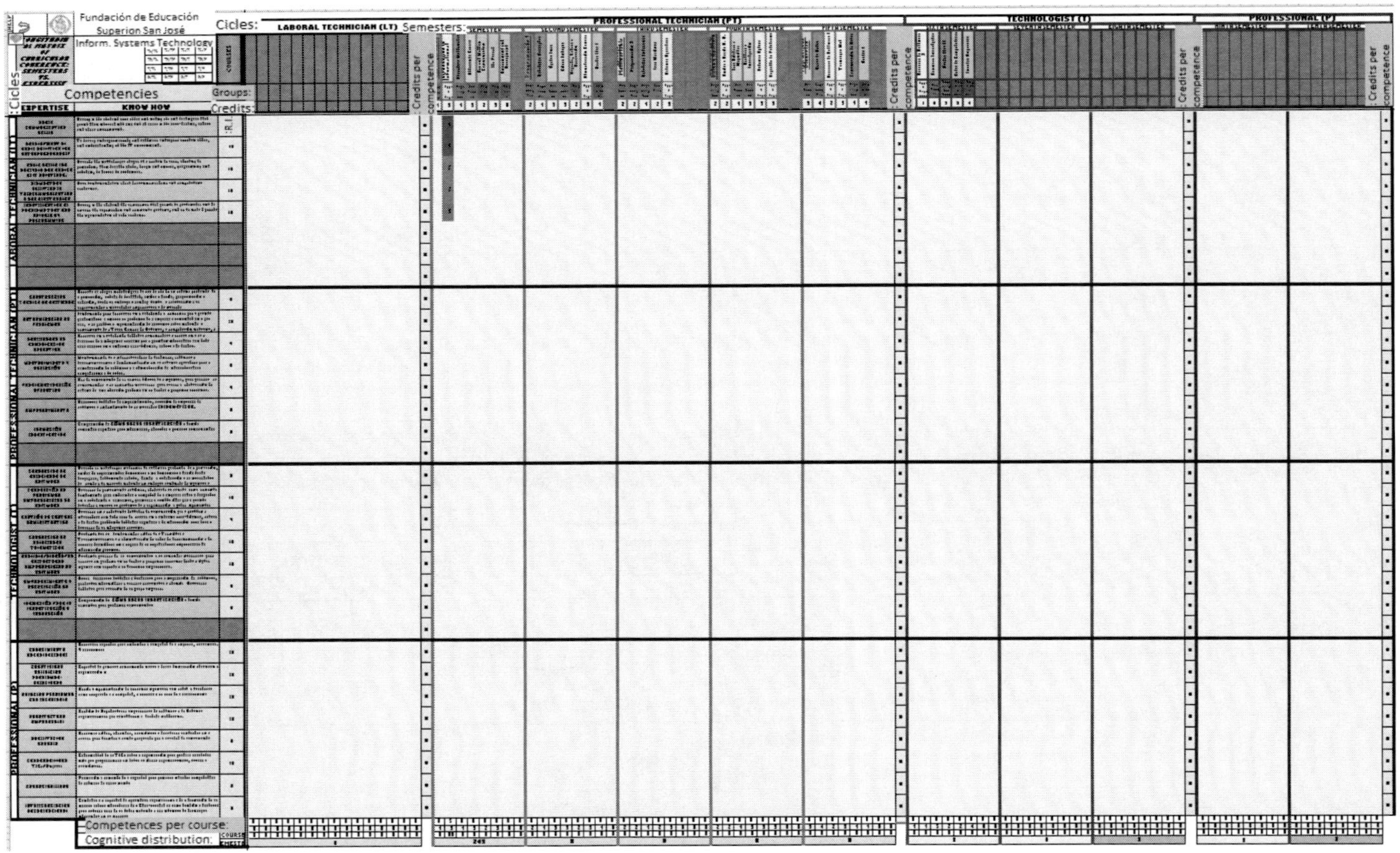

Figure 17. Main Curricular-Coherence Matrix.

is shown, and in the EVALUATORS is assigned by three evaluators or groups of evaluators; it's illustrated with a color code. This means that the correlation gives booth feedback and feed forward to the entire study program from all of its parts.

As consolidations, are presented in columns: (1) the total credits per cycle-competence which is cumulative through the program; and in rows: (2) the count of competencies feeding each course, and (3) the cognitive distribution per subject and per semester.

For the institution-administrator role, each of three evaluators in a sub-row, should grade the cross of each competence with each course, with an integer number between 0 and 4; the system calculates the average; and takes care of possible user mistakes.

12.3. Evaluators

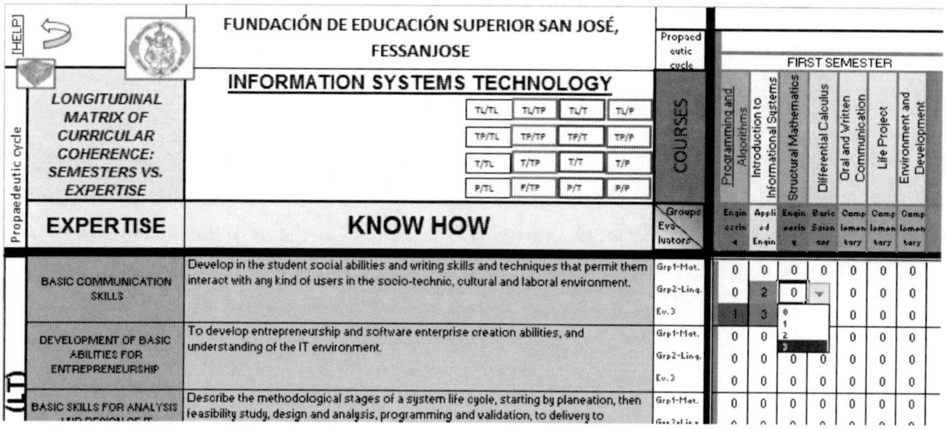

Figure 18. Assignement of fuzzy values.

12.4. Longitudinal

The two matrices (for edit and consult) can be navigated by locating the different propaedeutic-cycle pair crosses (example TL vs. PL or PL vs. P), via map buttons at the upper right corner.

The courses and the program structure can be consulted in the "COURSES.C" sheet; the academic aggregations of the courses can be seen illustrated by colors.

The student-role can use the system by consulting the Matrix and by personalizing it in the "STUDENT" sheet (Student Model), where registers his/her data.

The institution-administrator role can:

(1) Register and edit the competencies ("COMPETENCIES" sheet), maximum 8 per propaedeutic-cycle ,through the fields name ("EXPERTISE"), extended description ("KNOW HOW"), and "Relative Importance".

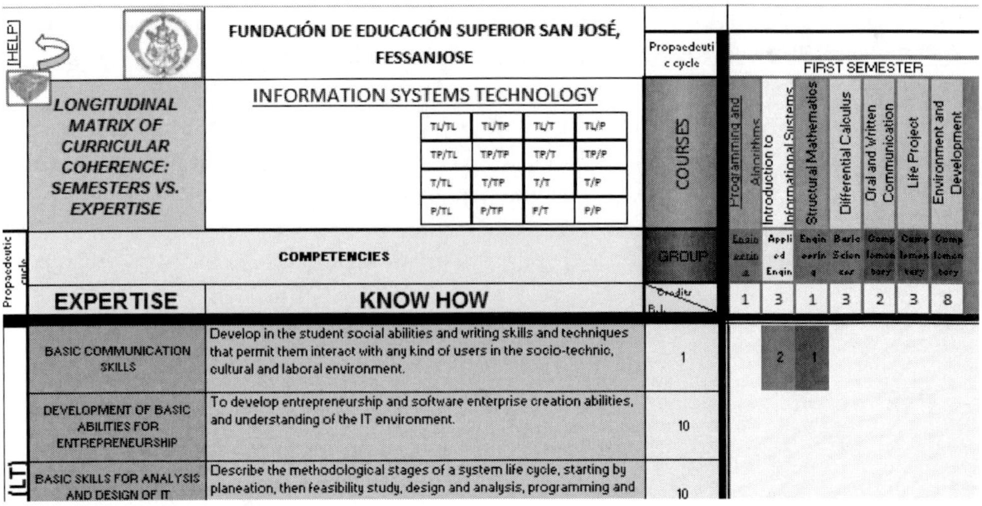

Figure 19. Dash-Board matrix.

(2) Register and edit the courses and their groups ("COURSES" sheet); firstly, writes the names of the groups, up to ten; then writes the names of the courses in a maximum of 8 per cycle, except 15 for the first; selects below from a drop-down list the group to assign the course to; and finally writes the number of credits.

(3) In the sheet "ADMIN", administrator can change the name of the study program, names of the propaedeutic cycles, ranges for competencies' relative importance, number of credits, possible incidence values, some student model fields options, and the names of the evaluators.

(4) Generate the final issue of the system in versions for the three roles.

The Summaries show to all users the results of: (1) credits per competence and per cycle, cumulative and total ("SUMMARY-CRED.COMP."); and (2) cognitive distribution per courses and semesters ("SUMMARY-COGNI.DIST"). Other summaries could be structured and added in development mode.

About the Authors

MARTHA ISABEL ROZO ARTEAGA, is Psychologist, graduated at St. Thomas University, BA in Early Childhood Education from University of Antonio Nariño also Bogotá. She is currently Director of the Department of Institutional Welfare San José Foundation for Higher Education, is also the leader of the group supporting institutional policy Higher Education Permanence at FESSANJOSE, developed since 2012 as part of "national agreement to reduce dropout top" of the Ministry of Education in Colombia education. She has published several papers currently in IEEE Xplore and also two books.

ALFONSO PEREZ GAMA, see short CV and photo on page 122.

CLAUDIA LUCIA CARO GOMEZ has BA Degree in Social Science of the City University Francisco Jose de Caldas of Bogota with extensive experience in consulting and implementing pedagogical projects, research and social. She also has a Master in Education and Social Development of the same university. Lecturer at the following: communication theory, semiotics, visual communication and communication skills, job: the curriculum problematized within the framework of meaningful learning. She is currently the Head of the Research Department of the FESSANJOSE, also is Director of graduate courses education, Education and Culture in the postmodernity. She has several publications IEEE Xplore and also is member of the San José - EIDOS International Research Group

GUILLERMO HOYOS GÓMEZ graduated in Colombia Autonoma University as a Systems Engineer, specialized in Software Engineering and Analysis and Design of Information Systems; Master in Development Process Data and has an Honorary Doctorate and the International Prize to the Education Excellence. He has over 20 papers published in IEEE Xplorer. He has held important administrative positions in companies and universities, exerting his leadership. He has been President of Colombian Association of Technical and Technological Institutions. He is currently the Chancellor of St. Joseph Higher Education Foundation, FESSANJOSE. Is member of the San José - EIDOS International Research Group. He has worked on several national and international research Projects.

LUIS GIOVANNI ROZO PARDO obtained his degree in Psychology from the National University of Colombia in 1996, and postgraduate degrees in Edumatics, form the Colombia Autonoma University in 1999, and in Technological Database Management, from SENA in 2013; has other university studies in systems engineering, philosophy, physical sciences and music. Was member of the Colombian Informatics Association (ACCIO) – Studies and Research Center from 1997 to 2009, mainly in the projects "CogniSociedad 2006 - XVII ACCIO Congress", "From Artificial Intelligence to Knowledge Engineering" and "Knowledge for the Society and Knowledge Industry", and as member of the curriculum design groups in programs about educational informatics and information systems architecture and administration for the universities: IDEAS, Magdalena, Santo Tomás and Technological of Chocó. Is member of the San José - EIDOS International Research Group from 2010, participating mainly in the projects: "FESSJPROP - iCoach" (2009), "Significant Experiences" (Ministry of Education), "Intelligent, Mathematical and Computational System of the Propaedeutic Cycles for Colombia", "Education Software

Architecture: Facing Student Desertion in Colombia Higher Education with an Intelligent Knowledge Based Coaching System" (2010) and "Transference" for COMFENALCO Technology University Foundation (2014) about curricular coherence and strategic planning and prospective for education map-route in student dropout. Has other professional experience in virtual education and development of cognitive and offimatics contents and tools. His main professional and research activities go around cognitive hyper-media fundamentals, technology and educational applications.

INDEX

#

A

B

C

D

E

F

G

H

I

K

Q

R

S

T

U

V

W

X

Y